HOW TO STUDY LAW

AUSTRALIA
LBC Information Services Ltd
Sydney

CANADA and USA
Carswell
Toronto

NEW ZEALAND
Brooker's
Auckland

SINGAPORE and MALAYSIA
Sweet & Maxwell (Asia)
Singapore and Kuala Lumpur

How to study law

Fourth Edition

ANTHONY BRADNEY, LL.B., B.A.
Lecturer in Law in the University of Leicester

FIONA COWNIE, B.A., LL.B., LL.M.
Barrister

JUDITH MASSON, M.A. Ph.D.
Professor, University of Warwick

ALAN C. NEAL, LL.B., LL.M., D.G.L.S., *Barrister*
Professor of Law in the University of Leicester

DAVID NEWELL, LL.B., M.Phil., *Solicitor*
Director, The Newspaper Society

LONDON
SWEET & MAXWELL
2000

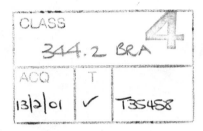
First Edition 1989
Second Edition 1991
Third Edition 1995
Reprinted 1997
Fourth Edition 2000

Published by
Sweet & Maxwell Limited of
100 Avenue Road, Swiss Cottage, London NW3 3PF
(http://www.sweetandmaxwell.co.uk)
Typeset by Dataword Services Limited of Chilcompton
Printed in Great Britain by Bookcraft (Bath) Ltd

A C.I.P. catalogue record for this book
is available from the British Library

ISBN 0421 717 203

ACKNOWLEDGMENTS

We are particularly grateful to the Law Society, Council of Legal Education, General Council of the Bar, and UCAS for their help with Chapter 8.

The authors and publishers wish to thank the following for permission to reprint material from publications in which they have copyright.

R. v. Jackson [1999] 1 All E.R. 572 and *Pickworth v. Imperial Chemical Industries plc* [1998] 3 All E.R. 462 reproduced by permission of the Butterworths Division of Reed Elsevier (U.K.) Ltd.

Blackwells for the article "Arresting Statistics: The Drift to Informal Justice in England and Wales" by Paddy Hillyard and David Gordon in the Journal of Law and Society.

Incorporated Council of Law Reporting for "Industrial Case Reports: *Pickford v. Imperial Chemical Industries PLC*".

Contents

PART 2

PART 3 81

PART 4

8. Where next? 185

Preface

The fourth edition of *"How to Study Law"* follows the structure that was established in previous editions. The book is for those who want to acquire the skills necessary to understand the law. We begin in Part 1 by providing the reader with a sketch of the law and the English legal system. We then move to the heart of the book, Parts 2 and 3, which is a series of chapters and exercises which describe the materials which the reader will use in studying law and demonstrate the techniques which are necessary if one is to successfully handle those materials. Part 4 looks at both the questions that one needs to consider when selecting a university law course and at the very varied careers that those versed in the law can follow.

"How to Study Law" is written for both the student studying alone and for those working in a group with a tutor. The exercises, which are an essential part of the book, are based on actual law reports, statutes and articles reproduced in their original form in this book. The exercises on primary material are all divided into two sections. The first section has questions with answers at the back of the book. The second section has no answers. The book is thus equally useful for the self-study student, who has no access to a tutor who can correct their work, and the tutor with a large class and a shortage of statutes, law reports or journals.

Chapter 7 is concerned with study skills. Study skills are often neglected by both students and tutors who prefer to concentrate on looking at pure legal or academic skills. We are convinced that most students would benefit from looking at techniques which will help them work not harder but more effectively. Law courses often contain a much larger quantity of material than courses in other disciplines. A student who has not considered how to make the best use of their time will find their studies that much the harder.

We are grateful to Jodie Sangster LL.B. LL.M. who helped with both Chapter 8 and Appendix I. We are all conscious that with this as with other editions this book is drawn not only from our own experience but from the help that our colleagues and our students have given us over the years. We are grateful to them for their assistance.

AGDB, FCC, JMM, CAN, DRN

PART 1

1 Sources of the law

DISCOVERING THE LAW

We could begin by asking "what is law?". Ordinary people regularly make law for their own circumstances. Freely-negotiated commercial contracts may bind them to behave in particular ways. By becoming members of a sports club or a trade union they agree to comply with a set of rules. Sometimes these forms of law will use the courts to enforce their arrangements. In other cases privately-instituted adjudication bodies are established; a third party being appointed to decide whether an agreement or rule has been broken or not. These kinds of arrangements may seem very different from the normal idea of law, especially if law is thought of mainly in terms of the criminal law. However, it is possible to see law simply as a way of regulating behaviour, of deciding what can be done and what cannot be done.

Most laws are not about something dramatic like murder but are, rather, about the everyday details of ordinary life. Every time a purchase is made, a contract is created. Both parties make promises about what they will do; one to hand over the goods, one to pay the price. In this and other ways, everybody is involved in law every day of their lives. In some cases the state steps in to say what people can do, perhaps by saying how they can contract or, more dramatically, by saying when they can kill each other. This is the kind of law, that which comes from the state, we most frequently think about. Most courses involving law are interested only in this one kind of law and that is what this book is about.

There are many generally acknowledged sources of English law. Some are more obvious than others. Thus, "the Queen in Parliament" (the House of Commons, the House of Lords and the monarch) is a vital source of modern English law. Here proposals for legislation (*Bills*) are presented to, debated by, and voted upon by the House of Commons and the House of Lords, finally receiving the assent of the monarch and thus becoming legislation (*Statutes* or *Acts*). It is also indisputable that judges are significant sources of law, since the English legal system places great emphasis upon judgments in previous legal cases as guidance for future judicial decision-making. There are, however, less obvious sources of English law. Some are direct: for example, in some circumstances the European Union may make law for England. Others are more indirect: thus customs of a particular trade may be incorporated into the law by the judges or Parliament or international law (the law between states) may be a basis for national law.

All of the above are sources of *legal rules*. What precisely it is that is meant by the term legal rules, is a subject much debated by philosophers of law. Generally speaking, when the term is used it indicates that a particular course of action should, or should not, be followed. Legal rules are said to be *binding*. This means if they are not followed some action in the courts may result. Some of the questions about the nature of law are discussed in Chapter 5, *"Law in Action/Law in Books"*.

It will suffice for present purposes if we consider just two of these sources of law: Parliament and the judiciary. In so doing, we will discover the central positions occupied within the English legal system by "statute law" and "judge-made law". There is a further explanation of international law and the law of the European Union in Chapter 2.

PARLIAMENT

Parliament creates law but not all the law that is created through Parliament is of the same kind. There is a need, in particular, to distinguish between various levels of legislation.

The legislation with which most people are familiar is statute law. Bills proposed in Parliament become Acts. These Acts may either be *General* or *Personal and Local*. Both of these are sometimes known as *primary legislation*. General Acts apply to everybody, everywhere within the legal system. In this context it is important to remember that there are several different legal systems within the United Kingdom; one for England and Wales, one for Scotland and one for Northern Ireland. A legal rule in a statute can only be changed by another statute. Any statute, no matter how important it seems, can be changed in the same way as any other.

Some Acts apply to all the legal systems; many apply only to one or two of them. Personal and local Acts apply either to particular individuals or (more usually) to particular areas. Thus, before divorce was part of the general law, it was possible to get a divorce by Act of Parliament. The most common example of local legislation is that which applies to individual cities. The law in Leicester is sometimes not the same as the law in London. General legislation is much more common than personal and local legislation.

Most legislation consists of a direct statement about how people should behave or indicates the consequences of certain behaviour. For example, a statute may define a crime and say what the punishment will be for that crime. Sometimes Parliament cannot decide exactly what the law should be on a particular point. It may not have the necessary expertise or it may be that the area is one where frequent changes are needed. In such cases Parliament may pass an Act giving somebody else the power to make law in the appropriate area. Such power is often given to government ministers or to local authorities. This is the most common example of what is known as *delegated* or *secondary legislation*. A person or body to whom legislative power is delegated cannot, as can Parliament, make law about anything. The Act (sometimes called *the parent Act*) will determine the area in which law can be made, it may say something about the content of the law, but the details of that law will be left to the person or body to whom legislative power is delegated. They may also have the power to change that law from time to time. Most delegated legislation is published as a statutory instrument. Although people are frequently unaware of this type of legislation it is very important, affecting most people's lives. For example, much of the social security system is based on delegated legislation.

The final type of legislation that we have to consider is the range of directives, circulars, and guidance notes produced by various State agencies and bodies such as the Inland Revenue, the Department of Social Security and the Department of Education and Employment. Some of these documents bind the people to whom they are addressed to behave in particular ways. Many are not legally binding. They do not compel people in the way that statutes or statutory instruments do. Even so, such documents are often very influential. In practice officials receiving them may always act in the way they indicate. Thus we might consider them all as a form of legislation.

In Chapter 4 you will find an explanation of how to find statutes and statutory instruments and in Chapter 5 an explanation of how you use them to find out where the law stands about something.

LEGISLATION IN PRACTICE

Even if we can find a statute the question still remains, "What will be its effect?". What will happen when somebody acts in a way which is contrary to the statute?

At this stage it is important to appreciate the relationship between the judges and statute law. The judiciary are bound by and, legally, must apply legislation, whether it is primary legislation or secondary legislation. However, an Act or piece of delegated legislation may be unclear or ambiguous. In some cases the difficulty will be resolved by applying one of the general Interpretation Acts. These are Acts which give a definition of words commonly found in legislation. Thus, for example, one Interpretation Act says that where a piece of legislation uses the word "he" this should be taken to mean "he or she" unless it is plain from the context that this should not be so. Some Acts have their own interpretation section, in which certain important words or phrases used in the Act are defined. However, if a difficulty cannot be resolved by such an Act or section; if the ambiguity or lack of clarity remains, it is for the judiciary to decide what the legislation means.

In order to discover the way in which legislation should be applied, the judges have developed a complex network of principles for statutory interpretation, which are designed to assist in the proper application of the law. These principles of statutory interpretation seek, it is said, to combine an interpretation of the natural meaning of the English language used to frame the particular statutory provisions with common-sense meaning and an avoidance of inconsistency. In particular, where primary legislation is involved, it is said that it is not the task of the judges to make law but merely to apply it. Nevertheless, there have been numerous occasions when the judges have been accused of "perverting the true intention" of Parliament. It must be evident that the very process of statutory interpretation always carries with it the risk of divergence between Parliament and the courts in the eventual conclusion reached.

Some of the principles which the judiciary use are very narrow. For example, they might apply only to the meaning of one phrase in a particular type of statute. Others are much broader. Books are written analysing the judicial approach to the interpretation of difficult legislation. At this point it is sufficient for you to know three broad principles. First, judges normally apply the actual words in the legislation not the words the legislator might have intended to use. Secondly, faced with ambiguity, the judges choose the least absurd meaning. Thirdly, when a statute is designed to remedy a problem, the statute will be interpreted in the light of that intent. Plainly these principles will leave many problems unresolved, including that of when to apply one rather than another principle. Leaving aside the difficulties caused in deciding what these principles of interpretation might mean, it is a matter of controversy whether they act as rules deciding what the judges do or provide rationalisations for what the judiciary have already decided.

JUDGE-MADE LAW

Not all legal rules are laid down in an Act of Parliament or some other piece of legislation. A number of fundamental rules are found in the statements of judges made in the course of deciding cases brought before them. A rule made in the course of deciding cases, rather than legislation, is called a rule of *common law*. A common law rule has as much force as a rule derived from statute. Many important areas of English law, such as contract, tort, crime, land law and constitutional law, have their origins in common law. Some of the earliest common law rules still survive, though many have been supplemented or supplanted by statute. Common law rules are still being made today, though as a source of new legal rules common law is less important than statute. Strictly speaking, the term common law is confined to rules which have been developed entirely by judicial decisions. It excludes new rules made by judges when they interpret statutes. The term *case law* covers both kinds of new rules.

The application of case law is easiest to understand when the issue presently before the court has been raised in some previous analogous case. In such a situation the court will look to see if there is a potential applicable rule in the reports of previously decided cases. Then they will decide whether they have to, or should, apply that rule. It is therefore vital that accurate and comprehensive records be kept of past court decisions and judicial pronouncements. Thus the importance of the numerous and varied series of Law Reports can be appreciated. Anybody entering a law library in England can hardly help being impressed at the volume of materials falling within this category of Law Reports. Row upon row of bound volumes, containing the judgments in thousands of past cases, dominate the holdings of any major English law library.

More information about the various kinds of Law Reports and how to use them can be found in Chapter 4. An explanation of how cases should be read is found in Chapter 5.

Cases are decided in court. Different kinds of legal disputes are decided in different kinds of courts. Sometimes it is possible to bring a legal dispute before two or more different kinds of court. In some situations, once a court has given judgment, it is possible to appeal against that judgment to another court. Some courts only hear appeals.

Not every judgment in every case is of equal importance. The weight which is to be given to them as guidelines for future judicial activity will depend upon two things. One is the level of the court in which that case was decided. In English law there is a principle of a *hierarchy of precedents*. Judgments given by superior courts in the hierarchy are binding on inferior courts.

A brief overview of the court structure seen from this hierarchical view appears below on page 7.

The highest, and thus most important court is the House of Lords. The results of cases heard in the House of Lords and in the Court of Appeal will normally be fully reported in the series of Law Reports as a matter of course. Other courts' judgments will either be reported only when they are considered important by those compiling the reports or, in the case of very lowly courts, will not be reported at all.

Even if a previous case is said to be binding, only some parts of the judgment are important. Lawyers distinguish two parts of a judgment: (a) the *ratio decidendi* and (b) the *obiter dicta*. Put most simply, the ratio decidendi is that part of reasoning in the judgment which is necessary in order to determine the law on the issue in the particular case before the judge. It is this which is *binding* on other courts in the hierarchy. The *obiter dicta*, on the other hand, is a term used to describe the remainder of the judgment.

Importance in Precedence

HOUSE OF LORDS (deals only with appeals)	Binds courts below but not itself
COURT OF APPEAL (deals only with appeals)	Binds courts below and normally binds itself

HIGH COURT
different divisions deal with different kinds of legal dispute (deals with both appeals and new cases)

FAMILY DIVISION	CHANCERY DIVISION	QUEEN'S BENCH DIVISION

Binds courts below but not itself

COUNTY COURT (deals with civil law disputes)	CROWN COURT (deals mainly with criminal law disputes)	Binds no-one

MAGISTRATES' COURT (main business—criminal, matrimonial and licensing matters)	Binds no-one

This is not binding but may be *persuasive*. In the absence of a binding ratio decidendi the court may be influenced by *obiter dicta*. These two terms are commonly shortened to *ratio* and *obiter*. There is a further discussion of this and other topics at this point in Chapter 5.

Thus, in asking whether a particular judgment is "important" from the point of view of influencing future decisions, and so representing the "state of the law" on any particular matter, we need to consider both its importance in terms of the court which delivered the judgment and whether the ratio decidendi of the case is sufficiently clear and relevant to future issues of law arising in later cases. The identification of the ratio decidendi is not always an easy matter. There is also great debate amongst academics as to what importance the obiter dicta in a previous case may or should have. Some academics, whilst accepting that terms like *ratio* and *obiter* are used in judgments, and whilst accepting that at least some judges think they construct their judgments on the basis of ratio and obiter in previous judgments, believe that important influences on decisions made by judges are to be found in the nature of matters such as the social background of judges, the economic circumstances of the time or even the very nature of language itself. In some instances there will be no binding precedent applicable to a problem before the court. No court may have been faced with the same issue or the courts which were faced with the issue may have been at the same point or lower in the hierarchy of courts. Even if a court is not bound by a previous judgment it may still consider that judgment to see whether or not it provides a good answer to the problem. The judgment may be persuasive. The importance of the previous case will then depend not simply on its position within the court hierarchy but upon factors such as the identity and experience of the individual judge or the composition of the bench of judges sitting to hear the case, the detail of the legal arguments put before the court, and whether the line laid down in the case has since been adopted by courts deciding subsequent cases.

When looking for the law created and developed by the judges, it will clearly be important to look at reports of cases decided in the higher levels of courts. Nevertheless, it should not be assumed that these are the only important courts. Only a very small proportion of all cases handled in the court system find their way to the Court of Appeal, let alone the House of Lords. The magistrates' courts are very much more important than the House of Lords in terms of the number of cases with which they deal. Nor would it be correct to assume that it is always the "important" cases which work their way through the appeal system, since much of the motivation for bringing an appeal will depend upon financial considerations which are often totally independent of the merits of the dispute in relation to which the case has been brought or the importance or complexity of the law to be applied to that dispute.

The legislature plainly makes new legal rules. Whether or not, in an effort to meet new developments, problems, and shifts in society's values, genuine departures from established rules of common law actually occur, is a matter of debate. The traditional notion is that common law rules do not alter to meet the requirements of society (or "public opinion"); it is the role of the legislator to remedy this through statutory intervention with specific legislation, and not for the judges to create new rules. The legislature makes law, the judiciary merely apply it. However, many academics and some judges would now argue that the judiciary sometimes do more than simply apply existing law; that in looking for rules of law in previous cases the judiciary subtly change the rules, consciously or otherwise, so that they produce the conclusions which they seek. If this is correct the judiciary are, in this sense, just as much legislators as Parliament.

COMMON LAW AND EQUITY

In the section above the term "common law" is used as a synonym for rules of law derived from judicial decisions rather than statute. This is a proper and common usage of the phrase. However another equally frequent sense of the word is as an antonym to "equity". English law has deep historical roots. The opposition of common law and equity refers to the system of rules which originally develop in different courts within the legal system. Common law rules arose first. Later, these rules were seen as being over-formal and concerned too much with the way a case was presented rather than with the justice in the issues at stake. Thus a less strict system of equitable rules was developed. In time, the rules of equity also became formalised. Eventually, the different courts were merged and now all courts can apply both the rules of common law and equity.

2 Divisions of law

INTRODUCTION

Legal rules can be divided up in many different ways. This chapter introduces some common ways of classifying law. Not all legal rules are of the same type. They show differences in purpose, in origin and form, in the consequences when the rules are breached, and in matters of procedure, remedies and enforcement. The divisions described below are of the broadest kind, chosen to highlight these kinds of differences in legal rules. One kind of division of legal rules has already been introduced, that between statute and case or common law. This division and the others now described overlap. For example, the legal rule defining murder originates in common law, not statute. It is a rule of criminal law rather than civil law; of public law rather than private law and of national law rather than international law.

There are ways, other than those discussed here, of dividing up the law. One way is to take the legal rules relating to a given topic, grouping them under a title such as "housing law" or "accountancy law" Categorising rules in this way can be very useful: for example, it is not necessary for a personnel manager to know the whole of the general law of contracts before becoming proficient in essential employment law. However, such subject groupings can also be confusing without some understanding of the basic differences between the rules.

CRIMINAL AND CIVIL LAW

One of the most fundamental divisions in law is the division between criminal and civil law. Newcomers to the study of law tend to assume that criminal law occupies the bulk of a lawyer's caseload and of a law student's studies. This is an interesting by-product of the portrayal of the legal system by the media. Criminal law weighs very lightly in terms of volume when measured against non-criminal (civil) law. There are more rules of civil law than there are of criminal law; more court cases involve breach of the civil law than involve breach of the criminal law. Law degree students will find that criminal law is generally only one course out of 12 to 15 subjects in a three-year law degree, although some criminal offences may be referred to in other courses.

Criminal law means the law relating to crime only. Civil law can be taken to mean all the rest. The distinction relies not so much on the nature of the conduct which is the object of a legal rule but in the nature of the proceedings and the sanctions which may follow. Some kinds of conduct give rise to criminal liability, some to civil liability and some to both civil and criminal liability. The seriousness of the conduct does not necessarily determine the type of liability to which it gives rise; conduct which is contrary to the criminal law is not always "worse" than conduct which is against the civil law. Few people would consider every criminal offence a moral wrong (except, perhaps, in the sense that every breach of the law might be thought to be a moral wrong). Equally, some actions which are purely breaches of the civil law might be considered breaches of morality. Nor is harm, in the sense of damage done to individuals, something which is found to a greater degree in the criminal law as against the civil law. The person who parks on a "double-yellow line" breaches the criminal law. The company which fails to pay for the goods that it has bought, thereby bankrupting another company, commits only a breach of the civil law. Who has done the greater harm? Concepts of morality have had some influence on the development of English law but historical accident, political policy and pragmatic considerations have played just as important a part in developing our law.

Some conduct which might be considered "criminal" gives rise only to civil liability or to no liability at all and some conduct which you may consider "harmless" may rise to both criminal and civil liability. It will be easier to see that "harm", "morality" and the division between criminal and civil law do not follow any clear pattern if you consider some fictitious examples. In considering them, ask yourself whether or not the conduct described should give rise to any legal liability; if it should, what form should that liability take and what should the legal consequences be which flow from the conduct described? Should any of the people be compensated for the harm done to them and, if so, by whom and for what? Should any of the characters be punished and, if so, for what reason and how? Who should decide whether or not legal proceedings of any variety should be instigated against any of the individuals? The probable legal consequences that follow from each example are found at the end of the chapter. Do not look at these until you have thought about the examples yourself.

Examples

1. Norman drinks 10 pints of beer. He drives his car into a queue at the bus station injuring a young woman and her child.

2. Sue, who is pregnant, lives with Chris. She smokes 50 cigarettes a day. Sue is also carrying on an occasional affair with Richard.

3. Robert agrees to pay Usha, a professional decorator, £500 if she paints his house. She completes the work to a very high standard. Robert, who is a millionaire, refuses to pay her.

Even when a person's actions clearly infringe either the criminal law or civil law, it does not necessarily mean that any actual legal consequences will follow. In criminal and civil cases persons with the legal right to take any legal action have a discretion as to whether or not they initiate legal proceedings. There is a difference between *liability* and *proceedings*. Conduct gives rise to liability. It is for someone else to decide whether or not to take the matter to court by starting proceedings.

In criminal proceedings *a prosecutor* prosecutes *the defendant*. The case is heard in the magistrates' court or the Crown Court, depending on the seriousness of the offence. The prosecutor will have to prove to the court, *beyond all reasonable doubt*, that the defendant committed the offence charged. The court will have to determine whether or not the defendant is guilty. In the magistrates' court it will be for the magistrates to determine this question, in the Crown Court it will be for the jury to decide questions of fact and for the judge to decide questions of law. A finding of "not guilty" will lead to the defendant's acquittal. A finding of "guilty" will lead to a conviction and may lead to a sentence of imprisonment or some other form of punishment such as a fine or probation.

One of the major objectives of the criminal law is to punish the wrongdoer for action which is deemed to be contrary to the interests of the state and its citizens. Criminal proceedings do not have as a major objective the provision of compensation or support for the victim of crime. It is significant that the exercise of the discretion to prosecute is seldom carried out by the victim of the crime. Criminal proceedings are normally initiated by the state or its agents and brought in the name of the Queen or the prosecuting officially.

In civil proceedings it is generally *the plaintiff* (the party harmed) (since April 1999 known as *the claimant*) who sues *the defendant*, although in some areas of the civil law other terms are used. For example, in the case of a divorce *the petitioner* sues *the respondent*. The case will usually be heard in either the county court or the High Court, depending on the nature of the case and the size of the loss involved. The plaintiff usually has to prove, *on the balance of probabilities*, that the events took place in the manner claimed. This is a lower standard of proof than in criminal cases. If the plaintiff proves their case, the court will make some kind of order. What this will be, will depend upon the kind of case and what the plaintiff has asked for. The basic choice before the court is whether to order the defendant to compensate the plaintiff for their loss by awarding damages, or to order the defendant to act, or refrain from acting, in some specific way in the future, or to make both kinds of orders. The function of civil law is to provide individuals with remedies which are enforceable in the courts, where they have suffered a wrong which is recognised by a statute or decided cases. The civil law creates a framework which delineates the rights and obligations of individuals in their dealings with one another. It is primarily founded on the law of contract and tort, which are mainly areas of common law. The law of contract determines which forms of agreement entered into between individuals are legally binding and on whom they will be binding. The law of tort covers categories of civil wrong, other than breach of contract, which may give rise to legal causes of action. It includes the law of negligence, trespass and libel and slander. Just as a set of facts can give rise to conduct which may result in both civil and criminal proceedings, so a set of facts can give rise to actions in contract and in tort. Most plaintiff's (or claimant's) primary motivation for bringing civil proceedings will be to obtain an effective remedy for the civil wrong which has been perpetrated. The fact that there is liability will not necessarily mean that they will take action. For example, there may be no point in suing a person for damages if you know they have no money.

The emphasis of the civil law has changed over the last hundred years with an increase in the role of the state and the importance of legislation as opposed to case law as the major source of law. Civil law does not just regulate relations between individuals covering such matters as their property transactions, but also deals with relations between the state and individuals. It covers unemployment and social benefit entitlement, tax and planning questions, and council tenants' relationships with their local authorities. All of these areas are covered by statute law which has created new rights and obligations. These are often enforced in tribunals as opposed to courts.

Statutory provisions have also been enacted in order to minimise the common law rights which have resulted from the judicial development of contract law and the notion of freedom of contract. For example, employment protection and landlord and tenant legislation give employees and tenants statutory rights which will often modify or override terms in their contracts which give their employers or landlords specific rights to dismiss or evict them.

NATIONAL, INTERNATIONAL AND EUROPEAN COMMUNITY LAW

The term "national" or "municipal" law is used to mean the internal legal rules of a particular country, in contrast to international law which deals with the external relationships of a state with other states. In the United Kingdom, national law is normally unaffected by international legal obligations unless these obligations have been transferred into national law by an Act of Parliament. European Community law, however, cuts across this conventional notion that national and international law operate at different and distinct levels. It is a form of international law in that it is in part concerned with legal relations between Member States, but European Community law may also directly affect the national law of Member States. It will therefore be considered separately from both national and international law.

National law

The system of national law has already been considered in Chapter 1.

International law

Public international law regulates the external relations of states with one another. It is a form of law very different from national law. There is no world government or legislature issuing and enforcing laws to which all nations are subject. The international legal order is essentially decentralised and operates by agreement between states. This means that the creation, interpretation and enforcement of international law lies primarily in the hands of states themselves. Its scope and effectiveness depends on the capacity of states to agree and the sense of mutual benefit and obligation involved in adhering to the rules.

International law is created in two main ways: by treaty and by custom. Treaties are agreements between two or more states, and are binding on the states involved if they have given their consent to be so bound. Customary law is established by showing that states have adopted broadly consistent practices towards a particular matter and that they have acted in this way out of a sense of legal obligation. International law is neither comprehensive nor systematic. Few treaties or customary rules involve the majority of world states. Most are bilateral understandings or involve only a handful of parties to a multilateral agreement.

Disputes about the scope and interpretation of international law are rarely resolved by the use of international courts or binding arbitration procedures of an international organisation. This is because submission to an international court or similar process is entirely voluntary and few states are likely to agree to this if there is a serious risk of losing their case of where important political or national interests are at stake. Negotiation is far more common. International courts are used occasionally, for example where settlement is urgent, or protracted negotiations have failed, where the dispute is minor or is affecting other international relations; in other words, in cases where failure to settle is more damaging than an unfavourable outcome. Where international law has been breached, an injured state must rely primarily on self-help for enforcement. There is no effective international institutional machinery to ensure compliance when the law is challenged. This means that in practice powerful states are better able to protect their rights and assert new claims.

Breaching established rules is one, rather clumsy, way of changing international law. In a decentralised system, change can only be effected by common consent or by the assertion of a new claim being met by inaction or acquiescence by others. The lack of powerful enforcement machinery does not mean that international law is widely disregarded. On the contrary, legal rules are regularly followed, not least because states require security and predictability in the conduct of normal everyday inter-state relations.

International law also plays an important role in the promotion of common interests such as controlling pollution, restricting over fishing, or establishing satellite and telecommunication link-ups.

A large number of global or regional international organisations have been established for the regulation and review of current inter-state activity. The best-known example, though perhaps not the most effective, is the United States, whose primary function is the maintenance of international peace and security.

In the United Kingdom, international law has no direct effect on national law and, on a given matter, national law may in fact be inconsistent with the United Kingdom's international obligations. The Government has authority to enter into treaties which may bind the United Kingdom *vis-à-vis* other states. However a treaty will not alter the law to be applied within the United Kingdom unless the provisions are adopted by means of an Act of Parliament. Customary international law may have been incorporated into national law but will enjoy no higher status than any other provision of national law and is, therefore, liable to be superseded by statute. However, it is a principle of judicial interpretation that, unless there is clear legal authority to the contrary, Parliament does not intend to act in breach of international law. In some other countries, international law is accorded a different status. In the Netherlands and Germany, for example, international law takes effect in municipal law and where these conflict international law prevails. The lack of direct application should not be taken to mean that international law is of no importance in United Kingdom courts or for United Kingdom citizens. National courts regularly decide domestic cases having presumed the existence and application of international law. For example, under the Vienna Convention of 1961, diplomats enjoy immunity from criminal prosecution. If a defendant claims immunity, a court must decide whether the defend ant falls within the terms of the treaty before proceeding further. Secondly, individuals may have rights under international law, enforceable not through national courts but through international institutions. The European Convention on Human Rights gives individuals the right to complain of breaches of the Convention to the European Commission on Human Rights which may then refer the case to the European Court of Human Rights. (These institutions should not be confused with European Union bodies: they are quite separate.) Although the United Kingdom ratified the Convention in 1951, it was only in 1966 that the United Kingdom agreed to the articles of the treaty which recognised the right of individual petition and the compulsory jurisdiction of the Court. The Human Rights Act 1999 gives an individual the right to enforce Convention rights in relation to public authorities. This right, however, is quite separate from the individual's right to make a complaint to the European Commission on Human Rights.

European Community law

In joining the European Communities in 1973, the United Kingdom agreed to apply and be bound by Community law, accepting that Community law would override any conflicting provisions of national law. Unlike other forms of international law, European Community law is capable of passing directly into national law; it is applicable in the United Kingdom without being adopted by an Act of Parliament. These principles were given legal effect by the passage of the European Communities Act 1972. The European Communities are made up of three organisations: the European Economic Community (EEC), the European Coal and Steel Community (ECSC) and the European Community for Atomic Energy (Euratom). Since the United Kingdom's entry the European Communities have been further enlarged. There are now 15 member states. Moreover, the European Communities are now part of the European Union, following the Treaty on European Union, signed at Maastricht. This section will concentrate on the implications of membership of the European Community for United Kingdom law.

The European Community is an international organisation established and developed by treaty between Member States. The basic framework was set out in the EEC Treaty of 1957 ("Treaty of Rome"), which defines the objectives of the Community, the powers and duties of Community institutions, and the rights and obligations of Member States. This treaty goes much further than just creating law which binds both Member States and Community institutions. It contains many detailed substantive provisions, some of which create rights for individuals which are enforceable directly in national courts. The EEC Treaty, and certain others which have followed it, are thus primary sources of Community law. The EEC has a number of major institutions: the Council of Ministers, the Commission, the Assembly (or European Parliament), the Court of Justice and the Court of First Instance. The terms of the various treaties give the EEC a powerful legislative, administrative and judicial machinery. The Treaty provides that further legislation may be made by the Council of Ministers and the Commission. This is called secondary legislation and takes three forms.

Regulations, once made, pass into the law of a Member State automatically. Regulations are "directly applicable," which means that Member States do not have to take any action (such as passing an Act of Parliament) to implement them or to incorporate them into national law. Regulations are intended to be applied uniformly throughout the Community, and override any conflicting provisions in national law.

Directives are binding on Member States as to the result to be achieved, but leave each Member State with a choice about the method used to achieve that result. Member States are given a transitional period in which to implement the directive. This may involve passing a new law, making new administrative arrangements, or, where national law already conforms with the directive, taking no action. The Commission can initiate proceedings against a Member State if it believes the steps taken do not achieve the desired result. Although directives are addressed to Member States, in some circumstances an individual may be able to rely directly on certain parts, whether or not the Member State has taken implementing action. This is when the relevant part lays down an unconditional obligation and grants enforceable individual rights.

Decisions can be addressed to Member States, individuals or companies. They are binding only on the person to whom they are addressed and take effect on notification.

Community law is applied in Member States by their system of national courts and tribunals. When a point of Community law is crucial to a court's decision, the court may refer the case to the Court of Justice for a preliminary ruling on the interpretation of the point in question. Courts against whose decision there is no appeal, (*e.g.*, the House of Lords) must make a reference to the Court of Justice when the case hinges on European Community law unless the Court has already ruled on that particular issue. Once the Court of Justice has given a preliminary ruling, the case is referred back to the national court from which it originated, which must then decide the case. The Court of Justice will only answer questions put to it about the interpretation of European Community law; it will not rule on national law or on conflict between national and European Community law or apply its interpretation to the facts of the case. These are all matters for national courts. The Commission may bring an action in the Court of Justice against a Member State for breach of a Community obligation, such as the non-implementation of a directive. Proceedings may be taken against the Commission or the Council for failing to act where the Treaty imposes a duty to act. There are also provisions for annulling legislation adopted by the Commission or Council, for example, where the action has exceeded the powers laid down by treaty.

PUBLIC AND PRIVATE LAW

Another distinction that may be drawn between different types of law is the division between "public" law and "private" law. Public law is concerned with the distribution and exercise of power by the state and the legal relations between the state and the individual. For example, the rules governing the powers and duties of local authorities, the operation of the National Health Service, the regulations of building standards, the issuing of passports and the compulsory purchase of land to build a motorway all fall within the ambit of public law. In contrast, private law is concerned with the legal relationships between individuals, such as the liability of employers towards their employees for injuries sustained at work, consumers' rights against shopkeepers and manufacturers over faulty goods, or owners' rights to prevent others walking across their land. The division of law into public and private law and civil and criminal law are two clear examples of categories which overlap. Thus, for example, some public law is civil and some is criminal.

The significance of the public/private law distinction operates at two levels. First, it is a very useful general classification through which we can highlight some broad differences, such as those in the purpose of law, in sources and forms of legal rules, and in remedies and enforcement. This is the way the idea of public/private law will be discussed here. However, the distinction is also used in a second, narrower sense; as a way of defining the procedure by which claims can be raised in court.

One way of thinking about a legal rule is to consider its purpose. The primary purpose underlying most private law rules is the protection of individual interests, whereas the aim of most public law provisions is the promotion of social objectives and the protection of collective rather than individual interests. The methods used to achieve these purposes also differ. A characteristic feature of public law is the creation of a public body with special powers of investigation, decision-making and/or enforcement in relation to a particular problem, whereas private law achieves its ends by giving individuals the right to take action in defence of their interests.

Many problems are addressed by both public and private law. Sometimes a single statute may include both private rights and liabilities alongside public law provisions. This can be seen both by looking at statutes characteristic of public law and by looking at an example in practice.

The Equal Pay Act and the Sex Discrimination Act both came into force in 1975. These Acts made it unlawful to discriminate on the grounds of sex in many important areas such as employment, education and housing. For the individual who had suffered discrimination, the Acts created new private rights to take complaints to industrial tribunals or county courts and claim compensation or other appropriate remedies. At the same time, the Equal Opportunities Commission was set up, with public powers and duties to investigate matters of sex discrimination and promote equal opportunities.

Example

Ann lives next door to an industrial workshop run by Brenda. The machinery is very noisy and the process discharges fumes which make Ann feel ill. This sort of problem is tackled by both public and private law in a number of different ways.

(i) As a neighbour, Ann may bring a private law action in nuisance, which is a claim that Brenda's activities unreason ably interfere with the use of Ann's land. Ann could claim compensation for the hard she has suffered and could seek an injunction to stop the harmful process continuing.

(ii) There are also public law rules which may be invoked whether or not an individual has or may be harmed, aimed at preventing the problem arising in the first place or controlling the situation for the public benefit. For example, when Brenda first started her workshop she would have needed to get planning permission from the local authority if her activities constituted a change in the use of the land. Planning legislation thus gives the local authority an opportunity to prevent industrial development in residential areas by refusing planning permission, or control it by laying down conditions. Other legislation gives the local authority powers to monitor and control various kinds of pollution and nuisances in their area, including noise and dangerous fumes. A further complex set of private rights and public regulations govern the working conditions of the workshop employees, who would also be affected by the noise and smells.

(iii) Public and private law also show differences in their origins and form. Some of the most important principles of private law are of ancient origin and were developed through the common law as individuals took their private disputes to court and demanded a remedy. The rules of private rights in contract, over land and inheritance, to compensation for physical injury or damage to property or reputation, were all first fashioned by judges in the course of deciding cases brought before them.

In contrast, most public law rules are of comparatively recent origin first originating in stature, not judicial decisions. There are obvious exceptions. Criminal law and the criminal justice system itself are prime examples where standards of behaviour are set by the state and enforced by a network of public officials with powers of arrest, prosecution, trial and punishment. Much of the early development of this field of public law lies in common law. An important function of public law has its roots in constitutional theory. The actions of public bodies are only lawful if there is a legal rule granting the body authority to act in a given situation. A private individual needs no legal authority merely to act. It is assumed that a person acts lawfully unless there is a legal rule prohibiting or curtailing that behaviour. Public law therefore has a facilitative function, for which there is no equivalent in private law, permitting a public body to take action that would otherwise be unlawful. A feature of much recent public law is a shift towards the grant of broad discretionary powers to public bodies. This means that the same legislative framework can be used more flexibly, accommodating changes in public policy as to the purposes to which the powers should be put or the criteria for the exercise of these powers. This characteristic form of modern public law contrasts quite sharply with the relatively specific rights and duties to be found in private law, and in turn affects the way public and private law can be enforced. All private law is enforced by granting individuals the right to take action in defence of a recognised personal interest. For example, a householder may make a contract with a builder over the repair of a roof, and may sue the builder if the work or materials are of a lower standard than was specified in the contract. Not all public law can be enforced by way of individual action.

The enforcement of public law can be viewed from two perspectives. First, public law can be enforced as when as official ensures that individuals or companies comply with standards set in statutes or delegated legislation, *e.g.* public health officials making orders in relation to or prosecuting restaurants. Secondly, the enforcement of public law can also be seen as the matter of ensuring public authorities themselves carry out their duties and do not exceed their legal powers. Here, the form of public law statutes, mentioned above, rarely ties a public body to supplying a particular standard of service, as a contract may tie a builder, but gives a wide choice of lawful behaviour.

Even where legislation lays a duty on a public authority, there may be no corresponding right of individual action. For example, under the Education Act 1996, local education authorities are under a duty to ensure that there are sufficient schools, in numbers, character and equipment, for providing educational opportunities for all pupils in their area. However, nobody can sue the authority if the schools are overcrowded or badly equipped. The only remedy is to complain to the Secretary of State, who can make orders if satisfied that the authority is in default of their duties. The mechanism for controlling standards of public bodies is generally by way of political accountability to the electorate or ministers rather than the legal process.

Some parts of public law do create individual rights and permit individual enforcement. In social security legislation, for example, qualified claimants have a right to certain benefits and may appeal against decisions of benefit to a tribunal. There is a procedure, special to public law, called "judicial review of administrative action" (often referred to simply as *judicial review*), whereby an individual may go to the High Court alleging unlawful behaviour on the part of a public body. However, in order to go to court, the individual must show "sufficient interest" in the issue in question (this being legally defined) and the court has a discretion whether to hear the case or grant a remedy. This is quite different from proceedings in private law, where a plaintiff does not need the court's permission for the case to be heard but has a right to a hearing if a recognised cause of action is asserted and also a right to a remedy of some kind if successful.

CRIMINAL LAW AND CIVIL LAW

Legal consequences in questions 1–3:

1. Norman's actions may give rise to both criminal and civil proceedings. He may be prosecuted for drink driving and related road traffic offences and, if convicted, will have a criminal record. All road traffic offences, including parking offences, are just as much part of the criminal law as murder is. He may also be sued by the woman or child who would wish to recover damages for the personal injuries they have suffered. Such an action would be a civil action. The same set of facts may give rise to both criminal and civil liability.

2. Sue has committed no criminal offence. Neither the unborn child nor Richard have any right of civil action for any harm they may consider Sue has done to them.

3. Robert has not committed any criminal offence. He is in no different a position in law to the person who has no money. Joan will be able to commence civil proceedings against him. She will be able to sue him for breach of contract. Robert's wealth makes it more likely that Joan will consider it worth suing him as she is more likely to be able to recover any damages. However, she will also have to remember that Robert will, if he wishes be able to hire the best lawyers so as to delay Joan's inevitable court victory.

3 | Law in action/Law in books

INTRODUCTION

This chapter is about the different kinds of questions that arise when studying law and the different techniques you need when studying them. You might think that studying law is purely a matter of learning a large number of legal rules. If this were the case only one kind of question would ever arise - what is the content of any particular legal rule? However, simply learning a large number of legal rules is not always a very useful way of learning about law. Learning the rules is like memorising the answers to a set of sums. It is of no help when the sums change. If all you do is learn a set of legal rules, when the rules change, when the law is altered, you are back where you started. At the very least, to use your legal knowledge, you also need to know how to find legal rules and how to find out if they have been changed. Thus, to the question "what is the content of the legal rule?" are added questions about how to find them.

Not everyone interested in law is interested in questions about the content of legal rules. For example, we might ask whether it is ever right to disobey the law. This is a question of ethics which might in part relate to the content of a legal rule but is much more about the nature of moral judgement. Equally questions about how the legal system works in practice are only partially concerned with the content of legal rules. Legal rules are about what should happen. Questions about practice are concerned with what does happen.

The various questions above are not merely different questions, they are different kinds of questions. Because they are questions about different things and because the different questions demand different techniques to answer them they are often put into separate categories. The terms for these categories vary. Some terms are more precise than others. We have taken one commonly drawn distinction, that between the law in action and the law in books, as the title for this chapter. This is because the distinction is a very basic one that can be applied to most areas of law. The law in action is that which actually happens in the legal system and is concerned with people's behaviour. The law in books is the system of legal rules which can be deduced from reading cases and statutes. A question about how defendants are treated in court is a question about the law in action. A question about the definition of theft in English law is a question about the law in books.

Although the distinction between the law in action and the law in books is both easy to see and useful to use it is also limited. Some questions about law seem to fit into neither category. For example, is our earlier question about disobedience to law a question about the law in action or the law in books? Information about what actually happens in the legal system will only tell us what people do, not whether their action is morally correct.

Equally, being told what the legal rule says is of little help in helping us assess whether we are correct to obey it or not. The question does not appear to fall into either category.

The distinction between the law in action and the law in books is broad but crude. More sophisticated categories provide narrower, more precise distinctions. Thus questions about the nature of law, which can include whether or not one has a duty to obey it, can be grouped together under the title the philosophy of law or jurisprudence. Such categories are not firmly fixed and may be defined by different people in different ways. Thus some people would use the term the sociology of law to refer to all questions about the operation of the legal system in practice. Others would distinguish between questions about the relationship between law and other social forces and questions about how effective a legal rule is. They would see the first kind of question as falling within the sociology of law and the second as coming under the heading socio-legal studies. It is more important to be able to identify the different kinds of questions than give them the labels.

DIFFERENT QUESTIONS MEAN DIFFERENT ANSWERS

Knowing that there are different kinds of questions asked when studying law is of intellectual interest but does it have any further significance? What happens if you fail properly to identify the kind of question that you are asking? We can answer these questions by looking at one way in which different kinds of questions are commonly confused.

For many years it was assumed that legal rules which laid down what should happen were an accurate guide to what actually happened. The law in action was thought to be a reflection of the law in books. It was accepted that there were divergencies but these were thought to be on a small scale and of no importance. However, academics have now shown that there is often a very great difference between legal rules and the practice in the legal system. One example of this can be seen in the area of criminal justice, when people are arrested and taken to the police station for questioning.

The Police and Criminal Evidence Act 1984 (generally referred to as "PACE") lays down a large number of rules relating to the treatment of suspects who are detained in police stations. The purpose of these rules is to try and provide a balance between providing safeguards for the person who is being questioned and enabling the police to carry out a thorough investigation. One of the rules which PACE contains is that the suspect must be told of his/her right to seek legal advice. However, researchers have found that most people do not receive legal advice at the police station. This can happen because many suspects do not appreciate how important it is to have legal advice at an early stage in criminal investigations. However, another significant reason influencing suspects in their decision not to seek legal advice is that the police may use a number of "ploys" to discourage suspects from taking advice, including minimising the significance of what is happening by saying the suspect will only be there for a short time, or emphasising what a long time the detainee will have to wait until their legal adviser arrives. Merely looking at the law in the books could only tell us what is supposed to happen; that suspects are entitled to be told about their right to seek legal advice. It is only when we look at the law in action that we can understand how the law really works in practice; in this case, we come to understand that merely giving a right to people does not mean that they will understand how important it is to exercise that right, nor does giving a right ensure that it will necessarily be implemented in the way it was intended.

The difference between the law in action and the law in books in this area is important for several reasons. First, confusing the different kinds of questions resulted in an inaccurate description. People accepted the wrong kind of material as evidence for their answers, and as a result thought that the law worked in practice in much the same way as the legal rules suggested it should. Secondly, because of that misdescription, those involved in advising others on the law may have given misleading advice. Finally, those involved in considering whether or not the law and legal system are effective and just looked not at the real legal system but at a shadowy reflection of it.

WHICH KIND OF QUESTION AM I ASKING?

Somebody has been divorced and you are asked how their financial affairs will be settled by the courts. Are you being asked what the relevant rules are, or what will actually happen in court, or both? Outside your course of study it may be very difficult to sort out what kind of question you are being asked. For study purposes the task will generally be simpler. The kind of question that you are being asked is likely to be indicated by the nature of your course as a whole. Some kinds of courses are more usually taught with one kind of question in mind than another. For example, courses on "land law" or the "law of contract" are more often concerned with the law in books than the law in action. These kinds of courses are sometimes termed 'black-letter' law courses. Courses on Family Law often include a great deal of material which tells us about the law in action. This kind of course is often described as 'socio-legal'.

Even when it is clear what kind of question your course is generally concerned with problems may still arise. It is not only important to know the kind of question that you are interested in. You must also be able to identify the kind of question that the author of a book or article which you are using is interested in. Are they trying only to analyse the legal rules, the cases and statutes in a particular area of law, or are they also interested in exploring how the law works in practice? If you know the type of answer they are trying to give you will be in a better position to judge the quality of their argument and, thus the value of their work. Even when you have identified the kind of question an author is most interested in you will also have to be careful to see that other kinds of question are not introduced. For example, it is not uncommon to find a book largely devoted to discussion of the content of legal rules also including a few remarks on the value or justice of those rules. There is nothing wrong with this if the author realises that a different kind of question is being addressed and uses the appropriate material to answer it. Unfortunately this is not always so.

ARE THERE REALLY DIFFERENT QUESTIONS?

There are some people who would argue that it is misleading to distinguish between different questions in the way we have done above. Some would argue that all the distinctions drawn are wrong. Others would argue that only some of them are invalid. Are there really different questions? One argument that might be advanced is about the distinction between the law in action and the law in books. In our earlier example we saw that there was a difference between the legal rule laid down in the Court of Appeal and the actual practice studied. If we assume that the practice of all courts was the same as the court studied, and if this practice continued for many years, what would it mean to say that the legal rule was that which was laid down by the Court of Appeal? People would only be affected by what happened in practice, which would always be different from that which the legal rules said should happen. Could we really say that the legal rule had any significance? If the legal rule has no significance, then surely all we ought to study is what happens in practice, ignoring questions about the law in books?

Other more complicated forms of the above argument exist. Some people would argue that when a judge makes a decision that decision is influenced by the judge's social background, political views and education. The result of any case is therefore not solely determined by the neutral application of legal rules but by factors personal to the particular judge in the case. If this is so, then what kinds of questions will discussion about the content of legal rules answer? If we are to advise people how to act so as to win cases in court what we need to discuss is not, or not only, the content of legal rules but, rather, who are the judges and what their background is. If we want to find out what the law is we have to ask a whole series of questions other than those about ratios or statutes.

In a similar fashion not everyone accepts that questions about the morality of law and questions about the content of law are different. For these people, the very idea of an immoral law, which is a law that, because it is immoral, should not be obeyed, is a contradiction in terms. They think that all law must have an irreducible minimum moral content. Without that content the "law," in their view, is merely a collection of words that make a command which may be backed by the physical power of the state but do not have the authority of law.

The authors of this book would accept that the distinctions drawn in previous sections are open to question. The relationship between the different questions, if there are different questions, may be more complicated than the simple divisions above. However most books and most courses in law draw the kinds of distinction outlined. At this early stage in your study of law it will be enough if you understand them. Even if later you come to reject all or some of them, you will still find yourself reading material which is based upon them.

ANSWERING QUESTIONS

This chapter has drawn a distinction between three types of question; those concerned with the nature of law, those concerned with the content of legal rules and those which address the operation of law and legal system in practice. Each type of question has a technique appropriate for answering it.

Questions about the nature of law are those which are most difficult to answer. The questions are basic ones, appearing to be very simple. For example, how is law different from other types of command? What is the difference between a gunman telling me to do something and the state, through law, telling me to do some thing? Are both simply applications of power or is there something fundamentally different between them? Neither the content of particular legal rules nor the operation of the law in practice provide any answer. Arguments in this area are abstract and philosophical. In advancing and judging such arguments it is necessary to see that all the terms are explained and that the argument is coherent. Arguments used here must also match the world they purport to explain. In practice these simple conditions are very difficult to meet.

The ultimate source for answers to questions about the law in books is the law reports and statutes which have already been discussed in Chapter 1. Only these sources will give you a definitive answer to any question you are asked. You are told how to find these materials in Chapter 4 and how to use them in Chapter 5. In some cases you may not have either the time or the resources to consult original materials. In such instance you can look at some of the various commentaries on the law. These vary in size, depth of coverage and price. Different commentaries serve different purposes. Some are student texts. Others are written for specific professions or occupations. Most cover only a limited area of law. However there are some general guides to the law and some encyclopedias of law. The best encyclopedia of general English law is Halsbury's Laws of England. This has a section on almost every area of law. Most good reference libraries will have a copy of this, and your library may also contain some of the other commentaries which are available. All commentaries try to explain legal rules. You should select one suitable to your interests. However, always remember that a commentary is one person's opinion about the law. It may be wrong. You can only be sure what the rule is if you consult the original cases and statutes.

Finding out how the law works in practice is frequently much more difficult than deciding what a legal rule means. It is easy to find opinions about how things work. Almost everybody who has contact with the law, even if only through reading about it in the newspapers, has an opinion on such questions. However, such opinions have little value. At best they are the experience of one person. That experience may be unusual or misinterpreted by that person. What we are trying to understand is how the legal system works, not the anecdotes of one person. Thus, to answer this kind of question, we need to turn to the materials and techniques of the social scientist.

SEEING THE LAW IN ACTION

One obvious source of detailed information about the legal system is statistical analyses. "You can prove anything with statistics" is a hostile comment suggesting that nothing at all can be proved with statistics. However, is this so? What use are statistics to anyone studying law?

Information about the number of cases handled by a court shows in specific terms what the court's workload is. Changes from year to year may indicate some effects of changes in the law and practice. Statistics here can be used descriptively to provide a clearer picture than general phrases such as "some," "many" or "a few." Statistical tests can also establish that there is a relationship, a correlation, between different things. For example, the length of a sentence for theft may correlate with the value of the items stolen or the experience of the judge who heard the case. This means that the sentence will be longer if, for example, more items are stolen or the judge is more experienced. Statisticians have produced tests to show whether, given the number of examples you have, there is a strong correlation or not. Where this correlation fits with a theory (sometimes termed a hypothesis) it provides evidence tending to confirm the theory. Such confirmation is important; without it we have little to establish the effect the law has, being forced to rely on personal knowledge of individual instances of its application and having to assume that these have general truth. Empirical study of the operation of law may reveal areas for improvement. It can also confirm that measured by particular standards, the court are working well.

If we want to use statistics where will we get them from? Government departments collect and print a large number of statistics relating to their operations. A comprehensive index to these, the Guide to Official Statistics, is published by the Office for National Statistics (ONS). Some of these official statistics provide background information for the study of the operation of law. Thus the ONS publishes details of the size, composition and distribution of the United Kingdom population. This information is essential if one is to be sure that other changes do not merely reflect population changes. The Department of Social Security provides figures for the number of social security claimants and the Department of Health provides figures for the number of children in the care of local authorities. The Home Office produces the annual criminal statistics as well as information about the police forces and immigration. The Lord Chancellor's Department produces the civil judicial statistics which contain figures for the work of the civil and all appellate courts. Most official statistics are collected from returns filed by local offices of the relevant departments. The content of these is determined by what the department needs to know about its activities and also by what Parliament has asked it to report on. Even minor changes in the collection of official statistics means that it is often impossible to make comparisons over a period of years. The information collected in one year is about something slightly different from that in other years. Moreover, because of the way in which information is collected and the purpose of collecting it, these statistics can only answer a few of the questions about the way the law operates. For example, the judicial statistics list the number of cases brought each year in the County Court, broken down according to the type of claim. They provide little or no information about the applicants, the specific point of law relied on or whether the judgment was successfully enforced.

Official statistics, as a source of information, are limited. They provide information about things of importance to those who collected them. These are not necessarily the things which are important to the researcher. Government departments, the research councils and some private bodies sponsor research into specific areas of law. Small scale research is often undertaken without sponsorship. Although this research may be based upon official statistics it may involve first collecting the necessary statistics and then deciding what they mean. The researchers must collect the data they need for each project. They have to design the study, that is to select the methods they will use and choose the sample to ensure that they have all the information relevant to their chosen topic. There is a more detailed discussion of some of these issues in Chapter 6, "Reading Research Materials"

The collection of statistics is only one way of describing law and the legal system. Statistics are useful for describing things like numbers of events but are poor for describing things like motivations. If researchers want to find out more about the reasons *why* the law affects people in certain ways, or *how* it affects them, they will have to carry out different types of research. This may involve interviewing people or even directly observing what is happening in the area in which they are interested. In each case the researchers must decide how they can carry out their research so as to ensure that the material they collect is an accurate reflection of the world as a whole.

Socio-legal research has enabled us to understand in a whole range of situations the way in which the law works in practice. It has revealed, for example, how barristers' clerks affect the working lives of barristers, why businesspeople often prefer to avoid taking their disputes to court, and how the practice of environmental health officers affects the way in which Local Authorities deal with industrial pollution. Socio-legal research offers us the opportunity to extend our knowledge of the law and the legal system far beyond the boundaries of the law in the books, showing us how legal rules are affected by the political, economic and social contexts in which law operates.

Whatever kind of question you are dealing with it is important that *you* decide what the answer is. Merely being able to repeat a passage from a book on legal philosophy, a paragraph from a judgement or the conclusion to a survey is not the same as knowing the answer. If you do not understand the answer you will neither be able to remember nor apply it.

PART 2

4 Finding cases and statutes

In Chapter 1 the importance of cases and statutes as sources of law was explained. This chapter explains how you find reports of cases and copies of statutes and how you make sure that they are up-to-date. Statutes and cases are sources of law, from them it is possible to derive the legal rules in which you are interested. Chapter 5 will explain in more detail how this is done.

FINDING CASES

The task of discovering case reports is considered here for three different sets of circumstances:

(a) Where a well-stocked and supported library is available.

(b) Where some research or library facilities are available, but without access to a fully-equipped law library

(c) With the aid of on-line computerised retrieval facilities.

Most readers will have different facilities available at different times. For example, a reader who has access to a fully-equipped law library can only use it during opening hours. Equally, even if computer facilities are available it may not always be appropriate to use them. It is important that you are aware of the different ways in which to find cases so that you can decide which is the best method to use at any particular time.

USING FULL LAW LIBRARY NON-ELECTRONIC RESEARCH FACILITIES

The traditional, and still the most comprehensive, form of research in relation to law reports is performed in law libraries containing a wide selection of materials and a variety of support systems, indexes, catalogues, access to databases, etc., designed to assist the researcher in the task of locating and using particular items. Such libraries are found in academic institutions, such as Universities, as well as in professional institutions such as the Inns of Court. In some cases, it is possible to use such libraries even if you are not a member of the institution. What follows in this chapter is an attempt to introduce the reader to the major series of law reports, and to indicate basic methods of locating and checking up-to-date material and of up-dating earlier materials. A helpful guide for those interested in more sophisticated use of the whole range of facilities made available in major law libraries is to be found in How to Use a Law Library, by J. Dane and P. Thomas. In particular, that work contains detailed explanations of how to use the various indexes and catalogues available in such libraries, and thus provides a more comprehensive guide on the "mechanics" of locating and using legal materials than is offered here. Law reports go back over 700 years, although most of the case reports you will find in a normal law library have been decided during the last 150 years. Reports are divided into different series. These series do not necessarily reflect any systematic attempt to present the reports of decided cases (e.g. by subject-matter covered), but tend, instead, to indicate the commercial means by which such reports have been made available. Thus, older cases can be found in series which bear the title of the name (or names) of the law reporter(s). Such a series is the nineteenth century series of Barnewall and Alderson (Bar & Ald). (All law reports have abbreviations which are used when discussing them. Whenever a series is first mentioned here its usual abbreviation will be given, in brackets, as above. Appendix II is a list of useful abbreviations, including those to the main law reports.) The range and variety of these older cases is enormous, although some help has now been provided to modern legal researchers with some of the old series reprinted in a collection under the title of The English Reports (E.R.). In 1865, the Incorporated Council of Law Reporting introduced The Law Reports, a series which was divided according to the different courts of the day. The Council has continued the current divisions of the reports, are different. Today one can find the following divisions:

(a) Appeal Cases (A.C.)—reports of cases in the Court of Appeal, the House of Lords and the Privy Council.

(b) Chancery Division (Ch.)—report of cases in the Chancery Division of the High Court and cases appealed from there to the Court of Appeal.

(c) Queen's Bench (Q.B.)—reports of cases in the Queen's Bench Division of the High Court and cases appealed from there to the Court of Appeal.

(d) Family Division (Fam.)—reports of cases in the Family Division of the High Court and cases appealed from there to the Court of Appeal. (Until 1972 the Family Division was the Probate, Divorce and Admiralty Division (P.).)

This series is the closest to an "official" series of case reports. If a case is reported in several different series and there is a discrepancy between the different reports it is The Law Reports which should normally be followed. There is, nowadays, a wide range of privately-published law reports. Most of these series concentrate upon a particular area of legal developments, (e.g., the law relating to industrial relations, or the law concerning road traffic). However, there are two series which publish cases dealing with decisions affecting a wide range of legal issues. These general series, with which most students of law will quickly become familiar, are the Weekly Law Reports (W.L.R.) and the All England Law Reports (All E.R.). Each of the series above reports fully any case contained in its volumes. There are, in addition, some sources which provide a short summary of, or extracts from, judgments given. In addition to these general series, it is possible to find short reports of case developments in a variety of sources. The most up-to-date of these sources are those newspapers which print law reports. Most of the quality daily newspapers contain law reports as well as news items on matters of legal interest. *The Times* has contained such reports for the longest time and is regarded as being the most authoritative source of such reports. Case-note sections published in legal periodicals, such as the New Law Journal (N.L.J.) or the Solicitors Journal (S.J. or Sol. Jo.), are also a good source of such summaries. There have always been specialist series of reports concerned either with one area of law or one type of occupation. In recent years, the numbers of such series has increased. If your interest is not in law as a whole but in particular areas of law, one of these series of reports may be a valuable tool. Indeed, sometimes such series are the only source for a report of a particular case. However, such series should be used with caution. First, these reports may not be as accurate as the series discussed above. Secondly, they represent not reports of the law but reports of such law as the publishers of the series think important. Their greater selectivity may be useful in giving you a guide as to what is important, but dangerous if you think cases not reported in the series must be irrelevant. Helpful lists of such reports can be found in law dictionaries.

USING LAW REPORTS

Every case which is reported in a series of law reports can be referred to by way of the names of the parties concerned in the action. Thus, where a court action is brought by somebody called Harriman in dispute with somebody called Martin, the case may be referred to as *Harriman v. Martin*. However referring to a case just by name does not tell the reader the date of the case nor does it indicate the series of where it can be found. There may be more than one case involving a Harriman and a Martin. Thus, in addition to its name, each reported case has a unique reference. This normally includes (although not always in the same order): A reference to

(1) The title of the series of law reports in which the report is found.

(2) A date (year) reference. Some series have a volume number for each year. Where the date reference tells you the year in which the case was reported the date is normally enclosed in square brackets.

(3) The volume number (if there is more than one volume of the particular law reports series in the year concerned).

(4) The page or paragraph number where the report of the case is located.

If the case of *Harriman v. Martin* is reported in the first volume of the Weekly Law Reports for 1962, at page 739, the reference would be [1962] 1 W.L.R. 739. This is sometimes called the case citation. Knowing this reference or citation, it is possible to go directly to the shelves of the law library find the volume and turn directly to the report of the case. If you know only the names of the parties in the case, you will need first to find the citation. Although each volume has an index, searching this way is inefficient and time-consuming. It is quicker to look in a general reference manual, known as a case citator. The commercial reference service Current Law provides the most widely used citator. Here is a brief description of the Current Law Case Citator. The Current Law Case Citator works through a combination of three separate reference items:

(1) Three hard-bound citators covering the periods 1947–1976 and 1977–1988 and 1989-1995.

(2) Laminated volumes covering the period from 1996 (a new, up-dated version of this volume is issued every year).

(3) "Monthly Parts," which are issued regularly in pamphlet form, for the current year. These are replaced by a volume for the year.

All three items complement one another to ensure up-to-date references are located (see below). Entries in the Current Law Case Citator are listed by title of case, arranged alphabetically. Thus, to find the law reports reference to the case of *Harriman v. Martin* you need to turn to the alphabetical heading under "Harriman".

This indicates: *Harriman v. Martin* [1962] 1 W.L.R. 739; 106 S.J. 507; [1962] 1 All E.R. 225, C.A . . . . Digested 61/1249: Referred to, 72/2355.

From this information, we discover not only the law reports reference to the first volume of the Weekly Law Reports for 1962, at page 739, but also that there are reports of the same case in:

106 S.J. 507 *i.e.* the 106th volume of the Solicitors Journal at page 507 and:
[1962] 1 All E.R. 225 *i.e.* the first volume of the All England Reports for 1962 at page 225.

We are also informed that the court which delivered the decision reported at those locations was:

C.A. *i.e.* the Court of Appeal.

Next, we are told that a "digest" (a brief summary) of the case has been included in a companion volume to the Current Law Case Citator at:

62/1249 *i.e.* in Current Law Year Book for 1962 at paragraph 1249.

Finally, we are told that the case was "referred to" (in another case) and that that case is to be found at:

72/2355 *i.e.* in Current Law year Book for 1972 at paragraph 2355.

It now only remains to find one of these volumes in the law library, and to turn to the right page for a report on the case of *Harriman v. Martin*. You can use this method to find an alternative reference for the case where someone else is using the volume of the report you need.

UP-DATING CASES

It is not enough to know merely what was said in a particular case in order to know its importance. It is also necessary to know whether a case has been used or referred to subsequently by the judges, or, indeed, whether it has been expressly approved or disapproved of by a later court. If a case is approved by a superior court (see the diagram on p. 7) (and that approval is part of the ratio of that later case) then the case will take on the status of the later decision. Thus a decision of the High Court approved by the Court of Appeal will take on the status of a Court of Appeal decision. Even if the approval forms part of the obiter within the later judgment this will be significant, indicating the way in which the court is likely to decide once the matter becomes central in a decision at that level. Disapproval of a case is similarly important. This information can be discovered by using the Current Law Case Citator. A case can be regarded as reliable (or, at least, not unreliable) where it has been "referred to," "considered," "explained," "followed," "approved" or "applied." On the other hand, considerable care must be taken with a case which has been "distinguished," while cases which have been "disapproved" or "overruled" are unlikely to prove reliable for future purposes.

Example

If, for example, in January 2000, we had looked for information on *Taylor v. Anderton* (which was decided in 1995), we would have found the following:

1. From the *Current Law Case Citator* for 1989–1995

Taylor v. Anderton (Police Complaints Authority Intervening); *sub nom.* Taylor v. Chief Constable of Greater Manchester [1995] 1 W.L.R. 447; [1995] 2 All E.R. 420; (1995) 139 S.J.L.B. 66; (1995) 92(11) L.S. Gaz 37; *The Times*, January 19, 1995; *The Independent*, February 28, 1995, C.A. . . . .
Digested, 95/4123

This tells us the various locations of reports of the case, as explained above. It also indicates that this case is reported under two different names. The court which decided the case is indicated (as explained previously) as C.A. (*i.e.* the Court of Appeal), and we are told there is a digest of the case in the *Current Law Year Book* for 1995 at para. 4123.

2. From the laminated volume *Current Law Case Citator* 1996-1997:

Taylor v. Anderton . . . *Applied* 96/1366; *Considered* 97/472

96/1366   *i.e.* a digest entry for the case of *R. v. Sec of State for Home Dept. ex parte Cleeland* for which there is no official report only a Crown Office (C.O.) transcript number.
97/472   *i.e.* a digest entry for the case of *Kelly v. Commissioner of Police for the Metropolis*, which is reported in *The Times*, August 20, 1997.

3. From the laminated volume *Current Law Citator* 1998:

The next thing to do is to consult any later volumes for the *Current Law Case Citator*. In our example, in January 2000, there is only the 1998 volume. There is no entry for *Taylor v. Anderton* in this volume so we can deduce that there was no mention of it in any case included in *Current Law* in 1998.

4. From the *Current Law Monthly Parts* for 1999:

Finally, in order to bring ourselves as up-to-date as possible using the *Current Law* system, we must look at the *Monthly Parts* for 1999. These are cumulative, *i.e.* in formation in the Table of Cases in the later Parts includes entries in any of the earlier

Parts for the same year. Cases which are included in the *Current Law* system in previous years are given in lower case, those recorded for the first time in capitals.

On looking at the December 1999 *Monthly Part* we find a reference:

Taylor v. Anderton [1995] 1 W.L.R. 447 . . . Jun 57.

We then need to consult the *Monthly Part* for June 1999 at paragraph 57.

—   *i.e.* a digest entry for *Goodridge v. Chief Constable of Hampshire* [1999] 1 All E.R. 896 a case where *Taylor v. Anderton* was applied.

USING LIMITED LIBRARY FACILITIES

The problems of finding and using cases and law reports where limited resources are available are significant. Clearly, it will not be possible to find reports of all the cases which you may need, since the available reports may only be found in series which are not at your disposal. By the same token, you may not have access to reference manuals, such as *Current Law Case Citator* or similar. You may have access to one of the general series of law reports. This will often be a set of All England Law Reports. Many public reference libraries possess a set of these law reports. If this is the case, some searching for cases can be done using the indexes contained in those volumes; though this will, of course, be time consuming. Alternatively, if you are concerned only with a limited specialist area you may have access to a specialised series of law reports. Whatever your source of available material, however, it is of paramount importance that you familiarise yourself with the specific indexing and cross-referencing system adopted by that source. If you do this, you will be able to use the material, in the most efficient manner. It will also be important to discover whether you can access some means for updating the material contained in your sources. The use of a citator, as explained above, is clearly of major benefit, for the consolidation of information within one reference item avoids the necessity of searching through a range of separate volumes and series. Amongst possible sources of updated information might be the general legal periodicals, such as the New Law Journal or the Solicitors Journal (both of which have been referred to above). Many public libraries subscribe to one of these, or to other relevant periodicals. Where your needs relate to a specific area, the periodicals available for that area may be of assistance in obtaining up-to-date information. For example, many personnel management journals contain information about employment law cases. All of these will probably refer you to sources of information which you do not have but they will also enable you to make the most efficient use of those sources which are available. A further common source of information will be text-books on the subject about which you are seeking information. The important rule here is to check that you have access to the most recent edition of the book, and to bear in mind that case-law may have developed after the date of the book was written. Most books dealing with the law will contain a statement in the "Foreword" stating the date on which the information given in the book is said to be current. You may have access to a case-book or cases and materials book. Such books are generally concerned with a specific topic, for example "contract law," and contain edited material relevant to the area. These books can be a very useful source where you have access only to limited library facilities. However, they suffer from several deficiencies. First, the reader relies on the editor of the volume to choose the material. The editor's reasons for selecting material may not fit your needs. Secondly, the material presented may only be given in part. Again, the reader must trust that the editor has not given misleading extracts. Finally, the reader has no means of up-dating the material. In some areas of law encyclopedias are produced. These are similar to case-books, although they are generally more detailed. Publishers of this kind of work often supply an up-dating service. Increasingly, encyclopedias are produced in a looseleaf form and the reader will substitute new pages as supplements are issued. (The use of encyclopedias is considered at the end of this chapter.)

USING ELECTRONIC RETRIEVAL FACILITIES

To complete this section on finding and using reports of cases, mention must be made of the important and fast-developing range of computerised databases.

"On-line" Services

There are two major, commercially marketed, legal databases which are widely used in universities and by practitioners, LEXIS and WESTLAW. LEXIS covers English case-law, materials from Commonwealth jurisdictions and some European materials. WESTLAW covers the USA but is being developed to include European and English materials. To use either of these systems effectively some training is necessary in the way the information contained is organised and the methods used to search them.

In general LEXIS and WESTLAW both contain the full text of cases but the format is somewhat different from that in traditional printed law reports. As well as providing access to a vast collection of published legal materials LEXIS and WESTLAW also include unreported cases *i.e.* cases which have yet to be included in law reports and cases for which there is no other full text report. However, in general cases are not included in published series of reports because they are of less significance.

The vast size and wide range of coverage of both LEXIS and WESTLAW does not mean that every search is conducted in the whole of the database. Rather, the user first selects which parts or libraries are to be used—thus, for example, the text of an English case will be found in the library of English cases not with American or European materials.

It should also be noted that a range of similar "on-line" services are available through various organisations which enable users to gain access to legal materials and case-law from many foreign systems and in a range of foreign languages. Searching for a case using an electronic retrieval system is done on the basis of selecting "key words." The user asks where a specific term or "string" of letters and/or numbers occurs in the database. The system indicates the number of cases in which that term or is to be found. The user can then narrow down the number of "responses", by further limiting the selected "key word". This is done by requesting the system to indicate where the original "key word" or "string" is to be found in conjunction with another "string." Eventually, the number of occasions on which the requested string or strings is to be found on the database will be small enough for the user to take a look at those instances which have been identified. At this stage, it is possible for the user to ask for the text of the reports containing the requested string(s) to be displayed on the screen. The full text of a law report may be requested, or there may just be a call for a selected portion of the report, such as the title, the decision, or the names of the lawyers acting in the case. Any information displayed on the user's computer screen can be printed simultaneously, and used as a record of the "search". It is possible to search on the basis of names, (*e.g.* asking for the occasions on which "Harriman" appears, with a view to locating the case of *Harriman v. Martin*) dates, courts, or subject-matter. The sophistication of any search under taken using this method depends in large measure upon the ability of the user to ask for matching of sufficiently specific and relevant "key words." Access to systems for on-line electronic retrieval of legal information offers the experienced user the possibility of making detailed and exhaustive searches in relation to known cases or around particular subject areas. It also makes possible speedy searches of law reports series, as well as offering access to the facilities of a large, well-equipped and constantly up-dated law library via the internet.

Cases on the net

There are many internet sites with discussions of law and legal issues; it is far easier to explore legal developments across the world via the internet than it was using only the printed word. Comprehensive services with the full text of a large number of cases are only available on subscription but there are free services which provide access to a more limited range of materials, including some full reports. It is also possible to follow news stories about legal issues via the internet. A wide range of materials relating to law is available on the British Government's web site:

www.open.gov.uk

This is arranged by department and organisation, *e.g.* the Home Office, the Lord Chancellor's Department and the Houses of Parliament. All decisions of the Judicial Committee of the House of Lords made since 1996 are published free on the internet on the day the judgment is given. They can be found at:

www.parliament.the-stationery-office.co.uk

A firm of law reporters, Smith Bernal, provides access to its Court of Appeal transcript archive which covers over 20,000 cases and is updated once a year. To find a case in this database you need to know its title, the number, the date or the court. This database can be found at:

www.smithbernal.com

Selected judgments from the Court of Appeal and the High Court are to be found at:

www.courtservice.gov.uk

Both *The Times* and the *Law Society Gazette* provide their law reports (usually edited versions) on their free web sites but these do not as yet contain archives of their older reports.

www.the-times.co.uk
www.lawgazette.co.uk

Cases of the European Court of Human Rights in Strasbourg are available on its website:

www.echr.coe.int

FINDING AND UP-DATING STATUTES

Statutes are published individually but law libraries and some large public libraries have bound collections which include all the statues for each year. Statues passed since 1995 are available on the internet at:

http://www.hmso.gov.uk/act/htm

With statutes there are three main problems. Is the statute in force? Has the statute been repealed by Parliament (*i.e.* replaced by some other statute)? Has the statute been amended by Parliament (*i.e.* had part of its contents altered by Parliament)? Having started out with a provision in an Act of Parliament (either in the form in which it was originally passed, or in a form amended subsequently and stated to be effective at a given date), it is necessary to use one of the "citator" systems in order to discover the most up-to-date changes (if any) which have affected that provision. There are several different ways of updating a statute, all of which are explained in detail in How to Use a Law Library. The following example shows how to update a relatively recent statutory provision using the Current Law Legislation Citator.

Let us take Children Act 1989, s.8(4). In its original form, this provision was set out as follows:

Residence, contact and other orders with respect to children

8.—(1) . . .

(2) . . .

(3) . . .

(4) The enactments are—

    (a) Parts I, II and IV of this Act;

    (b) the Matrimonial Causes Act 1973;

    (c) the Domestic Violence and Matrimonial Proceedings Act 1976;

    (d) the Adoption Act 1976;

    (e) the Domestic Proceedings and Magistrates' Courts Act 1978;

    (f) sections 1 and 9 of the Matrimonial Homes Act 1983;

    (g) Part III of the Matrimonial and Family Proceedings Act 1984.

If we assume that, in January 2000, we want to discover whether there have been changes to the wording of section 8(4) it is first necessary to turn to the volume of the *Current Law Legislation Citator* which covers the period following the enactment of the Children Act 1989. In January 2000 this was the volume for 1989–1995.

The *Current Law Legislation Citator* is arranged in chronological order, by year and then by Chapter number for each Act. Chapter numbers are fully explained at page 53 but briefly, they are a unique way of identifying a statute. Each statute has its own Chapter number. For the Children Act 1989 this is Chapter 41. To find whether there have been any amendments we turn to 1989, and eventually reach Chapter 41. We now need to look for our required provision (section 8). The entry gives us details of many cases but makes no reference to any amendments. Our search must be continued in later volumes.

In the *Current Law Legislation Citator* for 1996–1998 there are the following entries:

s.8, amended: 1996 c.27 Sch.8 para.41, Sch. 8 para.60.
s.8, repealed (in part): 1996 c. 27 Sch. 10.

The section was amended by Schedule 8 of the statute whose reference is 1996 Chapter 27. It was also repealed in part by Schedule 10 of the same statute.

We now need to continue our search beyond 1998 by checking the more recent volumes of the *Current Law Legislation Citator* so that we can make sure that we have the correct wording. By January 2000 there had been no further amendments of section 8.

Once we have a complete list of amendments we need to find the relevant provisions. We can find the names of the statutes either by looking at the relevant year volumes for statute series or by looking at the chronological index at the front of the *Current Law Statute Citator*.

Our search will lead us to discover that:

(1) section 8 has been amended by Schedule 8 paras 41 and 60 of the Family Law Act 1996.

(2) it was repealed in part by the Family Law Act 1996, sched 10.

We can now turn to the Family Law Act 1996 and find out the current wording of section 8(4):

Residence, contact and other orders with respect to children

8.—(1) . . .
(2) . . .
(3) . . .
(4) The enactments are—

(a) Parts I, II and IV of this Act;

(b) the Matrimonial Causes Act 1973;

(c)

(d) the Adoption Act 1976;

(e) the Domestic Proceedings and Magistrates' Courts Act 1978;

(f)

(g) Part III of the Matrimonial and Family Proceedings Act 1984.

(h) the Family Law Act 1996.

(5) . . .

We will also see that other amendments have been made to section 8(3) and a new subsection (5) has been added.

This method will not only allow us to see whether a statute has been amended. It will also enable us to find out if and when a statute has come into force. Thus, by using the method above, it is possible to see if a relevant "commencement order" has been made, or if part or all of a statute has been brought into effect by means of a Statutory Instrument. Finally, using the method above will also give us the citation of any case interpreting the section in the statute.

HOW TO USE ENCYCLOPEDIAS

Encyclopedias are not, in the strictest sense, a source of law (although they may contain sources of law). Cases and statutes are sources of law; judges use these to decide what the outcome of a case is to be. However, for some people encyclopedias will be the only material they have available. Different encyclopedias vary in form and content. They do not all contain the same kind of material nor are they ordered in the same way. Therefore it is not possible to give a series of rules saying how encyclopedias should be used. What follows are points that a reader should consider when first using any encyclopedia of law. The first thing to look at is the kind of material that the encyclopedia contains. One advantage of an encyclopedia can be that it brings together a wide variety of material about particular subject matter. Thus, you may find the encyclopedia which you are reading contains all the statutes in a particular area, all the statutory instruments, government circulars and other non-statutory material, references to relevant cases (with some description of their contents) together with some discussion of the application of legal rules in the area. On the other hand the encyclopedia may contain only some of the material or may extract some of it. For example, instead of having all of a statute you may find that you have only parts of it. Even if the encyclopedia claims to be fully comprehensive, remember that it is no more than a claim. The editors of the encyclopedia may feel that they have included all relevant statutes; others may disagree with them. It is always as important to be aware of what you do not know as what you do know. Relying on an encyclopedia means that there may be gaps in your knowledge of the particular area of law. However, you may have to rely on the encyclopedia because it is the only source available. Equally, you may find it quicker to use an encyclopedia and consider the advantage of speedy access more important than any element of doubt in your knowledge of the area. Most encyclopedias reproduce at least some of the material which they cover. They contain extracts of a statute, statutory instrument, or whatever, rather than the whole. Here the problem is that, in extracting their material, the editors of the encyclopedia limit your knowledge of the law. You rely on them to extract that which is relevant and cannot check the matter for yourself. As a source of law, the less comprehensive an encyclopedia is the less useful it will be. However, the more comprehensive an encyclopedia is the slower it may be to use. Before using the encyclopedia you need to consider the kind of question which you are trying to answer. If the question is a very broad and general one about the framework of some area of law you may find an encyclopedia with less detail easier to use. However, if you are trying to answer a very detailed point, perhaps applying the law to a very precise factual situation, you need the most comprehensive encyclopedia that you can find. Most encyclopedias, and increasingly many other books about law, are now issued in looseleaf form. This means that the publisher issues supplements to the encyclopedia on a regular basis. These supplements, which contain descriptions of changes in the law, are then substituted for the pages which discuss the out-of-date law. The advantage of the looseleaf form over ordinary books is that it means the encyclopedia is more likely to be accurate. When using looseleaf encyclopedias check when it was last up-dated. You will usually find a page at the front of the first volume of the encyclopedia gives you this information. The technique for finding out about points of law in an encyclopedia will vary depending upon the encyclopedia being used. Some are organised according to different areas of law within the subject of the encyclopedia. Others have different volumes for different kinds of material; one volume for statutes, one for discussion of the law and so forth. Most will have both indexes and detailed contents pages. Most encyclopedias have a discussion of how they should be used at the beginning of their first volume. Always consult this when first using an encyclopedia. The development of electronic sources is also changing the way legal encyclopaedias are accessed. A law library may not have a copy of a particular encyclopaedia but instead but instead subscribe to a service which enables it to be accessed and searched via the internet.

FINDING AND USING MATERIAL ON THE LAW OF THE EUROPEAN COMMUNITIES, THE EUROPEAN UNION, AND THE EUROPEAN ECONOMIC AREA

All basic material in relation to the European Communities, the European Union, and the European Economic Area is published in English. However, some material is not made available in all of the official languages of the European Communities immediately. What is said here refers specifically to English language versions of such material. The Official Journal of the European Communities is the authoritative voice of the European Communities, and is used to publish daily information. The Official Journal (the O.J.) is divided into two major parts (the L and C series). There are also separately published notices of recruitment, notices and public contracts and the like, which are published in a Supplement and in Annexes. Twice a year the O.J. issues a Directory of Community legislation in force and other acts of the Community institutions.

LEGISLATION

The L series (Legislation) contains the text of Community legislation. The series is arranged by Volume, starting in 1958, and by issue number sequentially throughout the issue year. Thus, the text of Council Directive 95/45 of September 22, 1994 on the establishment of a European Works Council or a procedure in Community-scale undertakings and Community-scale groups of under takings for the purposes of informing and consulting employees is to be found in the Official Journal of September 30, 1994.

The Volume number for 1994 is Volume 37.

The issue number of the OJ L series for September 30, 1994 is L254.

The text of the Directive is set out on page 64 and thus the page reference is p. 64.

The official reference for the Directive will be OJ No L254, 30.9.1994, p. 64.

INFORMATION AND NOTICES

The C series (Information and Notices) contains, amongst a host of other items, key extracts ("the operative part") from judgments of the Court of Justice of the European Communities (the ECJ, sitting in Luxembourg) and the Court of First Instance (which also sits in Luxembourg). Where the language of the particular court being reported is not English, the C series will include a "provisional translation": the definitive translation being found in the separately published Reports of Cases before the Court. There is also brief coverage of actions brought before the ECJ by Member States against the Council of the European Communities, as well as questions referred to the ECJ by national courts of Member States. Also, to be found in the C series will be Preparatory Acts in the course of being made into legislation by the European Communities. Thus, for example, the Official Journal for February 19, 1994 contains the text of an Opinion delivered by the Economic and Social Committee on a proposal for a Council Regulation on substances that deplete the ozone layer.

The Volume Number for 1994 is Volume 37

The issue of the OJ C series for February 19, 1994 is C 52
The text of the proposed Decision is item 3 in issue C 52, and so the reference is 03
The full reference for the Opinion is OJ 94/C 52/03.

OTHER MATERIALS

Whilst the Official Journal is the best official source of information about Community law it should be noted that a wide range of documentation does not find its way into the Official Journal and other sources may have to be considered for those wanting a comprehensive list of European materials. Other materials in particular, mention should be made of so-called "COM" documents, which often contain important proposals for future legislation. These are issued by the Commission with a "rolling" numerical reference by sequence of publication during a particular year. Consequently, there is no systematic numbering of such "COM Docs" a matter which frequently gives rise to criticism about the accessibility of important documentation in the legislative field. By way of example, an important recent Communication concerning the application of the Agreement on social policy, presented by the Commission to the Council and to the European Parliament on December 14, 1993, is simply designated:

COM(93) 600 final.

Where quotations "COM Docs" are proposed legislation they will appear in the Official Journal C series but the "COM Doc" also includes an explanatory text.

Various other series, apart from the "COM" series, are also to be found in relation to a range of spheres of activity within the European Communities. Judgments of the European Court of Justice are reported in two series of law reports. One series is that "formally" published by the European Communities itself the European Court Reports (E.C.R.). The other series is the privately produced Common Market Law Reports (C.M.L.R.). Both can be found in the normal manner. In addition to these specialised law reports series, an increasing number of judgments delivered by the European Court of Justice are now reported as a normal part of general law report series.

EUROPEAN COMMUNITY MATERIALS ON THE INTERNET

The official internet site of the European Community is found at:

europa.eu.int

From here it is possible to access all the institutions of the European Union in any of the official languages of the European Union. The Official Journal (O.J.), the Reports of the European Court of Justice and the European Parliament can all be found at this site. A useful way of finding legislation is to access the "legislative observatory" of the European Parliament.

COMMUNITY LEGISLATION TRANSPOSED INTO UNITED KINGDOM LAW

Where the European Community legislation has been transposed into United Kingdom law by means of Statutory Instruments (S.I.s), it is possible to discover the relevant references by using the *Current Law* system. The *Current Law Statutory Instrument Citator* is contained in a bound volume with the *Legislation Citator.* Appendix 3 covers Statutory Instruments enforcing European legislation from 1989 to 1995. Subsequent years are covered in the laminated volumes.

Since the method of accessing these provisions is from the starting point of the United Kingdom Statutory Instrument reference, the facility is of limited usefulness. In order to discover whether a particular piece of Community legislation has been transposed into United Kingdom law by a Statutory Instrument, it is necessary to read through all of the references until reaching the relevant title of the Community legislation. Nevertheless, this is one of the few generalised methods of linking Community legislation with the relevant United Kingdom counterpart, and will doubtless be improved as researchers increasingly attempt to make use of the *Current Law* facility.

An alternative method of finding the relevant Statutory Instruments is via the Web:

www.legislation.hmso.gov.uk

This site includes UK Statutes and Statutory Instruments and can be searched using a key word for the topic sought.

5 | Reading cases and statutes

This chapter will explain how you should use the primary sources for legal rules, cases and statutes. You will find a specimen case report and a specimen statute in each section. In addition, there are further examples of case reports in the exercise section of this book (Cases I and II). Skill in the use of the techniques described here can only be acquired with practice. For this reason the exercises in Part III of the book enable you to build a range of experience in handling the material contained in cases and statutes.

READING A CASE

The contents of law reports are explained here so that you can start to read cases, understand the law which they contain, and make useful notes about them. You will find the court structure, and how cases are decided, explained in Chapter 1. You will find a copy of a case, *R. v. Jackson*, on pp. 42–44. All specific references in this section will be to that case. The copy is taken from the All England Law Reports, which are the most commonly available law reports. However, if you have access to other kinds of law reports you will find that they look very much the same as the All England Law Reports. By way of example, in the exercises section of this book there are also to be found law reports taken both from the Court Service internet site (in transcript form) and from a law reports series known as the Industrial Cases Reports. The techniques discussed here will be just as useful in reading other series of law reports and court transcripts. The different series of law reports and their use has been explained in Chapter 4.

The case is the criminal law case of *R. v. Jackson*. Lawyers pronounce this "Regina (or "The Queen" or "King", or "The Crown") against Terry". Most criminal cases are written like this. In civil cases, the names of the parties are usually given, as in *Donoghue v. Stevenson*, the case being pronounced "Donoghue and Stevenson".

R v Jackson

a

COURT OF APPEAL CRIMINAL DIVISION
ROSE L.J., BUTTERFIELD AND RICHARDS JJ
28 APRIL, 1998

Criminal law—Appeal—Leave to appeal—Practice—Single judge granting leave on b
some grounds but refusing leave on others—Need for leave of full court to pursue
grounds in respect of which leave refused.

Where, on an application for leave to appeal to the Court of Appeal, Criminal
Division, the single judge grants leave on some grounds but specifically refuses leave
on others, counsel for the appellant must obtain the leave of the full court if he   c
wishes to pursue the grounds in respect of which leave has been refused (see
p. 574g. post).

Notes
For appeal against conviction or sentence following trial on indictment, see 11(2)   d
Halsbury's Laws (4th edn reissue) paras 1352, 1355.

Cases referred to in judgment
R v Bloomfield [1997] 1 Cr App R 135, CA.
R v Chalkley, R v Jeffries [1998] 2 All ER 155, [1998] QB 848, [19983] WLR 146, CA.

e

Appeal against conviction
Stephen Shaun Jackson appealed with leave of the single judge against his
conviction on 25 July 1995 in the Crown Court at Croydon before Judge Crush
and a jury of theft. The facts are set out in the judgment of the court.

Marc Willers (assigned by the *Registrar of Criminal Appeals*) for the appellant.   f
Hugh Davies (instructed by the *Crown Prosecution Service*, Croydon) for the Crown.

ROSE LJ delivered the following judgment of the court. On 25 July 1997 in the
Crown Court at Croydon, this appellant was convicted by the jury of theft, on the
first count in the indictment. He was acquitted of charges of false accounting on
counts 2, 3 and 4. The trial was a retrial, the jury on an earlier occasion having   g
acquitted in relation to certain counts on the then indictment, but failed to agree
in relation to the counts upon which the second jury adjudicated. He appeals
against his conviction by leave of the single judge, which was granted in relation
to the first of the two matters which Mr Willers, on behalf of the appellant, seeks
to canvass before this court.   h
   For the purposes of this appeal, the facts can be briefly stated. The appellant
was the proprietor of a minicab firm. Insurance brokers, Thompson Heath &
Bond (South East) Ltd (to whom we shall refer as 'THB') devised a scheme to
enable minicab drivers to pay for their motor insurance by instalments. That
scheme was underwritten by others.   j
   The scheme allowed the premiums to be collected from the minicab drivers on
a weekly basis, and passed on to THB each month. THB then paid the
underwriters.
   It was the Crown's case against the appellant that, while he acted as agent for
THB, to collect weekly premiums from the drivers, between February 1991 and
March 1994, he failed to declare to THB the full amount that he had collected,

a and that he kept a sum of money, in the region of £100,000, for himself and spent much of it on luxury items for his own benefit.

While he was acting in this way, the appellant, it was common ground, devised a form called a Bank 1 form, on which to record payments made by him to THB. At the original trial, the judge had ordered disclosure of Bank 1 forms by the prosecution but, save for one example of such a form, which was in the

b appellant's possession at the time of the first trial, no such disclosure had been made. Between the first trial and the retrial, however, those documents, which had apparently been in the possession not of the prosecuting authorities but of THB, were disclosed to the defence and were available to them at the time of the retrial.

A submission was made to the trial judge, Judge Crush, by Mr Willers then, as now, appearing for the defendant, that the second trial should be stayed as an

c abuse of the process of the court. The ground of that submission was that it would not be fair to try the appellant a second time, because the Bank 1 forms had not been available during the first trial and, if they had been, the first jury might have acquitted. The learned judge rejected that submission. That rejection forms the ground of appeal in relation to which the single judge gave leave and which Mr

d Willers has placed in the forefront of his argument in this court.

Mr Willers accepts that, although the judge at the first trial ordered disclosure and no disclosure took place, that was because the documents had simply not at that stage been found, although they were in the possession of THB.

Mr Willers did not, during the course of the first trial, make any further application, non-disclosure not having been made, either for the jury to be

e discharged, or otherwise.

Mr Willers does not suggest that, at the first trial or subsequently, there was any bad faith on the part of the prosecution in relation to the non-disclosure. He submits that, during the cross-examination of Det Sgt James at the second trial, it emerged that he had left with THB the responsibility for looking through the vast

f number of documents and passing to the police those which they thought relevant. Although Mr Willers does not suggest that gave rise to bad faith by the officer, he submits that it would have been better had the officer looked through the documents himself.

By the time of the second trial, however, Mr Willers accepts that the defence had all the documentation that they required, including all the Bank 1 forms. But,

g he submits, if there was a real possibility of acquittal at the first trial had those forms then been available, it was unfair for the second trial to take place, and the judge should have acceded to the defence application to stay the second trial for abuse of process.

Mr Willers accepted that his submission came to this that, despite the fact that

h all the relevant material was before the second jury who convicted, this court, in ruling upon the safety of that conviction, should speculate that the first jury, faced with all the relevant material, might have acquitted; and therefore it was unfair to proceed with the second trial. Mr Willers referred to the decision of this court in *R v Chalkley, R v Jeffries* [1998] 2 All E.R. 155, [1998] QB 848. In the course of

j giving the judgment of the court in that case, Auld LJ commented, adversely, on an earlier decision of this court, differently constituted, in *R v Bloomfield* [1997] 1 Cr App R 135, which had attracted some criticism from the editors of the third supplement to *Archbold's Criminal Pleading, Evidence and Practice* (1997 edn) para 7–45. We make that comment because the argument originally advanced in skeleton form on behalf of the appellant relied, in part, on this court's decision in *R v Bloomfield*.

On behalf of the Crown, Mr Davies submits that the safety of the appellant's *a* conviction depends on the evidence at the second trial, which was followed by an admirably succinct summing up by the learned judge, following a trial which, for reasons which are not manifest, had lasted a considerable number of weeks.

Mr Davies draws attention, in relation to the safety of that conviction, to a number of letters written by the appellant after these apparent defalcations came to light, the first of them, it was common ground, on 21 March 1994 to a man *b* called Andrew Orchard. That letter was written on the day that the defendant left this country, for a period of some seven months in the Canary Islands. The appellant also wrote letters to his sister, Jackie, and to his partner, David. Each of those letter, in various ways, comprises a series of admissions of criminal mis- behaviour of present materiality, coupled with expressions of regret. In the course of the thal, the appellant sought to explain those letters away on the basis of a state of *c* confused mind when he had written them.

In our judgment, it is wholly impossible to accept Mr Willers' submission either that the judge was wrong to rule as he did in refusing a stay, or that that refusal gives rise to any lack of safety in this appellant's conviction. It frequently happens that new evidence comes to light between the time of a first trial when a jury *d* disagrees and a second trial. Such evidence may be favourable to the prosecution or to the defence. But the verdict of the second jury does not become unsafe because it was unfair for there to be a second trial. Indeed, pursuing Mr Willers' argument to its logical conclusion, wherever fresh evidence appears between a first and second trial, it would be unfair, at least if the evidence assisted the defence, to have a second trial at all. That is a submission which we roundly reject. *e* The learned judge was, in our view, correct to refuse the stay on the basis of the application made to him. That refusal, in the light of the overwhelming evidence before the second jury, cannot, in any event, be regarded as rendering the verdict of the second jury unsafe.

The second matter which Mr Willers sought to canvass related to a criticism of the *f* learned judge's direction in relation to dishonesty and the character of the defence case. It is said that the judge misdirected the jury and failed to put the defence case adequately in relation to the way in which money was spent on luxuries.

It is fair to say that Mr Willers sought the leave of this court to pursue the interrelated grounds in relation to that aspect of the case, the learned single judge having refused leave to argue those grounds. For the avoidance of doubt, where, *g* in granting leave to appeal on some grounds, the single judge has specifically refused leave to appeal on other grounds, the leave of this court is required before counsel may argue those other grounds. As we have said, Mr Willers sought the leave of this court. We have read the passage in the summing up in the transcript of which he complains. It is to be noted that, in answer to a question from the *h* jury, the judge gave a dear direction as to dishonesty, relevant to this case, in identical terms to that which he had given at the outset of his summing up.

Nothing in the passage of the summing up about which complaint is made, in our view, renders it arguable that there was any misdirection. Accordingly, as to that aspect of the case, we refused leave to pursue an appeal on that basis. *j*

For the reasons given, this appeal is dismissed.

Appeal dismissed.

Carlone Stomberg   Barrister.

Underneath the name of the case at "**a**" you will see three pieces of information. First, you are told the court in which the case was heard. In this case, it was the Court of Appeal, Criminal Division. It is important to know which court heard a case because of the doctrine of precedent (see pages 6–8 for an explanation of the doctrine of precedent).

The report then gives the names of the judges who took part in the case. This information is used to help evaluate the decision. Some judges are known to be very experienced in particular areas of law. Their decisions may be given extra weight. Finally, you are told when the cases was heard and when the court gave its decision. In the House of Lords this process is called "delivering opinions", but in other courts it is known as "giving judgment".

The material in italics, at "**b**" on the first page of the report, is written by the editor of the report. It indicates the subject-matter of the case and the issue which it concerned. The subject index at the front of each volume of law reports includes a similar entry under the first words.

The next section , at "**c**", is called the *headnote*. It is not part of the case proper, and is prepared by the law reporter, not by the judges. The headnote should summarise the case accurately giving references to important parts of the court's opinion or judgment and any cases cited. Because it is written when the case is reported, the headnote may stress or omit elements of the case which are later thought to be important. Therefore, care should be taken when using the headnote.

The notes, just below "**d**", direct the reader to appropriate volumes of *Halsbury's Laws of England* and/or *Halsbury's Statutes of England*. *Halsbury's Laws* is an encyclopedia of law and provides a concise statement of the relevant law, subject by subject, including references to the main cases and statutes. *Halsbury's Statutes* gives the complete text of all statutes together with annotations which explain them. Although law students and others may need to research the law using *Halsbury* it is not necessary to turn to reference works when reading every case. In most instances, the background law will be sufficiently explained by the judge. In our case of *R. v. Jackson* the reference is confined to *Halsbury's Laws*.

At "**e**" there is a list of all the cases referred to by the judge. Where counsel have cited additional cases to which the judges did not refer, this will be given in a separate list under the heading "cases also cited".

At "**e**" to "**f**" you will find a full history of the proceedings of the case. This indicates all the courts which have previously considered the case before the present one. The final sentence of this section indicates where a full account of the facts of the case may be found.

Below "**f**" you will find the names of the counsel (the barristers) who appeared in the case. In the case of *R. v. Jackson* the barristers on both sides were what are known as "junior counsel". Senior counsel are called "Q.C.s" (Queen's Counsel), or "K.C.s" (King's Counsel) when the monarch is a King.

Not all series of law reports have marginal letters as this one does. When they do, these letters can be used to give a precise reference to any part of the case. Thus, the beginning of Lord Justice Rose's judgment is [1999] 1 All E.R. 572g.

Whilst the matters above provide an introduction to the case, the substance is to be found in the judgments. Every law case raises a question or series of questions to be answered by the judge(s). In civil cases, some of these will be questions of fact (in criminal cases these will be answered by the jury). For example, it may be necessary to know at what speed a car was travelling when an accident occurred. In practice, the answers to these factual questions are very important. Once they have been settled, the legal issues in the case may be simple. However, when it comes to the study of law, it is only the legal questions which matter.

For the judge(s) in a case, therefore, there are two clearly distinguishable processes which have to be gone through when hearing the matter and reaching a judgment. First, there is the process of making "findings of fact". Then, in the light of those findings of fact, there is the process of making "findings on the law". The key questions which are posed to the judge(s) in this context are referred to as "the issues in the case".

Lawyers and students of law are concerned primarily not with the outcome of a case but with the reasoning which the judge gave for the conclusion. The reasoning is important because within it will be found the *ratio decidendi* (often referred to simply as "the ratio"). The ratio is that part of the legal reasoning which is essential for the decision in the case. It is the ratio which is binding under the doctrine of precedent and which is thus part of the law. The ratio and the reasons for the decision are not necessarily the same thing. Not all of the reasons given for the decision will be essential. In courts where there is more than one judge, each may give a separate judgment (as can be seen from the examples in the exercises section of this book). If they do, each judgment will have its own reasons, and thus its own ratio. The judges must agree a conclusion to the case (although they may do so only by majority). However, they do not have to have the same reasons for their decision. If they have different reasons the judgments have different ratios and, thus, the case itself may have no ratio. Lawyers will rarely agree that a case has no ratio at all.

Finding the ratio in a case is crucial. It is also the most difficult part of reading cases, particularly when the case involves several judgments. The ratio is the essence of the case and, thus, may not be found simply by quoting from a judgment. Discovering the ratio involves skills of interpretation—understanding and explaining what judges meant, how they reached their conclusions—in order to see the common ground. Although the ratio is the law, it cannot be divorced entirely from the facts. Facts which are essential for a decision provide the conditions for the operation of the rules and are, thus, part of the rule itself. Deciding which are essential, as opposed to subsidiary, facts takes skill and practice. Lawyers frequently disagree on exactly what the ratio to a decision is. Some, for example, may view it broadly, seeing the decision as having few conditions but laying down a general rule. Others may take a narrower approach, suggesting that only in very limited circumstances would a decision bind a future court. Subsequent cases often help to clarify what the ratio of a previous case is accepted as being.

The editors of a law report write what they consider the ratio to be in the headnote. They may be wrong. Even if their interpretation is plausible when they write it, a later case may take a different view. For these reasons, statements of law in the headnote cannot be relied on.

If we look at *R. v. Jackson* we can see that some of the things that we are told in the judgment are irrelevant for the purposes of constructing the ratio. The case before the Court of Appeal concerns a question relating to "leave to appeal". Thus, for example, the fact that the accused collected money on a weekly basis, rather than monthly, is of no account. Similarly, the fact that he failed to declare to the insurance brokers the full amount that he had collected is not significant for the purposes of the Court of Appeal on the question concerning "leave to appeal". However, for the original trial judge in the Crown Court, when the charges brought against the accused were of "false accounting", this would have been a very significant matter.

You will see that in the case of *R. v. Jackson* Lord Justice Rose (Rose L.J.) delivers a judgment which is the "judgment of the court". This therefore reflects the shared views of himself, Lord Justice Butterfield and Lord Justice Richards. You should compare this with the judgments and opinions set out in the cases contained in the Exercises at Part III of this book. Having set out the history of the case (at page 572g–h), Lord Justice Rose then gives a brief outline of the relevant facts for the purposes of the appeal (at page 572h–573d). This is followed by a summary of the submissions made by the counsel for each party (at page 573d–574c). You will see that counsel are said to have "submitted" certain things and to have "accepted" other matters during the course of their arguments before the Court of Appeal. Having dealt with these matters by way of preliminary presentation, Lord Justice Rose then moves on to the conclusions of the Court of Appeal. It is here that we look for the reasons and the ratio in the case.

The first matter considered (set out at page 574c–e) is the court's view on a proposition put by counsel for the appellant. You will gather that the Court of Appeal has little sympathy for the argument put forward, and in quite strong terms (at page 574e) "roundly rejects" the proposition that "wherever fresh evidence appears between a first and second trial, it would be unfair, at least if the evidence assisted the defence, to have a second trial". This leads the Court of Appeal to the conclusion that (i) the trial judge acted correctly in refusing to "stay" the trial of the accused, and (ii) anyway, given the evidence before the second jury in this case, that the verdict of that second jury could not be regarded as in any way "unsafe" (see page 574e–f). These conclusions are specific to this case, although the first one follows from the view expressed by the court on counsel's (roundly rejected) proposition. The narrow ratio of the case may thus be discovered by looking at that view, which was essential for reaching the eventual decision delivered by the Court of Appeal.

However, it is the "second matter" dealt with by the Court of Appeal which has drawn the attention of the law report editor to this case. At page 574f–g you will see that the court is faced with a question of what permission (or "leave") is required in order for an appeal to be made against particular aspects of a case. The eventual decision of the Court of Appeal (not to allow an appeal to be pursued on the basis of an alleged misdirection in the trial judge's summing up) is set out at page 574j, and the reasons for arriving at this decision are explained at page 574h. However, in order to reach that decision, the court has had to decide in what circumstances an appeal such as this may or may not be pursued. In this case the Court of Appeal goes further than to pronounce merely in relation to the specific case before it, relating to Jackson, the accused. Here, the court makes a general statement "for the avoidance of doubt", which is intended to clarify the situation for all future cases where this issue arises (set out at page 574g–h). That ratio, indeed, is also the part of the judgment which has been extracted by the editor of the law reports series to form the headnote which we have already looked at (at page 572c).

R. v. Jackson contains only a single judgment. That judgment is a short one. If one had a longer judgment (and most judgments are longer) or multiple judgments in the same case, the task of constructing a ratio would be much more difficult. When one has to consider one judgment and its obscurities in the light of other judgments the process of analysing the law becomes even more uncertain. In order to appreciate some of the problems of constructing a ratio in a less straightforward case, therefore, you should apply the techniques discussed here to the law reports contained in the exercises section of this book.

A court must follow the ratio of any relevant case which is binding on it under the doctrine of precedent. Thus, the question arises, when is a case relevant? A case in the same area must be followed unless it can be "distinguished" on the basis of its facts. If the facts of the case cannot be distinguished—if, as it is commonly put, the case is "on all fours"—then it must be followed. The process of distinguishing cases is really just another way of deciding what the ratio of the case is. If the material facts necessary for the operation of the legal rule in the first case are not found in the second, or are different, there is no precedent. Just as lawyers differ about what the ratio to a case is, so they differ about whether a case is binding in a particular situation or not. Indeed, it is suggested by some commentators that judges sometimes distinguish cases on "flimsy grounds" simply to avoid having to follow precedents which they find unwelcome.

That in the judgment which is not part of the ratio of the case is said to be the *obiter dictum*. This is usually referred to as the *"Obiter"*. Obiter is said to have "persuasive authority". That which was said obiter in a court such as the House of Lords may be very persuasive indeed for a relatively inferior court such as a County Court. Moreover, remarks made obiter may indicate which way the law is developing, or which kinds of arguments judges find particularly persuasive. Equally, judges are not always very careful about differentiating between ratio and obiter.

The remainder of this section provides some guidance on how to study cases. The first question a student should ask about a case is "Why has this case been set?". The purpose of studying cases is to obtain an understanding of the relevance of the case to the area of law being studied. Some cases will be more important than others. A leading House of Lords decision will require more time and closer examination than a decision which is merely illustrative of a point mentioned in a lecture or included in a problem. Where a case has developed or defined an area of law it is usually helpful to start by reading what the textbook writers say about it. Where more than one case has to be read on the same point of law, they should, if possible, be read in chronological order and each one digested before moving on to the next. If the subject under consideration is not an area of substantive law, such as tort or contract, but procedure or precedent, different aspects of the case will be important. In reading the case it is essential that the relevance of the case is borne in mind.

A second question to ask when reading cases is, "How much time is available?" Try to spend more time on important decisions and important judgments, even if you have to rely on a headnote or a textbook when it comes to the others. Do not spend the greater proportion of your time reading cases which have been overruled or which have novel or interesting facts but no new point of law. The headnote is helpful when allocating time. Treat judgments in the same way as you treat cases. Do not waste your time reading judgments which merely repeat something you have already read. Spend more time on the leading judgments than on the others. Again, the headnote will be helpful for this. Some judgments are more clearly written than others. Some judgments are shorter than others. Neither clarity nor brevity necessarily means that the judgment is more important. Choose what you read because it is the best for your purposes, not because it is the easiest!

Notes on any case should start with the case name and any references. They should then include:

(1) a brief statement of the facts of the case;

(2) the history of the case;

(3) the point of law under consideration;

(4) the decision with the reasons for it, together with any names of cases relied upon.

One side of A4 paper should provide enough space for this basic information, leaving the reverse side free for individual notes form judgments and, where necessary, any comments. Some students prefer to keep notes of cases on file cards. These are easier to refer to quickly, but less can be put on them.

When reading judgments in order to make notes, look for agreement and disagreement on each of the points relevant to your study. It is often useful to make separate notes on each of the points raised by the case and then see what different judges said about them. In particular, too, do not forget to make it clear in your notes whether a judge was dissenting or not.

You can get practice in distilling notes for your own purposes by working with the law reports set out in the exercises section of this book (Cases I and II).

HOW TO READ A STATUTE

This section will explain how you should read statutes. The way in which statutes are created is explained on pages 4–5. Looking for a particular legal rule in a statute can be confusing. Some statutes are over 100 pages long, although most are shorter. The language they use often appears complicated and obscure. If you understand the structure of a statute and follow a few simple rules in reading them, statutes will become much clearer.

A copy of a statute, the House of Lords Act 1999, is reproduced below. All subsequent references here are to this statute.

You can find statutes in a number of different ways. Not all of the statutes which you find will look the same as the one which we have reproduced for you. One way to find a statute is to buy it from Her Majesty's Stationery Office, the official stockist for Government publications, or one of its agents. These copies look much the same as the one which we have reproduced, but they have, in addition, a contents list at the beginning. This is also the case in relation to statutes which you may find on the internet—principally at the website of Her Majesty's Stationery Office (HMSO) at *http://www.hmso.gov.uk*. The House of Lords Act 1999, for example, could be downloaded from the internet at *http://www.hmso.gov.uk/acts/acts1999/19990034.htm*. Statutes are also printed in a number of different series with different volumes for each year. The copy of the House of Lords Act 1999 which you are referring to is taken from such a series published by the Incorporated Council of Law Reporting. Some series of statutes are printed in an annotated form. This means that the statute is printed with an accompanying explanatory text, telling you what the statute does. If you use an annotated statute, remember that only the words of the statute are definitive. The explanatory text, although often helpful, is only the opinion of the author.

c. 34

ELIZABETH II

House of Lords Act 1999

①

1999 Chapter 34

②

An Act to restrict membership of the House of Lords by virtue of a hereditary peerage; to make related provision about disqualifications for voting at elections to, and for membership of, the House of Commons; and for connected purposes.

③

[11th November 1999]

④

BE IT ENACTED by the Queen's most Excellent Majesty, by and with the advice and consent of the Lords Spiritual and Temporal, and Commons, in this present Parliament assembled, and by the authority of the same, as follows:—

⑤

1. No-one shall be a member of the House of Lords by virtue of a hereditary peerage.

Exclusion of hereditary peers.

⑥

Exception from section 1.

2.—(1) Section 1 shall not apply in relation to anyone excepted from it by or in accordance with Standing Orders of the House.

(2) At any one time 90 people shall be excepted from section 1; but anyone excepted as holder of the office of Earl Marshal, or as performing the office of Lord Great Chamberlain, shall not count towards that limit.

(3) Once excepted from section 1, a person shall continue to be so throughout his life (until an Act of Parliament provides to the contrary).

(4) Standing Orders shall make provision for filling vacancies among the people excepted from section 1; and in any case where—

(a) the vacancy arises on a death occurring after the end of the first Session of the next Parliament after that in which this Act is passed, and
(b) the deceased person was excepted in consequence of an election,

that provision shall require the holding of a by-election.

(5) A person may be excepted from section 1 by or in accordance with Standing Orders made in anticipation of the enactment or commencement of this section.

(6) Any question whether a person is excepted from section 1 shall be decided by the Clerk of the Parliaments, whose certificate shall be conclusive.

Removal of disqualifications in relation to the House of Commons.

3.—(1) The holder of a hereditary peerage shall not be disqualified by virtue of that peerage for—

(a) voting at elections to the House of Commons, or
(b) being, or being elected as, a member of that House.

(2) Subsection (1) shall not apply in relation to anyone excepted from section 1 by virtue of section 2.

Amendments and repeals.

4.—(1) The enactments mentioned in Schedule 1 are amended as specified there.

(2) The enactments mentioned in Schedule 2 are repealed to the extent specified there.

Commencement and transitional provision.

5.—(1) Sections 1 to 4 (including Schedules 1 and 2) shall come into force at the end of the Session of Parliament in which this Act is passed.

(2) Accordingly, any writ of summons issued for the present Parliament in right of a hereditary peerage shall not have effect after that Session unless it has been issued to a person who, at the end of the Session, is excepted from section 1 by virtue of section 2.

(3) The Secretary of State may by order make such transitional provision about the entitlement of holders of hereditary peerages to vote at elections to the House of Commons or the European Parliament as he considers appropriate.

(4) An order under this section—

(a) may modify the effect of any enactment or any provision made under an enactment, and
(b) shall be made by statutory instrument which shall be subject to annulment in pursuance of a resolution of either House of Parliament.

Interpretation and short title.

6.—(1) In this Act "hereditary peerage" includes the principality of Wales and the earldom of Chester.

(2) This Act may be cited as the House of Lords Act 1999.

SCHEDULES

SCHEDULE 1

AMENDMENTS

Peerage Act 1963 (c.48)

1. In section 1(2) of the Peerage Act 1963 (disclaimer of certain hereditary peerages) for the words from "has" to the end there shall be substituted the words "is excepted from section 1 of the House of Lords Act 1999 by virtue of section 2 of that Act".

Recess Elections Act 1975 (c.66)

2. In section 1 of the Recess Elections Act 1975 (issue of warrants for making out writs to replace members of the House of Commons whose seats have become vacant), in—

    (a) subsection (1)(a), and

    (b) paragraph (a) of the definition of "certificate of vacancy" in subsection (2),

    for the words "become a peer" there shall be substituted the words "become disqualified as a peer for membership of the House of Commons".

SCHEDULE 2

REPEALS

Chapter	Short title	Extent of repeal
1963 c.48.	The Peerage Act 1963.	In section 1(3), paragraph (b) and the word "and" immediately preceding it. Section 2. In section 3, in subsection (1)(b), the words from "(including" to "that House)" and, in subsection (2), the words from "and" to the end of the subsection. Section 5.

THE DIFFERENT PARTS

① This is the *short title* of the Act, together with its year of publication. When you are writing about a statute, it is normal to use the short title and year of publication to describe the statute. Sometimes, when a statute is referred to constantly, the short title is abbreviated. Thus, the Disability Discrimination Act 1995 is often referred to as "the D.D.A. 1995". If you work in a particular area of law, you will quickly learn the standard abbreviations for that area.

② This is the *official citation* for the statute. Each Act passed in any one year is given its own number. This is known as its *chapter number*. Thus you can describe a statute by its chapter number and year. The citation "1999 Chapter 34" could only mean the House of Lords Act 1999. "Chapter" in the official citation may be abbreviated to "c.", as in the top right hand corner of your copy of the statute. This form of official citation began in 1963. Before that, statutes were identified by the "regnal year" in which they occurred, followed by their chapter number. A regnal year is a year of a monarch's reign. Thus, "30 Geo 3 Chapter 3" refers to the Treason Act 1790, which was passed in the 30th year of King George III's reign. It is much easier to remember and use the short title of an Act rather than its official citation.

③ This is the *long title* of the Act. The long title gives some indication of the purpose behind the Act. It may be of some use in deciding what the Act is all about. However, the long title may be misleading. For example, the long title of the Parliament Act 1911 indicates that the Act is part of a process of abolishing the House of Lords although, nearly nine decades later, that institution is still in existence, even though the House of Lords Act 1999 has introduced restrictions upon membership of the institution by virtue of a hereditary peerage. Long titles are sometimes vague and may conflict with the main body of the Act. In the event of such a conflict, the legal rule is that expressed in the main body of the Act.

④ This indicates when the *royal assent* was given and the House of Lords Bill 1999 became an Act. Statutes become law on the date when they receive the royal assent *unless the Act says otherwise*. The statute itself may say that it becomes law on a fixed date after the royal assent, or it may give a Government Minister the power to decide when it becomes law. When a Minister brings a statute into effect after the date on which it has been passed a "commencement order" must be made. This is a form of delegated legislation. Statutes do not have a retrospective effect unless the Act expressly says so.

⑤ This is known as the *enacting formula*. It is the standard form of words used to indicate that a Bill has been properly passed by all the different parts of the legislature.

⑥ By each section you will find a short explanation of the content of that section. These *marginal notes* may help you to understand the content of the section if it is otherwise unclear.

The main body of the statute which follows is broken up into numbered *sections*. Each section contains a different rule of law. When you refer to a rule of law contained in a statute, you should say where that rule of law is to be found. This enables others to check your source and to see whether or not they agree with your interpretation of the law. Instead of writing "section", it is usual to abbreviate this to "s." Thus, "section 1" becomes "s.1". Sections are often further subdivided. These sub-division are known as *subsections*. When you wish to refer to a subsection, you should add it in brackets after the main section.

Example

> Q. How many people are excepted from s.1 of the House of Lords Act 1999?
>
> A. 90 people at any one time. See s.2(2) House of Lords Act 1999.

In larger statutes, sections may be grouped together into different *Parts*. Each Part will deal with a separate area of law. Looking for the correct Part will help you to find the particular legal rule that you want.

Some statutes have one or more *Schedules* at the end. The content of these varies. Some contain detailed provisions which are not found in the main body of the act. Others are merely convenient reminders and summaries of legal rules, and changes to legal rules, found elsewhere in the Act.

Example

> In the House of Lords Act 1999 there are two Schedules. The first Schedule says which sections of previous statutes have been changed (amended) by the 1999 Act. This Schedule sets out the detailed effect of the amendments, which are given their legal effect by virtue of s.4(1) of the Act. The second Schedule sets out which sections of a previous statute have been repealed by the 1999 Act. Those repeals are given their legal effect by virtue of s.4(2) of the Act.

References to Schedules are often abbreviated as "Sched.". Where a Schedule is divided up, the divisions are known as *paragraphs*, and can be abbreviated as "para.".

USING A STATUTE

Your use of statutory material will vary. Sometimes you will be referred to a particular section or sections of a statute in a case, article, or book that you are reading. In other instances, a new statute will be passed which you need to assess as a whole in order to see how it affects those areas of law in which you are interested. In either case, when first reading statutory material, you may be able to gain some help in deciding what it means from commentaries.

Commentaries are explanations of the law written by legal academics or practitioners. Annotated statutes, which were discussed earlier, are one useful source of such commentaries. You may also find such commentaries in books and articles on the area of law in which the statute falls. Always remember that a commentary represents only one author's opinion of what the statute says. In the case of a very new statute there will probably be no commentary. Therefore, you will need to be able to read a statute yourself, so that you can assess the value of other people's opinions and form your own view when there is no other help available.

When reading a statute, do not begin at the beginning and then work your way through to the end, section by section. Statutes do not necessarily use words to mean the same things that they do in ordinary conversation. Before you can decide what a statute is about you need to know if there are any special meanings attached to words in it. These special meanings can be found in the Act, often in sections called *definition* or *interpretation sections*. These are frequently found towards the end of the Act. For example, in the House of Lords Act 1999, there is a guide in s.6(1) to the interpretation of the expression "hereditary peerage" when used in the context of the Act. An Act may have more than one definition section. Sometimes, Parliament, when laying down a particular meaning for a word, will say that the specified meaning will apply in all statutes in which that word appears. Unless a statute specifically says this, however, you should assume that a definition in a statute applies only the use of the word in that statute.

You are now in a position to decide what new legal rules the statute creates. Some people begin this task by reading the long title of the Act to give themselves some idea of the general aim of the statute. Although this can be helpful, as we saw above in the section on the different parts of the Act, it can also be misleading.

Statutes should be read carefully and slowly. The general rule is that a statute means precisely what it says. Each word is important. Because of this, some words which we use loosely in ordinary conversation take on special significance when found in a statute. For example, it is important to distinguish between words like "may" and "shall", one saying that you *can* do something and the other saying that you *must* do something. Conjunctives, such as "and", joining things together, must be distinguished from disjunctives, such as "or", dividing things apart.

Example

Section 26A(1) of the Race Relations Act 1976 provides that:

> "It is unlawful for a barrister or barrister's clerk, in relation to any offer of a pupillage or tenancy, to discriminate against a person —

> (a) in the arrangements which are made for the purpose of determining to whom it should be offered;
> (b) in respect of any terms on which it is offered; or
> (c) by refusing, or deliberately omitting, to offer it to him."

As a result, a barrister or a barrister's clerk will discriminate unlawfully if they do *any one* of the acts spelled out in (a) *or* (b) *or* (c).

This would be a very different provision if it had said that it was necessary for all three of the acts (a) *and* (b) *and* (c) to be present before discrimination occurrred. As the law stands, any one of the acts listed will make the actor guilty of unlawful discrimination. If a conjunctive were substituted, then it would be necessary to show all three acts in order for unlawful discrimination to be established.

So far, the emphasis has been upon closely reading the particular statute. You should also remember that the statute should be read in the context of the general Acts, rules and principles of statutory interpretation discussed in Chapter 1.

One further thing to remember when reading a statute is that the fact that it has been printed does not mean that it is part of the law of the land. It may have been repealed. It may not yet be in force. Re-read pages 34–36 if you cannot remember how to find out if a statute has been repealed. Go back and read about the royal assent on page 53 if you cannot remember how to find out if a statute is in force.

STATUTORY INSTRUMENTS

What statutory instruments are, the way in which they are created, and the purposes which they have, are discussed on page 4.

Statutory instruments should be read in the same way as statutes. However, whilst statutes make relatively little reference to other sources, statutory instruments, because of their purpose, make very frequent reference either to other statutory instruments or to their parent statute. The legislative power has been given only for a limited purpose, the statutory instrument is a small part of a larger whole. For this reason, you will find it much more difficult to understand a statutory instrument if you do not have access to the surrounding legislation. Before reading a statutory instrument, it is vital that you understand the legislative framework into which it fits.

6 | Reading research materials

Chapter 4 explained that one of the ways of answering questions about law was the use of the research methods of the social scientist. Because this kind of research is the only way in which some questions about law can be answered, it is important that those interested in law can understand it.

In order to understand research into law you have to understand how and why it is written in the particular way that it is. Once you can understand the structure of the material, you will be able to see whether or not it helps to answer the questions in which you are interested.

Haphazard approaches to research are likely to be unsuccessful, the information gathered being too unrepresentative of the world at large and, therefore, too inaccurate for any conclusions to be drawn safely. Good research is done systematically. Research methods are highly developed.

There are three sources of information about how and why the law operates: records, people and activities. There are also three principal methods used in socio-legal research. The researcher may read records, interview people (or send questionnaires), or observe activities.

RECORD READING

The researcher reads the records and collects the required information, which is then either written down or noted on a prepared recording sheet. The researchers must ensure that the information collected from each record is as accurate and as complete as possible. This may involve searching through disordered files of letters and notes or simply copying the details from a form, such as a divorce petition.

INTERVIEWS AND QUESTIONNAIRES

Interviews are conducted in person; questionnaires are given, or sent, to the respondents to complete. It is important, in so far as is possible, to ask the same questions in the same way each time so as to get comparable information. Questions may be "open-ended," allowing the respondent to reply in his or her own words, or be "closed," requiring selection of the answer from a choice given by the interviewer. The style and wording of the question is selected to fit the data sought. Whatever the questions, the interview must be recorded. This may be done by using a tape recorder or by the interviewer noting the replies. Interviews are most useful for finding out what reasons people have for what they have done and for exploiting their feelings. If questions are asked about the future, the answers can only indicate what respondents currently think they would do. It has also been established that recollection of past events may be inaccurate, particularly about dates, times and the exact sequence of events. Interview and questionnaire design requires considerable skill, as does interviewing itself. If it is to reflect the respondent's views rather than those of the researcher.

OBSERVATION

The observer attends the event and records what occurs there. The observer may be an outsider, for example, a person watching court proceedings from the public gallery. Alternatively, the observer may be a person actually taking part in the events being described, for example, a police officer researching into the police force. Observation needs to be done systematically and accurately in order to avoid bias. Observers cannot record everything that they see. They must be careful that they do not record only what they want to see and neglect that which is unexpected and, perhaps, thereby unwelcome. One great difficulty in noting observations lies in deciding what to note down and what to omit. What seems unimportant at the time the notes were taken may take on a greater significance when a later analysis is made. It is important that the observer's record is contemporaneous, otherwise the data is weakened by what has been forgotten.

For any particular piece of research, one method may be more suitable than another, because of the nature of the data sources or the approach which the researcher wishes to take. If, for example, you want to research into the reasons magistrates have for their decisions, there is little point in reading records of what those decisions were. Here, the best place to start would be to interview magistrates. No single method can be said to provide the truth about every situation; some would argue that no method can provide the truth about any situation, for no one truth exists. Each method provides information based on the perceptions of the people who provide it, the record keepers, the interviewers or the observers.

Choice of research method depends not only what information is sought but also on practicalities. The researcher may not be given access to records or permitted to carry out interviews. Professional bodies and employers are not always willing to let their members or staff participate in research. This may be because they consider the research unethical (perhaps requiring them to divulge information given in confidence), because they are too busy, because they do not see the value of the research or because they wish to conceal the very information in which the researcher is interested. Thus, for example, it is unusual for researchers to be able to interview judges about cases, although there is nothing to prevent them sitting in the public gallery and watching cases from there.

For many research studies more than one method is used to obtain a complete picture. However, practical matters, including budget and time limits, may mean that not every avenue of enquiry is pursued. What is important is that the methods chosen are appropriate to the subject of study, the approach of the researcher and the conclusions drawn.

SAMPLING

Looking at every case is not normally practical in detailed social research. Instead, the researcher takes a sample of cases. Thus, one may interview some lawyers or some defendants or observe, or read records at some courts. If a completely random sample is taken, then it should have the characteristics of the population as a whole. A sample of judges should, for example, include judges of the different ages, backgrounds and experience to be found amongst the judiciary. However, if a characteristic is very rare a sample may not contain any example of having that characteristic. Thus, a 10 per cent sample of judges (*i.e.* contacting every tenth judge) might well fail to include any women judges since there are very few of them. The size of sample and method of sampling must be chosen to fit with the study. In a study of attitudes of clients to lawyers there is clearly no point in interviewing only successful clients. The number of people refusing to take part in a study is also important. Researchers will try to obtain a high response rate (over 75 per cent) and also attempt to find out if those who refuse are likely to be different in any material way from those who agree to participate in the study.

RESEARCH FINDINGS

The account of any research will usually include some background information about the subject, the purpose of the study (the questions to be answered) and the methods used. Findings presented in words should cause no difficulty to the reader, but numbers may be quite confusing. Where comparisons are made, it is usually thought better to use either *proportions* or *percentages* rather than actual numbers. It is then important to be clear what the percentage represents: for example, was it 20 per cent of all plaintiffs or 20 per cent of successful plaintiffs. Some researchers do not give the actual figures, but prefer to use words such as "some," "most" or "the majority." This is not very helpful, since a word like "majority" can mean anything from 51 per cent to 99 per cent. There is a variety of ways of presenting figures so as to make them clearer. *Tables* (lists of figures) are commonly used because they make it easier to compare two or more categories or questions. Graphic presentation, using bar charts (histograms), pie charts or graphs, can create a clear overall impression of a complex set of figures.

Figure 1 below is a *bar chart*. It shows clearly the different numbers of the three offences where guns were used. It also shows for each the relative proportion in which

Figure 1 Notifiable offences in which firearms were reported to have been used, by type of offence and type of weapon

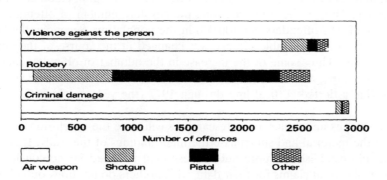

England and Wales 1982

Violence against the person

Robbery

Criminal damage

0   500   1000   1500   2000   2500   3000
Number of offences

Air weapon   Shotgun   Pistol   Other

particular types of gun were used. As can be seen from this example, the greatest advantage of a bar chart is the way in which it makes a quick visual comparison of information easy.

Figure 2 is a *pie chart*. The whole circle represents 100 per cent of the particular group. The segments represent different percentages. In this example, the exact percentages represented in the different segments have been printed on to the chart. This is not always done. Different circles represent both different types of original sentence and different courts in which that sentence was imposed. The segments themselves indicate what happened to people who breached their original sentence: for example, by committing a further crime whilst on probation.

Figure 2 Person breaching their original sentence or order by type of sentence or order imposed for the breach

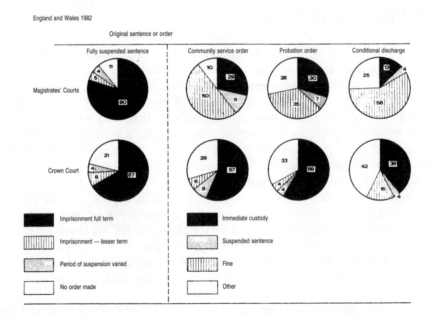

Figure 3 is a *graph*. This is probably the best way of showing a trend over time. The graph is designed to show the rise in the number of females found guilty of indictable (basically, serious offences). There are two major problems in doing this. One is that an increase in numbers caused by an increase in the size of the population as a whole is not very interesting. Thus, rather than counting the absolute number of offenders, the graph shows the number of offenders per 100,000 in the population. Secondly, the law relating to who is guilty of an indictable offence was changed in the course of the period which the graph records. Thus, some of the increase in the number of offenders may be due to the fact that the categories of indictable crime have become different. The graph indicates this by showing a dotted vertical line through 1977 (the year in which the change took effect).

As well as graphs and tables, most researchers will state the conclusions that they have drawn from the material and summarise the main findings of the study. It is crucial that the data should establish no more and no less than is stated in the conclusions. Some researchers make great claims for their data, whilst others do not draw out all the answers

Figure 3 Females found guilty of, or cautioned for, indictable offences[1] per 100,000 population in the age group by age

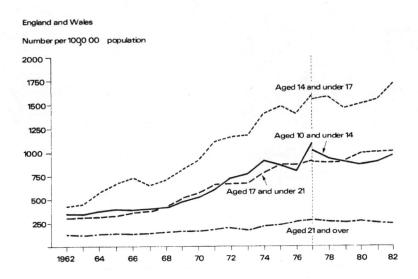

England and Wales

Number per 100,0 00   population

which it could provide. To avoid being persuaded by poor reasoning, look at the data and see what conclusions seem appropriate, then read the explanation given, and compare it with what you originally thought. A critical approach to any empirical research should always consider the following three questions. First, are the methods chosen appropriate? This includes both, "have the right questions been asked" and "have the right people (people who should know about the topic) been asked?" There may have been better sources of information available to the researcher, but were the ones used good enough for this study? Secondly, is the sample big enough and has it been properly drawn? Thirdly, does the data justify the conclusions which have been drawn? If it does not, can you see any other conclusions which it would justify?

Research often leaves as many questions raised as answered provided. Further studies may be indicated, interesting new areas which need to be explored. Studying this type of material will, hopefully, increase your interest and insight into the operation of law. It will not provide you with all the answers.

7 | Study Skills

STUDYING EFFECTIVELY

Whilst you need to be reasonably intelligent in order to be a successful student, you do not have to be a genius. However, if you are not in the genius category, you need to make the most of the ability you have. In other words, you need to study effectively. Studying effectively will not only give you the opportunity to try and improve your academic performance, but will also help to make studying a more enjoyable and satisfying experience. Successful study does not simply involve spending a lot of time reading books. Students who spend a lot of time on their work do not always receive high marks. The purpose of this chapter is to suggest some techniques which you can apply to the tasks which law students are asked to carry out, such as writing essays, reading cases and statutes, participating in seminars and sitting examinations. These techniques are intended to enable you to study effectively. If you are able to study effectively, you should be able not only to be successful in your academic work, but also to have sufficient time for a social life as well.

MANAGING YOUR TIME

One of the most valuable things you can learn as a student is how to manage your time. This, like the other skills discussed in this chapter, is what employers would call a "transferable skill," a technique which, once you have mastered it, you should be able to apply to numerous other situations.

As a law student, you will be expected to do a number of different things attend classes or lectures, prepare work for discussion in tutorials, seminars or classes, write essays. Often you will be given several of these tasks at once. Clearly you cannot do them all at the same time. You will have to plan your time, working out how much time is available, identifying what you need to do, how long it will take you and when you are going to do it, so that you can complete all the tasks before the relevant deadline.

Most people find that it is best to plan one or two weeks' activities at a time. Sometimes you will need to plan for longer, for example when you are planning your revision for examinations, but generally speaking it is best to plan for a smaller period. This means that if anything goes wrong with your planning, you do not have to wait for very long before you can adjust your ideas. It is best to make your plan as simple as possible. Your academic timetable gives you a good basis from which to start. You can just extend it into the evenings and the weekends.

Make a list of all the things you want to fit in. There will probably be more things on your list than you have time to do, so you will have to prioritise your list. Highlight those things which you must do, like attending compulsory classes. Then look at other tasks which have to be completed by a particular deadline, such as preparation for essays or tutorials. There may also be practical tasks which are important, such as getting a repair kit for your push bike. There are then the things you would like to do fairly soon, such as going round to see friends. Finally, there are a number of things which you would like to do at some point when you have time, such as writing to your brother. Number the items on your list, dividing them into three or four levels of priority. Once you have prioritised your list, you can fill in your timetable accordingly, putting the most important items in first. When you are working out your timetable, there are a number of general principles you need to bear in mind:

Do not try to study for long periods of time without a break.
You will find that making a coffee, going for a brief stroll or reading a newspaper for 10 minutes in between periods of study helps to relax you and enables you to extend your total period of study.

Be realistic when planning your time.
It is counterproductive to set yourself a deadline which you cannot possibly hope to meet. If you do not allow yourself sufficient time to do something, your timetable will not work properly, and you may start to feel depressed and frustrated. If your schedule is realistic, you will gain satisfaction from knowing you have achieved what you set out to do. Of course, everyone underestimates the time they need sometimes, but you should try to avoid this happening to you too often.

Recognise your own strengths and weaknesses.
If you are the sort of person who can stay in and write your essay on a Saturday afternoon when all your friends are going out together, so you have time to go to a party on Saturday evening, then you can build this into your timetable. On the other hand, if you are the sort of person who cannot wake up before midday, it is unrealistic to plan to write your essay at 8.30 a.m. every morning.

Find out if there are hidden institutional time constraints.
Your time management can be upset by the arrangements made by your institution. It is all very well planning to do lots of research for an essay during the vacation, but not if the library is going to be closed for three weeks. Equally, you may come across the problem of "bunched deadlines," where several of the courses you are doing require assessed work to be handed in on the same day. You can alleviate these problems by finding out about the library, computers, and other support services well in advance and by asking tutors to give you assignments in good time, but you may not be able to overcome such difficulties completely. If you are used to planning your time, however, you will be able to deal with the resulting pressure on your time much better than someone who has given no thought to such problems.

Plan to have some time off each week.
The aim of planning your time is to allow you to do your academic work to the best of your ability, but also to have some time left over to enjoy yourself and to relax.

LECTURES—LISTENING AND NOTETAKING

Lectures are generally seen as a cost-effective way of imparting the main ideas in an area to a large number of people. They also give the lecturer the opportunity to tell students about the latest developments in an area, and to explain any particularly complex parts of a subject. Lectures are often regarded as forming the backbone of a course and it is usually assumed that most students will attend them.

Lecturing style is closely related to the personality of an individual lecturer, so you are likely to come across a wide variety of lectures delivered in many different styles. Some will be excellent, some less so. As a student, you will need to develop a good technique for dealing with lectures, which you can then adapt to cope with the different lecturing styles you come across. Listening to a lecture can be a very passive experience. Students are not generally expected to interrupt a lecture by asking questions or making comments and not all lecturers include interactive elements in their lectures. It is therefore very easy to "switch off" and lose the thread of the lecture. In order to get the most out of lectures, you need to listen effectively and take good notes. Doing both of these things helps to make the experience less passive and also helps you to record the lecture in a way which will prove useful for future reference.

Listening effectively does not mean merely that you hear the lecture. It means that you listen actively. Taking notes will help you listen actively, because it provides the listening activity with a purpose. You should also listen reflectively; in other words, you should try to relate what you are hearing to your existing knowledge of the subject and think how the new information fits into it. A lecture can be very boring if the lecturer has a monotonous delivery, but as an effective listener, you need to train yourself to ignore poor delivery, and concentrate on the content of what is being said.

In order to help you concentrate in lectures, you need to eliminate as many distractions as possible. Make sure you are comfortable. Use a clipboard if there is no desk. Use a convenient size of paper, which gives you enough space to set out your notes clearly. Decide whether you prefer lined or unlined paper. If you have a series of consecutive lectures you may become uncomfortable because you are sitting for long periods; try to move your limbs slightly during the lecture and use any brief gaps between the lectures to get out of your seat and move around a bit.

Taking notes in lectures not only helps you to concentrate; it also means that you have a record of the content of the lecture which you can refer to in the future. Since one of the main purposes of taking notes is to use them in the future, it is important to devise a system of note-taking which produces a clear set of notes which you will understand when you come to look at them again, weeks or months after the original lecture. The following points may help you to achieve that goal:

Good presentation is important.
Use headings and sub-headings to emphasise the main points made, and to indicate changes in topics. Numbered points can provide a quick way of noting a large quantity of information. Underlining and the use of different coloured pens can direct your attention to particular points.

Review your notes as soon as possible.
It is important to review your notes while the lecture is still fresh in your mind. You may need to expand what you have written, or add headings, or do a little research on a point which you have not understood. Some people like to summarise their notes in diagrammatic form at this stage.

Arrive in reasonably good time.
Handouts and important announcements are often given out at the beginning
of lectures; you may be very confused if you miss them.

TUTORIALS AND SEMINARS

Tutorials involve small groups of students who meet regularly with an academic tutor to
discuss questions which have generally been set in advance by the tutor. Seminars are
similar, but usually involve larger groups of students; sometimes seminars may be led by
one or more of the students. These names for small group work are often interchangea-
ble, so you may find something labelled "tutorial" which is attended by 30 students. The
title is not important; it merely indicates a 'teaching event' which is usually smaller scale
and more interactive than a lecture. In both tutorials and seminars, all the students are
generally expected to have prepared the topic under discussion in advance and tutors
usually expect that all the students involved in the group will participate, by joining in
the discussion. The following points will help you get the most benefit from these
sessions:

Ensure you know what is expected of you.
Many tutors set specific work for tutorials and seminars. Ensure that you obtain
this in good time, so that you can prepare the topic properly. If you are
unprepared, and unfamiliar with the subject matter, participating in the
discussion is more difficult. Different tutors will run these groups in very
different ways. You will need to be adaptable, to fit in with different teaching
styles. Some tutors will make this easy for you, by having explicit "ground
rules," with others you will have to work it out for yourself.

Try to participate.
Often, you will attend tutorials and seminars with the same group of people for
a whole academic year. Clearly, the experience will be more pleasant if the
members of the group get on with each other, but this is essentially a learning
experience, so you have to balance your desire to be friendly with your learning
needs. No one wants to make a fool of themselves in front of a group of other
people, but if you do not try out ideas in discussion, you are not going to
develop your thinking, so a little bravery is called for. Try not to be so worried
about what the others will think that you do not participate at all. Everyone is in
the same situation, so people are generally sympathetic to contributions made
by others.

Consider making a contribution early in the discussion.
If you make a contribution to the discussion at a fairly early stage, it is likelier
to be easier than if you delay participating, for a number of reasons. In the early
stages of discussion, it is less likely that other people will have made the point
you have thought of. Tutors who are keen to involve the whole group may
single out people who have not said anything and ask them direct questions;
this is much less likely to happen to you if you have already made a
contribution. If you are less confident about talking in front of other people, the
longer you wait to say something, the more difficult you may find it to join in.

Think about the art of polite disagreement.

The aim of academic discussion is to try to develop the ideas you are considering. Often, this involves members of the group disagreeing with one another's ideas. Remember that you are challenging the argument which is put forward, not the person who is advancing it. It is also important to remember this when your ideas are challenged.

Expect to be challenged.

During group discussions, tutors will try to teach you not to make assumptions. Their aim is to help you to think critically and precisely. They will therefore challenge many of the things you say. Most people are not used to being challenged in this way, and the ability of tutors to question almost everything you say can seem unduly negative. However, if you are going to succeed in thinking rigorously, you need to be able to question your own ideas and those of other people, and tutors whose sessions are the most challenging may turn out to be the best ones you have.

Do not expect to take notes all the time.

If you take notes of everything that goes on in a tutorial or seminar, you will be so busy writing that you will not be able to participate in the discussion. Not only will you not be able to make an oral contribution, but notetaking also detracts from your ability to think about the points that are being made. Try to limit your notetaking to jotting down the main issues raised and the outline of any answer given. You can then read over your notes later and follow up any points of particular interest.

Learn to take advantage of small group learning situations.

It is much easier to learn in small groups than in huge lectures, because small groups should give you the opportunity to ask questions about aspects of the subject under discussion which you do not understand so well. Clearly, you do not want to dominate the discussion, or interrupt with too many questions, but small group situations do give you an opportunity to raise issues which are of particular concern to you.

STARTING TO RESEARCH A TOPIC FOR AN ESSAY, TUTORIAL OR SEMINAR

When you are preparing for a tutorial or seminar, or preparing to write an essay or problem answer, you will need to carry out some research, in order to find the information you need. In the case of tutorials and seminars, you will often be given specific reading lists, so some of the research has been done for you, but you will still need to use the information to the best advantage, in much the same way as you need to do when you are writing an essay or problem answer. Firstly, define the area you are interested in. This task will have been done for you in relation to tutorials and seminars, but you need to work it out for yourself in relation to essays and problems. Next, read the question carefully. Think about what you are being asked to do. Titles which invite you to "discuss" or "critically analyse" mean that you are expected to engage in reasoned argument about the topic; you are not being invited merely to describe something. One of the easiest traps to fall into is to fail to answer the question which is set because you are concentrating on conveying as much information as possible about the general area of law, rather than focusing on the specific aspect which is the subject of the question you are answering.

The first stage of the research process is to make a plan. A plan provides a structure for your argument and allows you to organise your arguments into a coherent whole. It is a vital stage of the research process and you need to produce one as soon as possible. You may want to do a bit of basic reading first, but generally, the plan should be one of your first tasks. When preparing for tutorials or seminars, your plan might be just a simple "shopping list" of the topics you have to cover, but if you have been asked questions which require you to look at a particular aspect of the subject, you will need a more elaborate plan, similar to that for an essay. Plans for problem answers are easier to produce than those for essays, because the events which make up the problem give you a structure for your plan. In all cases, plan the main points of your answer carefully first, and then fit in subsidiary points in the most logical places.

Example

A first plan for an essay entitled

"Discrimination in the legal profession is a thing of the past". Discuss.

Introduction—much discrimination on grounds of both race and sex in the past refer to numbers of women/members of ethnic minorities qualifying as solicitors and barristers, also women not able to qualify as solicitors till well into the twentieth century—see Bebb v. The Law Society.

Currently, still a lot of discrimination on grounds of sex—refer to small numbers of women partners in solicitors' firms, small numbers of female Q.C.s and small numbers of female judges. Also refer to research reports on women in the legal profession.

Equally, still a lot of discrimination on grounds of race—refer to small numbers of solicitors, barristers and judges drawn from ethnic minority communities, also research reports on racial discrimination at the Bar and in the solicitors' profession.

Conclusion—although it appears there is still a lot of discrimination on grounds of race and sex in the legal profession, it is arguable that the situation is improving—use statistics to show increased participation in the legal profession by women and by members of ethnic minority groups.

Use your plan flexibly. It is there to help you; you do not have to stick with your original plan too rigidly. If you can see a better way of organising your argument once you have done a bit of reading, then adjust the plan but do not abandon it. Many students fail to realise that a plan can go through several versions during the research process. It is unlikely that you will come up with the perfect plan immediately, so be prepared to be flexible. The plan in the example above is just a first draft. It provides a basic framework, but it does not contain enough ideas at this stage. The author needs to go and do some more reading before amending the plan in the light of the additional information. However, this is a good start.

Once you have made your plan, you will need to find out some more information about the topic involved. Often, your topic will have been referred to in reading lists or handouts used in classes, so this is a good place to start. Look on the reading lists for books and journal articles relating to your topic. If you are dealing with a completely unknown topic, try looking it up in the relevant student textbooks. Use the library catalogues to help you do this. You can also use any resources on electronic databases, CD Roms or the World Wide Web to which you have access. Either way, you will come up with some information to get you started. You can then look up material which is referred to in the relevant parts of the sources which you have located, and look up these references to give you some more information.

You need to ensure that you are using your library as effectively as possible. There may be leaflets designed to help readers find their way around the different catalogues; see if any of these are relevant to you. Some libraries have specialist librarians who are immensely knowledgeable and helpful. Try to help yourself first, but do not ignore the experts whose job it is to help you.

If you are researching a topic which many other people are working on at the same time, you need to be particularly skilled in using the library. Perhaps the books you really want to use are all out on loan. Do not despair! Consider the following techniques:

Use bibliographic sources

There are a number of publications which give details of all British books in print, arranged by subject, as well as by author and title. The Index to Legal Periodicals will help you to find articles in legal journals and there are similar publications relating to social science literature, often called 'Abstracts'. Using these sources will help you find a wider range of materials than those referred to on your reading lists. You may then be able to use these as alternatives to the ones which everyone else is using or which are unavailable when you wish to consult them.

Work backwards in time

Start with the most recent literature on your chosen topic, *i.e.* the latest books and the most recent issues of relevant journals. These items may not appear on reading lists, so may have been missed by others.

Search other nearby libraries

Many libraries now have the facility to allow you to search the catalogues of other libraries. Think of other libraries in the area which you could use and have a look in their catalogues to see if it would be worthwhile visiting them. Perhaps their students are not all doing the essay on offences against the person which your year has been set.

Use the references in the text

Academic writing contains a lot of references and footnotes. At first, this can be confusing, and you may tend to ignore them. However, when you are researching a topic, footnotes and references are an important source of further information. If you look up the material referred to in parts of an article or book that are directly relevant to your work, you will find that footnotes serve some important purposes.

(a) They give full references to articles or books which are just mentioned or summarised in the text. This is useful if the material referred to is relevant to your work, because you can then read the full text.

(b) They give references to other books or articles on the same topic, which put forward a similar argument (or the opposite one often indicated by the word contra in front of the reference). Again, you can extend your knowledge by following up the references.

(c) They give further explanation about points made in the text.

SOME GENERAL POINTS ABOUT DOING RESEARCH

When you are gathering and using written materials, remember that you must always read things for yourself. The insertion of a footnote in a piece of academic writing does not necessarily mean that the footnote is accurate. Sometimes, when you find the article or case report which is referred to, you discover that it cannot possibly be used as justification for the proposition which you have just read. In order to find out whether a footnote is accurate, you will need to look up the reference for yourself. You should not merely replicate a reference without looking it up for yourself.

When you are copying down references from the library catalogue, or any other source, it is important that you take down all the information which you will need. For a book, you will need the author, title, date of publication and edition, plus the reference number (usually a Dewey decimal reference number). Your reference should look something like this:

Bradney et al How to Study Law 1995 3rd edition 340.07 HOW

If you are finding a journal article, your reference will be something like:

Addison & Cownie "Overseas Law Students: Language Support and Responsible Recruitment" (1992) 19 JLS p. 467 PER 340 J 6088

If you do not take down a proper reference for items that you consult, you may find that you waste a lot of time desperately trying to remember which chapter of which book contained that really good quotation, which you now want to use to finish off your essay.

READING

Once you have used your reading list or some of the other bibliographic sources indicated above, you will have to decide whether the references you have found are going to be useful for you. As far as books are concerned, the catalogue will give you some basic information, such as the date of publication and the edition. Legal textbooks go out of date very quickly, so this is important information. If a book is old, it may be inaccurate. Equally, you should generally use the latest *edition* of a book; often your tutors will refer you to a particular edition, and this is the one you should use; you cannot merely substitute another edition. Much the same applies to articles in academic journals; since the law changes so rapidly, you have to exercise caution about using articles which were written more than a few years ago. In the case of both books and articles, you should check to ensure that the information you are relying on is still applicable.

You will also have to develop a strategy for dealing with the large amount of reading you will have to do. All students have to face this problem, but if you are studying law, you have a particular problem, because although by this stage you are an expert reader, you are unlikely to have had much experience, if any, of reading legal materials, such as case reports and statutes, so in this respect you are a novice again. The chapters in this book which deal with reading cases and statutes will help you develop an effective method of reading these new types of text, and once you have practised a bit, you will find that you can process them as quickly as other types of text, such as articles or textbooks, with which you are already familiar. There are many different ways of reading; for example, you can skim quickly through something, or you can read it slowly and carefully. In order to decide what kind of reading you should be doing at any particular time, you need to think about the purpose of your reading. You also need to be aware of the different techniques of reading and be able to use each type as it becomes relevant. The following key points will help you read the materials for your law course more effectively:

Titles are there to help you

When looking at a book, the title and contents pages will give you a broad outline of the information you will find. Subheadings within an article perform the same function.

Scan the text first

To check the relevance of a text, skim through it, looking for the key words and phrases which will give you the general sense of the material and enable you to decide whether it is relevant for your purposes.

Approach the text gradually

Even when you have decided that a particular chapter of a book or an article is relevant, check it out before you begin to take notes; you may not need to take notes on the whole chapter, but only a part of it; similarly, with an article. It is often suggested that you should read the first sentence of each paragraph to find out more precisely what the text is about.

Reading Statutes

As you have discovered in Chapter 5 of this book, statutes must be read carefully and precisely. At first, they can seem very complicated to read, because they are so detailed. When you read a section of a statute, try to establish the main idea first, then you can re-read it and fill in the details on the second reading. You might find it helpful to photocopy the parts of the statute which you have to read, so that you can use a pen or highlighter to mark the main idea. There is an example below:

Sale of Goods Act 1979 Section 11(3)

Whether a stipulation in a contract is a condition, the breach of which may give rise to a right to treat the contract as repudiated, **or a warranty**, the breach of which may give rise to a claim for damages but not to a right to reject the goods and treat the contract as repudiated, **depends in each case on the construction of the contract**; and a stipulation may be a condition, though called a warranty in the contract.

The main point which is being made is quite simple, and can be identified by reading the phrases in bold type "Whether a stipulation in a contract is a condition or a warranty depends in each case on the construction of the contract." Having established what the section is basically about, you can now go back and find out what the section says about the effect of a stipulation in a contract being classified as either a condition or a warranty.

NOTETAKING

Your next task is to extract the information which is relevant to the task you have to carry out. You will probably have gathered a number of different sources, and clearly you will not be able to remember everything they contain, so you are going to have to make notes. It is important that your notes are accurate and clear; if they are not, you will waste a lot of time trying to work out what they mean, and where you found a particular piece of information.

Always begin by asking yourself why you are taking notes. Look back at your plan and refresh your memory as to the question you are trying to answer. Remember that you can take different types of notes on different parts of a text detailed notes on the directly relevant parts, outline notes on other parts, while sometimes you will be able to read through without taking any notes at all.

Your notes will be more use to you if they are reasonably neat. Try to develop a standard way of recording the source you are taking the notes from, perhaps always putting it at the top right- hand corner of the page, or in the margin. You can use this reference for your bibliography, or for footnotes, or for your own use if you need to clarify a point at some later stage. In order to make it even easier to find your way around the original text, you might like to make a note of the actual page you have read, either in the margin, or in brackets as you go along. Here is an example of some notes on the first few pages of a chapter of a book:

H. Genn
Hard Bargaining 1st Edn.
Oxford Uni. Press. 1987.
344.6 GEN

Chapter 3 "Starting Positions" p. 34.
Structural imbalance between the parties. (p. 34) *One-shotter pl. v Repeat-player* def.
* (Exceptions, *e.g.* class action)
* *cf.* Galanter 1974

* Repeat players—advance intelligence, expertise, access to specialists, economies of scale.
* *cf.* Ross 1980

Distribution of personal injury work (p. 35)
* Pls huge variety of firms.
* Defs-insurance co/specialist firm
* Defs solicitors allowed few mistakes (p.36 top)
* Defs solicitors nurture relationship w insurance co.
* Contrast position of general practitioner.

When making notes, it might help to keep the following general points in mind:

Keep notes and comments separate.

It is a good idea to think critically about the content of what you are reading. However, if you want to make comments, keep these separate in some way, preferably on a separate sheet of paper. Otherwise, when you come back to the notes, you might find it impossible to distinguish your great thoughts from those of the original author.

Good presentation is important.

Remember that clear presentation of your notes is just as important when you are taking notes for an essay or seminar as it is when you are taking lecture notes. Use headings and sub-headings, and remember that underlining and the use of different coloured pens can direct your attention to particular points.

Consider using a different technique for noting cases.

Many tutors recommend that you help yourself to take brief notes of cases by using filecards, one card for each case. You can note the citation, the facts and the main points of the judgment using two sides of a card and then your notes of cases are in a very flexible form, so you can arrange them alphabetically, or by topic, or by date, depending on your particular needs.

Do you need to photocopy the bibliography?

When you are taking notes, you will often note down references to other articles or books referred to in the text you are reading. You will have to decide later whether you need to look these up, but many people find that it disturbs their train of thought to look up the full reference for each of these as they occur in the text. If that is the case, it is important to photocopy the bibliography of your source, so that you have a copy of the full reference in case you need to refer to it later.

WRITING ASSIGNMENTS

You will have begun to prepare your essay long before you start to write it. The first stage was to read the question carefully and make a suitable plan. You will have used this plan to help you when you were carrying out the research for your assignment. When you have gathered all the relevant materials and made the necessary notes, it is time to review your plan in the light of what you have discovered. Read through your notes, bearing in mind all the time the question you have been asked. Now you will be able to make a new plan, indicating not only the main points you are going to make, but also any arguments or pieces of information drawn from your research which you wish to include. Once you are satisfied with your revised plan, you can embark on the first draft of your essay. Before you start, consider the following points:

Make sure all your points are relevant.

Look at your plan. Every argument you make should relate to the question you have been asked. This is what makes it relevant.

Here is an example of a first plan for an essay whose title is

"Settlement of major litigation is a necessary evil." Discuss.
Settlement definition.
Settlement is necessary because (a) saves court time (b) saves expense (c) saves litigants' time.
But settlement is an "evil" because (a) litigants are not equally experienced and do not have equal resources (b) inexperienced litigants often go to lawyers who are not specialists in the relevant field and are not well advised (c) inexperienced litigants can easily be put under pressure, *e.g.* by payment into court, delays (often manufactured by the other side), worries about cost, risk-aversion.
Conclusion settlement is a necessary evil, but currently is so evil it is immoral and unacceptable.

Every point which is made relates directly to the quotation; this means that everything contained in the essay is relevant to the title set. The example given is only an initial plan. After some research, you would be able to expand some points, and to insert the names of books or articles which you could use to justify the points being made. But you would still ensure that everything fitted in to the basic plan, and related to the quotation, so that it remains relevant.

Remember the audience you are writing for.

When you write an academic essay, you can assume that you are writing for a reasonably intelligent reader who knows almost nothing about your subject. That means you have to explain clearly every step of your argument. At first, many students are ignorant of this convention. They know their essay is going to be marked by an expert, so they do not bother to include all the information about a topic, only to be told by their tutor "I cannot give you credit for anything, unless it is written down in your essay. It's no use keeping things in your head". Do not assume that your tutor will draw on their own knowledge to fill in any gaps in the assignment you have submitted; it is up to you to provide a full, clear picture of the topic you are writing about.

Do not make assertions.

In academic writing, you must always be able to justify what you say. You cannot make assertions, which is when you say something without providing any evidence which proves that what you say is accurate. You must always be able to give evidence or provide reasons for your statements. If someone writes "A police officer cannot stop and search a person unless he/she has reasonable suspicion that they will find stolen or prohibited articles" that is an assertion. There is no evidence that the statement is true, the author is just expecting us to take their word for it. After a little research, it is possible to rewrite the sentence in an academically acceptable way. "The Police and Criminal Evidence Act 1984 section 1(3) provides that police officers cannot stop and search people unless they have reasonable suspicion that they will find stolen or prohibited articles, or articles to which s.1.8A applies". If you are making a really important point in your answer, it may be appropriate to quote directly from the primary source (it might be a statute, decided case or academic article). Note that you do not need to quote large chunks of material, but just that which is relevant to the point you are making.

What kind of introduction?

The beginning of your essay is very important. Unless you have been instructed that you must have an introduction in a particular form, your essay might have more impact if you start straight away with a comment on the central point; "The Small Claims system is intended for use by litigants in person, although over the years serious doubts have been raised as to whether it achieves this objective" may be a more appropriate beginning than "This essay is about the small claims system in the County Court. It will address the following issues . . .". Try to interest your reader by indicating the main issue, but do not rehearse all your arguments in the first sentence or two. Openings such as "This essay discusses . . . " can be very boring. They can also give hostages to fortune. If you tell your reader that you are going to discuss X, Y and Z, they will expect you to do exactly that. Such promises can prove very difficult to fulfil.

Consider the style of your writing.

An academic essay is a formal piece of writing, so the style in which you write should not be too colloquial. Shortened forms of phrases, such as isn't and mustn't, are inappropriate. So is too much slang. However, pomposity is equally inappropriate. Phrases such as "I submit that . . ." are out of place. Advocates make submissions in court, but you do not make submissions in an academic essay. Aim for a clear, direct style, which conveys your arguments in a way which can be readily understood. Use paragraphs to indicate a change of subject, and keep sentences reasonably short. In general, academic writing, is written in an impersonal style, so writers do not use phrases such as "I think that . . ." They use alternative phrases, such as "This indicates that . . ."

Be prepared to write several drafts.

Before you arrive at the final version of your essay, you should have produced several drafts. You should read through each draft carefully, making additions and alterations which you then incorporate into the next draft. Although it is important to correct the spelling and the grammar in each draft, the primary reason for having several drafts is to give yourself the opportunity to examine your argument and make sure that it is as convincing as possible. Think about what you are saying. Have you justified all the points you have made? Does the argument flow logically from one point to another? Is the material relevant? Are you sure that you have made yourself clear?

Do not describe too much.

In general, the object of writing academic essays is to engage in critical analysis, *i.e.* thought and argument. Your tutors are not looking for detailed descriptions of subjects which they could, after all, read in any competent textbook. A certain amount of description is necessary, to explain what you are talking about, but the main emphasis in any academic piece of work will be on analysing. You are interpreting for the reader the significance of what you have described, and it is this process which is most important.

Acknowledge your sources.

During the course of your writing, you will often put forward arguments and ideas which you have discovered in books or articles. If you do this, you must acknowledge that the idea is not an original one. You can do this expressly in the text by saying something like "As Bradney argues in 'How to Study Law' at page 6 . . . " or you can use a footnote to indicate the source of the idea. What you must not do is to pass off someone else's idea as if it were something you had thought of for yourself. That is stealing their idea, and it is a practice known as plagiarism. Your tutor may supply you with further guidance to help you understand exactly what may be regarded as plagiarism; it is important that you understand what it is so that you can avoid plagiarising the work of others, even unintentionally. In academic life, where people's ideas are of the utmost importance, plagiarism is regarded as a form of cheating.

Ideally, you will use other people's ideas as a base from which to develop thoughts of your own, acknowledging their idea, and then going on to say something original about them. This is the kind of critical thinking which you are trying to develop.

WRITING PROBLEM ANSWERS

Sometimes, instead of setting you an essay to write, your tutors may give you a legal problem to solve. This will usually consist of a fictional scenario, in which a series of events is described. Various different characters appear in the scenario, and you may be asked to advise one or more of the characters, in the light of the events that have happened to them. An example is given below:

Bill called at Amanda's house, begging. Amanda told him to weed the garden for an hour. When he had finished, she gave Bill an overcoat and said to him, "You've done a good job; come back on Wednesday and I will give you £10." When Bill called on Wednesday, Amanda refused to give him any money. Advise Bill.

It is often said that it is easier to answer a problem than to write an essay, but this is largely a matter of personal preference. Problem answers are certainly easier in one sense, because they provide a framework for your answer by posing certain issues which you must answer. However, you still need to carry out the research and planning process described above when you are answering a problem question. You should also bear in mind the following points:

Problem answers do not need lengthy introductions.

The convention is that you need to introduce a problem answer by identifying the main issue in the problem, but you do not need a lengthy introduction.

All points of law must be justified by reference to authority.

Whenever you make a statement about the law, you must give the relevant legal authority, which might be a case or a section of a statute, for example, "When X wrote to Y saying that if he did not hear from Y, he would assume that Y agreed to the contract, this had no effect, because silence does not imply consent (*Felthouse v. Bindley* (1862) 11 C.B. 869)."

Socio Legal information is not relevant in a problem answer.
Strictly speaking, problem questions are just asking you to identify the relevant legal rules relating to the issues raised. There may be very interesting research studies on a topic, but these are not relevant to a problem answer so they should not be mentioned.

ASSESSMENT

It is likely that you will experience a number of different forms of assessment, including continuous assessment, based on written work submitted during the course of the academic year, and the traditional three hour unseen examination. The strategies discussed above will help you to cope with the various forms of continuous assessment which you are likely to meet. This section will therefore concentrate on strategies designed to help you cope with the traditional unseen examination.

Make a revision timetable in good time.
It is important to make a realistic revision timetable well in advance of the examinations, allocating a certain amount of time for each subject you have to prepare. Most people find it best to study each subject in turn, rather than finishing one before going on to the next one. This ensures that you will at least know *something* about each of the subjects you are studying, rather than knowing a lot about one subject, but being relatively unprepared for the other exams.

Make sure you get enough rest.
Studying hard for examinations is a very tiring experience. It is important to ensure that you get sufficient sleep and exercise, so that you remain as fresh as possible. Burning the midnight oil is not necessarily a sensible strategy. Try to work out a realistic schedule, which allows some time for rest and refreshment.

Reduce your notes to a manageable size.
At the beginning of the revision period, you are likely to find that you have a large amount of notes. It is a good idea to precis these, so that you end up with a manageable quantity of material to work with. As the examinations approach, most people reduce their notes, perhaps several times, so that they end up with a list of points which they know about each topic, and a whole topic can be covered comprehensively, but speedily.

Question-spotting is a risky strategy.
It is sensible to consider what sort of subjects might come up in the examination. Consulting old examination papers is a useful way of finding out what is expected of you in the exam. However, it is unwise to "question spot" too precisely. It is unlikely that you will be able to revise the whole course; indeed, this would often be a waste of effort, but you need to cover several subjects in addition to the three or four which you hope will come up, so that you have plenty of choice when it comes to deciding which questions you will answer in the examination. Remember that you need to be familiar with a range of subjects because:

(a) Your favourite topics might not come up at all.
(b) Some topics might come up, but in a way which is unfamiliar to you.
(c) Your favourite topic might be mixed up with another topic which you have not revised.

Consider practising timed answers.
If you find it difficult to write answers quickly, it is a good idea to spend some time before the examinations begin writing some answers in the same time that you will have in the examination. Use questions from old examination papers.

Make sure you are as comfortable as possible during the examination.
Before you enter the examination room, make sure you have all the pens, pencils, etc., that you need. Wear something comfortable, preferably several layers of clothing so you can discard some if the room is hot, or add additional layers if you are cold. Check whether you are allowed to take drinks or food into the examination room. If you are allowed to do so, it is a matter of personal choice whether you take advantage of this facility or not; some people find it helps to have a can of drink, others find it a distraction. Check that you know where you have to sit, and whether there are any attendance slips or other forms that you have to fill in. Ensure that you know whether or not you will be told when you can start the examination you do not want to sit there, waiting for an instruction which never comes.

Develop good examination technique.
In the examination, plan your time carefully. Provided that all the questions carry an equal number of marks, you should allow an equal amount of time for answering each question. Subdivide your time into reading the question, planning the answer, writing the answer and checking it. Planning is a very important part of good examination technique. If you spend a few minutes setting out a good plan, it will allow you to write a much fuller answer than if you are thinking out your answer as you go along, because all the basic thinking will be done at the planning stage, and you will be able to concentrate on writing a relevant answer. Bear in mind the following points:

Read the rubric carefully.
Make sure that you read the instructions at the top of the examination paper very carefully. The paper may be divided into different sections and frequently candidates must answer a certain number of questions from each section. Sometimes you will be asked to write certain questions in certain answer books.

Keep to the timing you have worked out.
Do not spend more than the time which you have allocated for each question. If you run out of time, leave that question and go on to the next one, returning to the unfinished question if you have some spare time later.

Answer the question.
Read the question carefully. To gain the maximum number of marks, your answer must be relevant to the question you have been asked. If you are

familiar with a topic on which a question is set, it is tempting to write down a version of your notes, which includes all you know about that topic, in the hope that you will get a reasonable number of marks. However, if you merely write all you happen to know about a topic, it is unlikely that you will be answering the question. You need to slant your information to the question, showing how the things you know relate to the precise question which you have been asked.

Answer the correct number of questions
Under pressure of time, some people fail to answer the whole examination paper by missing out a question. They often use the last few minutes to perfect their answers to the questions they have completed. This is not a good strategy. Examiners can only award marks for what is written on the examination paper. By not answering a question, you have forfeited all the marks allocated to that question. However, it is often said that the easiest marks to gain are the ones awarded for the beginning of an answer, so if you do run out of time, it is much better to use those final minutes to start the final question, rather than perfecting answers you have already finished.

Remember that examiners are human too.
When you are writing an examination paper, you often feel as if the examiner is the enemy "out there", determined to fail you. In fact, examiners do not want candidates to fail. They want to be fair, but they generally expect students who have done a reasonable amount of work to pass examinations.

INTERNATIONAL STUDENTS

The study skills discussed in this chapter are required by all law students. However, if English is not your first language you may feel that you would like some extra assistance with studying in the United Kingdom. Most institutions which welcome students from around the world have a support service which offers different classes covering a range of English Language and study skills, and you should try and find out about these at an early stage in your course. Many institutions also offer self-access materials, which you can go and use at a time which is convenient for you.

The support service will also be able to help you familiarise yourself with the particular types of teaching and learning situations which you will find in British educational institutions, what might be termed the "hidden culture" of learning, such as particular ways of writing essays or behaving in seminars, which might be different to those with which you are familiar at home. This sort of information can be very useful, as it is impossible to discover beforehand, however good your English is.

FURTHER READING

If you would like to find out more about any of the topics covered in this chapter, you will find that there are many books on study skills available. The following brief list includes books which cover a wide range of study skills.

R. Barnes, Successful Study for Degrees (2nd ed., 1995) Routledge.
S. Cottrell, The Study Skills Handbook (1999) Macmillan.
L. Marshall & F. Rowland, A Guide to Learning Independently (2nd ed., 1993) Open University Press.

PART 3

EXERCISES

This section of the book will test your understanding of the skills we have just described. Before attempting each exercise reread the appropriate chapter of this book. Each exercise is divided into two sections. Answers to Section A in each exercise are to be found at the back of this book. Do not look at these answers before you have tried to do the questions yourself. There are no answers to Section B in this book. You should discuss your answers to these questions with either your course tutor or with someone else you know who is studying law.

Exercise 1

STATUTES I

Start by re-reading the appropriate parts of Chapter 5 and then look at the Knives Act 1997. Then answer the questions. When answering the questions, make sure that you include the correct statutory reference.

Knives Act 1997

(1997 c. 21)

ARRANGEMENT OF SECTIONS

The offences

1. Unlawful marketing of knives.
2. Publications.

The defences

3. Exempt trades.
4. Other defences.

Supplementary powers

5. Supplementary powers of entry, seizure and retention.
6. Forfeiture of knives and publications.
7. Effect of a forfeiture order.

Stopping and searching

8. Powers to stop and search for knives or offensive weapons.

Miscellaneous

9. Offences by bodies corporate.
10. Interpretation.
11. Short title, commencement, extent etc.

An Act to create new criminal offences in relation to the possession or marketing of, and publications relating to, knives; to confer powers on the police to stop and search people or vehicles for knives and other offensive weapons and to seize items found; and for connected purposes.
[March 19, 1971]

The offences

Unlawful marketing of knives

1.—(1) A person is guilty of an offence if he markets a knife in a way which—

(a) indicates, or suggests, that it is suitable for combat; or

(b) is otherwise likely to stimulate or encourage violent behaviour involving the use of the knife as a weapon.

(2) "Suitable for combat" and "violent behaviour" are defined in section 10

(3) For the purposes of this Act, an indication or suggestion that a knife is suitable for combat may, in particular, be given or made by a name or description—

(a) applied to the knife;

(b) on the knife or on any packaging in which it is contained;

(c) or included in any advertisement which, expressly or by implication, relates to the knife.

(4) For the purposes of this Act, a person markets a knife if

(a) he sells or hires it;

(b) he offers, or exposes, it for sale or hire; or

(c) he has it in his possession for the purpose of sale or hire.

(5) a person who is guilty of an offence under this section is liable—

(a) on summary conviction to imprisonment for a term not exceeding six months or to a fine not exceeding the statutory maximum, or to both;

(b) on conviction on indictment to imprisonment for a term not exceeding two years or to a fine, or to both.

Publications

2.—(1) A person is guilty of an offence if he publishes any written, pictorial or other material in connection with the marketing of any knife and that material—

(a) indicates, or suggests, that the knife is suitable for combat; or

(b) is otherwise likely to stimulate or encourage violent behaviour involving the use of the knife as a weapon.

(2) a person who is guilty of an offence under this section is liable—

(a) on summary conviction to imprisonment for a term not exceeding six months or to a fine not exceeding the statutory maximum, or to both;

(b) on conviction on indictment to imprisonment for a term not exceeding two years or to a fine, or to both.

The defences

Exempt trades

3.—(1) It is a defence for a person charged with an offence under section 1 to prove that—

(a) the knife was marketed—

(i)   for use by the armed forces of any country;

(ii) as an antique or curio; or

(iii) as falling within such other category (if any) as may be prescribed;

(b) it was reasonable for the knife to be marketed in that way; and

(c) there were no reasonable grounds for suspecting that a person in whose possession the knife might come in consequence of the way in which it was marketed would use it for an unlawful purpose.

(2) It is a defence for a person charged with an offence under section 2 to prove that—

(a) the material was published in connection with marketing a knife—

(i)   for use by the armed forces of any country;

(ii) as an antique or curio; or

(iii) as falling within such other category (if any) as may be prescribed;

(b) it was reasonable for the knife to be marketed in that way; and

(c) there were no reasonable grounds for suspecting that a person into whose possession the knife might come in consequence of the publishing of the material would use it for an unlawful purpose.

(3) In this section "prescribed" means prescribed by regulations made by the Secretary of State.

Other defences

4.—(1) It is a defence for a person charged with an offence under section 1 to prove that he did not know or suspect, and had no reasonable grounds for suspecting, that the way in which the knife was marketed—

(a) amounted to an indication or suggestion that the knife was suitable for combat; or

(b) was likely to stimulate or encourage violent behaviour involving the use of the knife as a weapon.

(2) It is a defence for a person charged with an offence under section 2 to prove that he did not know or suspect, and had no reasonable grounds for suspecting, that the material—

(a) amounted to an indication or suggestion that the knife was suitable for combat; or

(b) was likely to stimulate or encourage violent behaviour involving the use of the knife as a weapon.

(3) It is a defence for a person charged with an offence under section 1 or 2 to prove that he took all reasonable precautions and exercised all due diligence to avoid committing the offence.

Supplementary powers

Supplementary powers of entry, seizure and retention

5.—(1) If, on an application made by a constable, a justice of the peace or sheriff is satisfied that there are reasonable grounds for suspecting—

(a) that a person ("the suspect") has committed an offence under section 1 in relation to knives of a particular description, and

(b) that knives of that description and in the suspect's possession or under his control are to be found on particular premises, the justice or sheriff may issue a warrant authorising a constable to enter those premises, search for the knives and seize and remove any that he finds.

(2) If, on an application made by a constable, a justice of the peace or sheriff is satisfied that there are reasonable grounds for suspecting—

(a) that a person ("the suspect") has committed an offence under section 2 in relation to particular material, and

(b) that publications consisting of or containing that material and in the suspect's possession or under his control are to be found on particular premises.

The justice or sheriff may issue a warrant authorising a constable to enter those premises, search for the publications and seize and remove any that he finds.

(3) A constable, in the exercise of his powers under a warrant issued under this section, may if necessary use reasonable force.

(4) Any knives or publications which have been seized and removed by a constable under a warrant issued under this section may be retained until the conclusion of proceedings against the suspect.

(5) For the purposes of this section, proceedings in relation to a suspect are concluded if—

(a) he is found guilty and sentenced or otherwise dealt with for the offence;

(b) he is acquitted;

(c) proceedings for the offence are discontinued;

(d) or it is decided not to prosecute him.

(6) In this section "premises" includes any place and, in particular, any vehicle, vessel, aircraft or hovercraft and any tent or movable structure.

Forfeiture of knives and publications

6.—(1) If a person is convicted of an offence under section 1 in relation to a knife of a particular description, the court may make an order for forfeiture in respect of any knives of that description—

(a) seized under a warrant issued under section 5; or

(b) in the offender's possession or under his control at the relevant time.

(2) If a person is convicted of an offence under section 2 in relation to particular material, the court may make an order for forfeiture in respect of or containing that material which—

(a) have been seized under a warrant issued under section 5; or

(b) were in the offender's possession or under his control at the relevant time.

(3) The court may make an order under subsection (1) or (2)—

(a) whether or not it also deals with the offender in respect of the offence in any other way; and

(b) without regard to any restrictions on forfeiture in any enactment.

(4) In considering whether to make an order, the court must have regard—

(a) to the value of the property; and

(b) to the likely financial and other effects on the offender of the making of the order (taken together with any other order that the court contemplates making).

(5) In this section "relevant time"—

(a) in relation to a person convicted in England and Wales or Northern Ireland of an offence under section 1 or 2, means the time of his arrest for the offence or of the issue of a summons in respect of it;

(b) in relation to a person so convicted in Scotland, means the time of his arrest for the offence or of his being cited as an accused in respect of it.

Effect of a forfeiture order

7.—(1) An order under section 6 (a "forfeiture order") operates to deprive the offender of his rights, if any, in the property to which it relates.

(2) The property to which a forfeiture order relates must be taken into the possession of the police (if it is not already in their possession).

(3) The court may, on an application made by a person who

(a) claims property to which a forfeiture order applies, but

(b) is not the offender from whom it was forfeited,

make an order (a "recovery order") for delivery of the property to the applicant, if it appears to the court that he owns it.

(4) An application to a sheriff must be made in such manner as may be prescribed by act of adjournal.

(5) No application may be made after the end of the period of six months beginning with the date on which the forfeiture order was made.

(6) No application may succeed unless the claimant satisfies the court

(a) that he had not consented to the offender having possession of the property; or

(b) that he did not know, and had no reason to suspect, that the offence was likely to be committed.

(7) If a person has a right to recover property which is in the possession of another in pursuance of a recovery order, that right—

(a) is not affected by the making of the recovery order at any time before the end of the period of six months beginning with the date on which the order is made; but

(b) is lost at the end of that period.

(8) The Secretary of State may make regulations, in relation to property forfeited under this section, for disposing of the property and dealing with the proceeds in cases where—

(a) no application has been made before the end of the period of 6 months beginning with the date on which the forfeiture order was made; or

(b) no such application has succeeded.

(9) The regulations may also provide for investing money and auditing accounts.

(10) In this section, "application" means an application under subsection (3).

Stopping and Searching

Powers to stop and search for knives or offensive weapons

8.—(1) Section 60 of the Criminal Justice and Public Order Act 1994 (powers to stop and search in anticipation of violence is amended as follows.

(2) For subsection (1) substitute—

"(1) If a police officers of or above the rank of inspector reasonably believes—

(a) that incidents involving serious violence may take place in any locality in his police area, and that it is expedient to give an authorisation under this section to prevent their occurrence, or

(b) that persons are carrying dangerous instruments or offensive weapons in any locality in his police area without good reason, he may give an authorisation that the powers conferred by this section are to be exercisable at any place within that locality for a specified period not exceeding 24 hours."

(3) Subsection (2) (exercise by chief inspector or inspector of power to give authorisation is repealed.

(4) In subsection (3) (continuation of authorisation)—

(a) for "the officer who gave the authorisation or to a "substitute" an officer of or above the rank of ";

(b) for "incident" substitute "activity";

(c) for "six" substitute "24".

(5) After subsection (3) insert—

"(3A) If an inspector gives an authorisation under subsection (1) he must, as soon as it is practicable to do so, cause an officer of or above the rank of superintendent to be informed."

(6) In subsection (9) (matters to be specified in authorisations) after "specify" insert "the grounds on which it is given and".

(7) In subsection (10), the words from "and similarly" to the end of the subsection are repealed.

(8) After subsection (10) insert—

"(10A) A person who is searched by a constable under this section shall be entitled to obtain a written statement that he was searched under the powers conferred by this section if he applies for such a statement not later than the end of the period of twelve months from the day on which he was searched."

(9) In subsection (11), in the definition of "offensive weapon", after "Act 1984" insert "or, in relation to Scotland, section 47(4) of the Criminal Law (Consolidation) (Scotland) Act 1995".

(10) After subsection (11) insert—

"(11A) For the purposes of this section, a person carries a dangerous instrument or an offensive weapon if he has it in his possession."

(11) Section 60 of the Act of 1994 is to extend to Scotland; and accordingly in section 172(8) of that Act (list of provisions that extend to Scotland), for "61 to 67 substitute" 60 to 67.

Miscellaneous

Offences by bodies corporate

9.—(1) If an offence under this Act committed by a body corporate is proved—

(a) to have been committed with the consent or connivance of an officer, or

(b) to be attributable to any neglect on his part, he as well as the body corporate is guilty of the offence and liable to be proceeded against and punished accordingly.

(2) In subsection (1) "officer", in relation to a body corporate, means a director, manager, secretary or other similar officer of the body, or a person purporting to act in any such capacity.

(3) If the affairs of a body corporate are managed by its members, subsection (1) applies in relation to the acts and defaults of a member in connection with his functions of management as if he were a director of the body corporate.

(4) If an offence under this Act committed, by a partnership in Scotland is proved—

(a) to have been committed with the consent or connivance of a partner, or

(b) to be attributable to any neglect on his part, he as well as the partnership is guilty of the offence and liable to be proceeded against and punished accordingly.

Interpretation

In this Act

10. "the court" means—

(a) in relation to England and Wales or Northern Ireland, the Crown Court or a magistrate's court;

(b) in relation to Scotland, the sheriff;

"knife" means an instrument which has a blade or is sharply pointed;

"marketing" and related expressions are to be read with section 1(4);

"publication" includes a publication in electronic form and, in the case of a publication which is, or may be, produced from electronic data, any medium on which the data are stored;

"suitable for combat" means suitable for use as a weapon for inflicting injury on a person or causing a person to fear injury;

"violent behaviour" means an unlawful act inflicting injury on a person or causing a person to fear injury.

Short title, commencement, extent etc.

11.—(1) This Act may be cited as the Knives Act 1997.

(2) This section comes into force on the passing of this Act.

(3) The other provisions of this Act come into force on such date as may be appointed by order made by the Secretary of State; but different dates may be appointed for different provisions and for different purposes.

(4) Any such order may include such transitional provisions or savings as the Secretary of State considers appropriate.

(5) The power—

(a) to make regulations under section 3 or 7, or

(b) to make an order under this section, is exercisable by statutory instrument.

(6) A statutory instrument made under section 3 or 7 shall be subject to annulment in pursuance of a resolution of either House of Parliament.

(7) Except for section 8, this Act extends to Northern Ireland.

Section A

1. What criminal offences does this Act create?

2. To which parts of the United Kingdom does it apply?

3. What further information do you require to know whether it is in force?

4. Jonathan, an arms trader has a stand at the Eurasian Arms Fair in London in order to sell weapons, including combat knives, to armies from overseas. Has he committed an offence under the Knives Act?

5. Dimitri has a business producing high quality sports knives for use by anglers and hunters. He advertises the knives in a specialist magazine, *Hunting Life* with the following text, 'Steel sharp blades, excellent for gutting and skinning. . . .' Has he, or the publisher of *Hunting Life*, committed an offence under the Knives Act?

6. Gurpul owns an ornamental sword and dagger. They are stolen from his house and are later found on offer at a car boot sale together with army surplus clothing and old army cap badges. Wally, the man selling these items, is arrested and charged with an offence under s.1(1) of the Knives Act. If Wally is convicted can Gurpul get his sword and dagger back?

Section B

7. What is the short title of this Act?

8. Why do you think this Act was passed?

9. Eric owns a combat knife which he bought before the Knives Act 1997 came into force. Does he commit an offence by continuing to possess it? Can he sell it to Tom?

10. Dorothy runs a dress-making business and also sells fabric, dress patterns, and dress-making equipment from her shop. She arranges a window display showing a dummy draped with black material and surrounded by scissors lying on blood red silk. One pair of scissors is cutting the fabric around the dummy's neck. A sign in the window announces 'The sharpest scissors ever! They will cut anything!' A neighbouring shop keeper has complained about this display. Has Dorothy committed any offences under the Knives Act? If so does she have any defences?

11. Stella has a business selling security and protection equipment, particularly to security officers. She knows that some items are also used by criminals. She wants to know whether she needs to take any new precautions when marketing or advertising her latest range of equipment which includes clubs, truncheons and stun guns.

12. Is it likely that the Knives Act will reduce the number of assaults with knives?

EXERCISE 2

STATUTES II

Dangerous Dogs Act 1991

(1991 C. 65)

ARRANGEMENT OF SECTIONS

SECT.
 1. Dogs bred for fighting.
 2. Other specially dangerous dogs.
 3. Keeping dogs under proper control.
 4. Destruction and disqualification orders.
 5. Seizure, entry of premises and evidence.
 6. Dogs owned by young persons.
 7. Muzzling and leads.
 8. Power to make corresponding provision for Northern Ireland.
 9. Expenses.
10. Short title, interpretation, commencement and extent.

An Act to prohibit persons from having in their possession or custody dogs belonging to types bred for fighting; to impose restrictions in respect of such dogs pending the coming into force of the prohibition; to enable restrictions to be imposed in relation to other types of dog which present a serious danger to the public; to make further provision for securing that dogs are kept under proper control; and for connected purposes.

[July 25, 1991]

Dogs bred for fighting

1.—(1) This section applies to—
(a) any dog of the type known as the pit bull terrier;
(b) any dog of the type known as the Japanese tosa; and
(c) any dog of any type designated for the purposes of this section by an order of the Secretary of State, being a type appearing to him to be bred for fighting or to have the characteristics of a type bred for that purpose.
(2) No person shall—
(a) breed, or breed from, a dog to which this section applies;
(b) sell or exchange such a dog or offer, advertise or expose such a dog for sale or exchange;
(c) make or offer to make a gift of such a dog or advertise or expose such a dog as a gift;
(d) allow such a dog of which he is the owner or of which he is for the time being in charge to be in a public place without being muzzled and kept on a lead; or
(e) abandon such a dog of which he is the owner or, being the owner or for the time being in charge of such a dog, allow it to stray.
(3) After such day as the Secretary of State may by order appoint for the purposes of this subsection no person shall have any dog to which this section applies in his possession or custody except—

(a) in pursuance of the power of seizure conferred by the sub section provisions of this Act; or

(b) in accordance with an order for its destruction made under those provisions; but the Secretary of State shall by order make a scheme for the payment to the owners of such dogs who arrange for them to be destroyed before that day of sums specified in or determined under the scheme in respect of those dogs and the cost of their destruction.

(4) Subsection (2)(b) and (c) above shall not make unlawful anything done with a view to the dog in question being removed from the United Kingdom before the day appointed under subsection (3) above.

(5) The Secretary of State may by order provide that the prohibition in subsection (3) above shall not apply in such cases and subject to compliance with such conditions as are specified in the order and any such provision may take the form of a scheme of exemption containing such arrangements (including provision for the payment of charges or fees) as he thinks appropriate

(6) A scheme under subsection (3) or (5) above may provide for specified functions under the scheme to be discharged by such persons or bodies as the Secretary of State thinks appropriate.

(7) Any person who contravenes this section is guilty of an offence and liable on summary conviction to imprisonment for a term not exceeding six months or a fine not exceeding level 5 on the standard scale or both except that a person who publishes an advertisement in contravention of subsection 2(b) or (c)—

(a) shall not on being convicted be liable to imprisonment if he shows that he published the advertisement to the order of someone else and did not himself devise it; and

(b) shall not be convicted if, in addition, he shows that he did not know and had no reasonable cause to suspect that it related to a dog to which this section applies.

(8) An order under subsection (1)(c) above adding dogs of any type to those to which this section applies may provide that subsections (3) and (4) above shall apply in relation to those dogs with the substitution for the day appointed under subsection (3) of a later day specified in that order.

(9) The power to make orders under this section shall be exercisable by statutory instrument which, in the case of an order under subsection (1) or (5) or an order containing a scheme under subsection (3), shall be subject to annulment in pursuance of a resolution of either House of Parliament.

Other specially dangerous dogs

2.—(1) If it appears to the Secretary of State that dogs of any type to which section 1 above does not apply present a serious danger to the public he may by order impose in relation to dogs of that type restrictions corresponding, with such modifications, if any, as he thinks appropriate, to all or any of those in subsection (2)(d) and (e) of that section.

(2) An order under this section may provide for exceptions from any restriction imposed by the order in such cases and subject to compliance with such conditions as are specified in the order.

(3) An order under this section may contain such supplementary or transitional provisions as the Secretary of State thinks necessary or expedient and may create offences punishable on summary conviction with imprisonment for a term not exceeding six months or a fine not exceeding level 5 on the standard scale or both.

(4) In determining whether to make an order under this section in relation to dogs of any type and, if so, what the provisions of the order should be, the Secretary of State shall consult with such persons or bodies as appear to him to have relevant knowledge or experience, including a body concerned with animal welfare, a body concerned with veterinary science and practice and a body concerned with breeds of dogs.

(5) The power to make an order under this section shall be exercisable by statutory instrument and no such order shall be made unless a draft of it has been laid before and approved by a resolution of each House of Parliament.

Keeping dogs under proper control

3.—(1) If a dog is dangerously out of control in a public place—

(a) the owner; and

(b) if different, the person for the time being in charge of the dog, is guilty of an offence, or, if the dog while so out of control injures any person, an aggravated offence, under this subsection.

(2) In proceedings for an offence under subsection (1) above against a person who is the owner of a dog but was not at the material time in charge of it, it shall be a defence for the accused to prove that the dog was at the material time in the charge of a person whom he reasonably believed to be a fit and proper person to be in charge of it.

(3) If the owner or, if different, the person for the time being in charge of a dog allows it to enter a place which is not a public place but where it is not permitted to be and while it is there—

(a) it injures any person; or
(b) there are grounds for reasonable apprehension that it will do so, he is guilty of an offence, or, if the dog injures any person, an aggravated offence, under this subsection.

(4) A person guilty of an offence under subsection (1) or (3) above other than an aggravated offence is liable on summary conviction to imprisonment for a term not exceeding six months or a fine not exceeding level 5 on the standard scale or both; and a person guilty of an aggravated offence under either of those subsections is liable—

(a) on summary conviction, to imprisonment for a term not exceeding six months or a fine not exceeding the statutory maximum or both;
(b) on conviction on indictment, to imprisonment for a term not exceeding two years or a fine or both.

(5) It is hereby declared for the avoidance of doubt that an order under section 2 of the Dogs Act 1871 (order on complaint that dog is dangerous and not kept under proper control)

(a) may be made whether or not the dog is shown to have injured any person; and
(b) may specify the measures to be taken for keeping the dog under proper control, whether by muzzling, keeping on a lead, excluding it from specified places or otherwise.

(6) If it appears to a court on a complaint under section 2 of the said Act of 1871 that the dog to which the complaint relates is a male and would be less dangerous if neutered the court may under that section make an order requiring it to be neutered.

(7) The reference in section 1(3) of the Dangerous Dogs Act 1989 (penalties) to failing to comply with an order under section 2 of the said Act of 1871 to keep a dog under proper control shall include a reference to failing to comply with any other order made under that section; but no order shall be made under that section by virtue of subsection (6) above where the matters complained of arose before the coming into force of that subsection.

Destruction and disqualification orders

4.—(1) Where a person is convicted of an offence under section 1 or 3(1) or (3) above or of an offence under an order made under section 2 above the court—

(a) may order the destruction of any dog in respect of which the offence was committed and shall do so in the case of an offence under section 1 or an aggravated offence under section 3(1) or (3) above; and
(b) may order the offender to be disqualified, for such period as the court thinks fit, for having custody of a dog.

(2) Where a court makes an order under subsection (1)(a) above for the destruction of a dog owned by a person other than the offender, then, unless the order is one that the court is required to make, the owner may appeal to the Crown Court against the order.

(3) A dog shall not be destroyed pursuant to an order under subsection (1)(a) above—

(a) until the end of the period for giving notice of appeal against the conviction or, where the order was not one which the court was required to make, against the order; and
(b) if notice of appeal is given within that period, until the appeal is determined or withdrawn, unless the offender and, in a case to which subsection (2) above applies, the owner of the dog give notice to the court that made the order that there is to be no appeal.

(4) Where a court makes an order under subsection (1)(a) above it may—

(a) appoint a person to undertake the destruction of the dog and require any person having custody of it to deliver it up for that purpose; and
(b) order the offender to pay such sum as the court may determine to be the reasonable expenses of destroying the dog and of keeping it pending its destruction.

(5) Any sum ordered to be paid under subsection (4)(b) above shall be treated for the purposes of enforcement as if it were a fine imposed on conviction.

(6) Any person who is disqualified for having custody of a dog by virtue of an order under subsection (1)(b) above may, at any time after the end of the period of one year beginning with the date of the order, apply to the court that made it (or a magistrates' court acting for the same petty sessions area as that court) for a direction terminating the disqualification.

(7) On an application under subsection (6) above the court may—

(a) having regard to the applicant's character, his conduct since the disqualification was imposed and any other circumstances of the case, grant or refuse the application; and

(b) order the applicant to pay all or any part of the costs of the application; and where an application in respect of an order is refused no further application in respect of that order shall be entertained if made before the end of the period of one year beginning with the date of the refusal.

(8) Any person who—

(a) has custody of a dog in contravention of an order under subsection (1)(b) above; or

(b) fails to comply with a requirement imposed on him under subsection (4)(a) above, is guilty of an offence and liable on summary conviction to a fine not exceeding level 5 on the standard scale.

(9) In the application of this section to Scotland—

(a) in subsection (2) for the words "Crown Court against the order" there shall be substituted the words "High Court of Justiciary against the order within the period of seven days beginning with the date of the order";

(b) for subsection (3)(a) there shall be substituted—"(a) until the end of the period of seven days beginning with the date of the order";

(c) for subsection (5) there shall be substituted—"(5) Section 411 of the Criminal Procedure (Scotland) Act 1975 shall apply in relation to the recovery of sums ordered to be paid under subsection (4)(b) above as it applies to fines ordered to be recovered by civil diligence in pursuance of Part II of that Act."; and

(d) in subsection (6) the words "(or a magistrates' court acting for the same petty sessions area as that court)" shall be omitted.

Seizure, entry of premises and evidence

5.—(1) A constable or an officer of a local authority authorised by it to exercise the powers conferred by this subsection may seize—

(a) any dog which appears to him to be a dog to which section 1 above applies and which is in a public place—

   (i) after the time when possession or custody of it has become unlawful by virtue of that section; or

   (ii) before that time, without being muzzled and kept on a lead;

(b) any dog in a public place which appears to him to be a dog to which an order under section 2 above applies and in respect of which an offence against the order has been or is being committed; and

(c) any dog in a public place (whether or not one to which that section or such an order applies) which appears to him to be dangerously out of control.

(2) If a justice of the peace is satisfied by information on oath, or in Scotland a justice of the peace or sheriff is satisfied by evidence on oath, that there are reasonable grounds for believing—

(a) that an offence under any provision of this Act or of an order under section 2 above is being or has been committed; or

(b) that evidence of the commission of any such offence is to be found, on any premises he may issue a warrant authorising a constable to enter those premises (using such force as is reasonably necessary) and to search them and seize any dog or other thing found there which is evidence of the commission of such an offence.

(3) A warrant issued under this section in Scotland shall be authority for opening lockfast places and may authorise persons named in the warrant to accompany a constable who is executing it.

(4) Where a dog is seized under subsection (1) or (2) above and it appears to a justice of the peace, or in Scotland a justice of the peace or sheriff, that no person has been or is to be prosecuted for an offence under this Act or an order under section 2 above in respect of that dog (whether because the owner cannot be found or for any other reason) he may order the destruction of the dog and shall do so if it is one to which section 1 above applies.

(5) If in any proceedings it is alleged by the prosecution that a dog is one to which section 1 or an order under section 2 above applies it shall be presumed that it is such a dog unless the contrary is shown by the accused by such evidence as the court considers sufficient; and the accused shall not be permitted to adduce such evidence unless he has given the prosecution notice of his intention to do so not later than the fourteenth day before that on which the evidence is to be adduced.

Dogs owned by young persons

6. Where a dog is owned by a person who is less than sixteen years old any reference to its owner in section 1(2)(d) or (e) or 3 above shall include a reference to the head of the household, if any, of which that person is a member or, in Scotland, to the person who has his actual care and control.

Muzzling and leads

7.—(1) In this Act—
(a) references to a dog being muzzled are to its being securely fitted with a muzzle sufficient to prevent it biting any person; and
(b) references to its being kept on a lead are to its being securely held on a lead by a person who is not less than sixteen years old.

(2) If the Secretary of State thinks it desirable to do so he may by order prescribe the kind of muzzle or lead to be used for the purpose of complying in the case of a dog of any type, with section 1 or an order under section 2 above; and if a muzzle or lead of a particular kind is for the time being prescribed in relation to any type of dog the references in subsection (1) above to a muzzle or lead shall, in relation to any dog of that type, be construed as references to a muzzle or lead of that kind.

(3) The power to make an order under subsection (2) above shall be exercisable by statutory instrument subject to annulment in pursuance of a resolution of either House of Parliament.

Power to make corresponding provision for Northern Ireland

8. An Order in Council under paragraph 1(1)(b) of Schedule 1 to the Northern Ireland Act 1974 (legislation for Northern Ireland in the interim period) which states that it is made only for purposes corresponding to the purposes of this Act—
(a) shall not be subject to paragraph 1(4) and (5) of that Schedule (affirmative resolution of both Houses of Parliament); but
(b) shall be subject to annulment in pursuance of a resolution of either House.

Expenses

9. Any expenses incurred by the Secretary of State in consequence of this Act shall be paid out of money provided by Parliament.

Short title, interpretation, commencement and extent

10.—(1) This Act may be cited as the Dangerous Dogs Act 1991.
(2) In this Act—

"advertisement" includes any means of bringing a matter to the attention of the public and "advertise" shall be construed accordingly;
"public place" means any street, road or other place (whether or not enclosed) to which the public have or are permitted to have access whether for payment or otherwise and includes the common parts of a building containing two or more separate dwellings.

(3) For the purposes of this Act a dog shall be regarded as dangerously out of control on any occasion on which there are grounds for reasonable apprehension that it will injure any person, whether or not it actually does so, but references to a dog injuring a person or there being grounds for reasonable apprehension that it will do so do not include references to any case in which the dog is being used for a lawful purpose by a constable or a person in the service of the Crown.

(4) Except for section 8, this Act shall not come into force until such day as the Secretary of State may appoint by an order made by statutory instrument and different days may be appointed for different provisions or different purposes.

(5) Except for section 8, this Act does not extend to Northern Ireland.

Dangerous Dogs (Amendment) Act 1997

(1997 C. 53)

ARRANGEMENT OF SECTIONS

An Act to amend the Dangerous Dogs Act 1991; and for connected purposes.
[March 21, 1997]

Destruction orders

1.—(1) In paragraph (a) of subsection (1) of section 4 (destruction and disqualification orders) of the Dangerous Dogs Act 1991 ("the 1991 Act"), after the words "committed and" there shall be inserted the words "subject to subsection (1A) below,".

(2) After that subsection there shall be inserted the following subsection-

"(1A) Nothing in subsection (1)(a) above shall require the court to order the destruction of a dog if the court is satisfied—

that the dog would not constitute a danger to public safety; and where the dog was born before 30th November 1991 and is subject to the prohibition in section 1(3) above, that there is a good reason why the dog has not been exempted from that prohibition."

(3) In subsection (2) of that section, the words "then, unless the order is one that the court is required to make" shall cease to have effect.

(4) In subsection (3)(a) of that section, the words "where the order was not one that the court was required to make" shall cease to have effect.

Contingent destruction orders

2. After section 4 of the 1991 Act there shall be inserted the following section—
"Contingent destruction orders
4A.—(1) Where—

(a) a person is convicted of an offence under section 1 above or an aggravated offence under section 3(1) or (3) above;

(b) the court does not order the destruction of the dog under section 4(1)(a) above; and

(c) in the case of an offence under section 1 above, the dog is subject to the prohibition in section 1(3) above, the court shall order that, unless the dog is exempted from that prohibition within the requisite period, the dog shall be destroyed.

(2) Where an order is made under subsection (1) above in respect of a dog, and the dog is not exempted from the prohibition in section 1(3) above within the requisite period, the court may extend that period.

(3) Subject to subsection (2) above, the requisite period for the purposes of such an order is the period of two months beginning with the date of the order.

(4) Where a person is convicted of an offence under section 3(1) or (3) above, the court may order that, unless the owner of the dog keeps it under proper control, the dog shall be destroyed.

(5) An order under subsection (4) above—

(a) may specify the measures to be taken for keeping the dog under proper control, whether by muzzling, keeping on a lead, excluding it from specified places or otherwise; and

(b) if it appears to the court that the dog is a male and would be less dangerous if neutered, may require it to be neutered.

(6) Subsections (2) to (4) of section 4 above shall apply in relation to an order under subsection (1) or (4) above as they apply in relation to an order under subsection (1)(a) of that section."

Destruction orders otherwise than on a conviction

3.—(1) After section 4A of the 1991 Act there shall be inserted the following section—
"Destruction orders otherwise than on a conviction
4B.—(1) Where a dog is seized under section 5(1) or (2) below and it appears to a justice of the peace, or in Scotland a justice of the peace or sheriff—

(a) that no person has been or is to be prosecuted for an offence under this Act or an order under section 2 above in respect of that dog (whether because the owner cannot be found or for any other reason); or

(b) that the dog cannot be released into the custody or possession of its owner without the owner contravening the prohibition in section 1(3) above,

he may order the destruction of the dog and, subject to subsection (2) below, shall do so if it is one to which section 1 above applies.

(2) Nothing in subsection (1)(b) above shall require the justice or sheriff to order the destruction of a dog if he is satisfied—

(a) that the dog would not constitute a danger to public safety; and

(b) where the dog was born before November 30, 1991 and is subject to the prohibition in section 1(3) above, that there is a good reason why the dog has not been exempted from that prohibition.

(3) Where in a case failing within subsection (1)(b) above the justice or sheriff does not order the destruction of the dog, he shall order that, unless the dog is exempted from the prohibition in section 1(3) above within the requisite period, the dog shall be destroyed.

(4) Subsections (2) to (4) of section 4 above shall apply in relation to an order under subsection (1)(b) or (3) above as they apply in relation to an order under subsection (1)(a) of that section.

(5) Subsections (2) and (3) of section 4A above shall apply in relation to an order under subsection (3) above as they apply in relation to an order under subsection (1) of that section, except that the reference to the court in subsection (2) of that section shall be construed as a reference to the justice or sheriff."

(6) In section 5 of the 1991 Act (seizure, entry of premises and evidence), subsection (4) (which is superseded by this section) shall cease to have effect.

Extended, application of 1991 Order

4.—(1) Where an order is made under section 4A(1) or 413(3) of the 1991 Act, Part 111 of the Dangerous Dogs Compensation and Exemption Schemes Order 1991 (exemption scheme) shall have effect as if—

(a) any reference to the appointed day were a reference to the end of the requisite period within the meaning of section 4A or, as the case may be, section 4B of the 1991 Act;

(b) paragraph (a) of Article 4 and Article 6 were omitted; and

(c) the fee payable to the Agency under Article 9 were a fee of such amount as the Secretary of State may by order prescribe.

(2) The power to make an order under this section shall be exercisable by statutory instrument which shall be subject to annulment in pursuance of a resolution of either House of Parliament.

Transitional provisions

5.—(1) This Act shall apply in relation to cases where proceedings have been instituted before, as well as after, the commencement of this Act.

(2) In a case where, before the commencement of this Act—

(3) the court has ordered the destruction of a dog in respect of which an offence under section 1, or an aggravated offence under section 3(1) or (3), of the 1991 Act has been committed, but

    (a) the dog has not been destroyed, that destruction order shall cease to have effect and the case shall be remitted to the court for reconsideration.

(3) Where a case is so remitted, the court may make any order in respect of the dog which it would have power to make if the person in question had been convicted of the offence after the commencement of this Act.

6.—(1) This Act may be cited as the Dangerous Dogs (Amendment) Act 1997.

(2) This Act does not extend to Northern Ireland.

(3) This Act shall come into force on such day as the Secretary of State may by order made by statutory instrument appoint.

Section A

1. When did section 4A of the Dangerous Dogs Act 1991 come into force?

2. To what parts of the United Kingdom do these two Acts apply?

3. Does the Dangerous Dogs Act 1991 define "dangerous dogs"?

4. Peter is the proud owner of a pit bull terrier, Pugsy. When the Dangerous Dogs Act 1991 came into force Peter moved to Ireland with Pugsy. He is now planning to return to England and wants advice about whether he can bring Pugsy with him.

5. Peter returns to England with Pugsy but has failed to apply for an exemption. The local park keeper saw Pugsy in the park off his lead and told the police. Peter is being prosecuted for allowing his dog to be in a public place without a lead and an application has been made for Pugsy's destruction. Advise Peter about the court's powers if he is convicted.

6. Barbara is exercising her dog, Becks, in the park when it suddenly sees another dog, rushes towards it and its owner, a seven year old boy, and begins to fight with the other dog. The boy attempts to separate the dogs and is bitten by Becks.

    (i) what offence, if any, has Barbara committed?
    (ii) Would it make any difference if Barbara was not walking the dog herself but had paid, Stan, a professional dog walker to exercise Becks for her?
    (iii) who would be liable if the dog fight occurred because the boy's dog rather than Becks was out of control?

7. What were the main changes to the Dangerous Dogs Act 1991 introduced by the 1997 Act?

Section B

8. Once the destruction of a dog has been ordered how long must elapse before the dog can be destroyed?

9. Who pays for the dog's care between the making and carrying out of the order for destruction?

10. Why was it thought necessary to amend the Dangerous Dogs Act? What sources of information would help find reasons for the reform?

11. How would you find out whether any other types of dog had been prohibited under s.2?

12. William has been breeding pit bull terriers at his remote farm ever since the Dangerous Dogs Act 1991. He has generally sold the puppies through friends but occasionally he has placed a postcard in a newsagent's window announcing, "For sale £1000 each, very special puppies, unobtainable elsewhere." William is arrested and charged with an offence under s.1(2). The newsagent is also charged. Advise the newsagent whether he can be convicted, and if so, what the penalties are.

13. Martha owns a large friendly dog called Bill. One day when she is walking down the road with Bill he slips his lead, runs into a garden where a child is playing and jumps ups, licks the child's face and knocks him over onto the grass. The child's mother is very angry and wants Martha to be prosecuted and Bill to be destroyed.

   (i) What offence, if any has Martha committed?
   (ii) What must be established if Bill is not to be destroyed?

14. Kurt, a security officer has a pet German Shepherd dog, Buster, which he also uses for his work. One night when he is patrolling a factory complex he sees a man climbing over the fence into the complex. He lets Buster off his lead and tells it to stop the man. Buster catches the man and starts to bite his leg. The man threatens to prosecute Kurt for having a dangerous dog. Advise Kurt.

Drafting exercise

15. Draft an amendment to the Dangerous Dogs Act 1991 which reverses the presumption that a dog whose owner has been convicted on an offence in sections 1 or 3 should be destroyed.

EXERCISE 3

CASE 1

Before:

THE MASTER OF THE ROLLS
LADY JUSTICE HALE
and
LORD MUSTILL

CHIEF CONSTABLE OF WEST YORKSHIRE POLICE &   **Appellant**
ORS
– V –
R N KHAN   **Respondent**

EATRF 1999/0003/A1

February 24, 2000

The Court Service (Civil Judgments)

MR DAVID BEAN QC & MR DAVID JONES (instructed by Mr A K Hussain, Solicitor, West Yorkshire Police for the Appellants)
MR JOHN HAND QC & MISS MELANIE TETHER (instructed by Russell Jones & Walker, Leeds LS1 2HA for the Respondent)

Judgment: Approved by the court for handing down (subject to editorial corrections)

Lord Woolf MR:

1. This appeal raises a short but by no means easy point to resolve under the Race Relations Act 1976 ("RRA 1976"). As the relevant statutory provisions contained in the Sex Discrimination Act 1975 ("SDA 1975") are materially in identical terms it applies to that legislation as well. The issue involved can be encapsulated by asking: What should be the proper approach to selecting an appropriate comparator in determining complaints that a person has been victimised under either of the Acts?

Background

2. The appeal is from the judgment of the Employment Appeal Tribunal ("EAT") who gave judgment on 28 July 1998 dismissing the appellant's appeal from two decisions of an Employment Tribunal ("ET"), the first on 22 April 1997 and the second on 30 July 1997. The decisions were that the appellant had unlawfully victimised the respondent within the meaning of s.2 of the RRA 1976 and the respondent was awarded £1,500 damages.

3. The respondent was a Police Sergeant in the West Yorkshire Police. He believed that the appellant had discriminated against him on racial grounds by failing to support his application for promotion to Inspector. For this reason on 1 September 1996 he made a complaint to the ET alleging such discrimination. Subsequently in October 1996 the respondent completed an application form for an appointment as Inspector in the Norfolk Police. The Norfolk Police requested the employer's observations and recommendations on the suitability of the respondent for that post. The appellant's response was:

> "Sergeant Khan has an outstanding Industrial Tribunal application against the Chief Constable for failing to support his application for promotion.
>
> In the light of that, the Chief Constable is unable to comment any further for fear of prejudicing his own case before the Tribunal."

4. The Norfolk Police's request for the respondent's last two staff appraisals and a copy of any computer printout on the appellant's personnel system was refused. On learning of this the respondent amended his application to the ET to add a complaint of victimisation.

5. In fact the respondent was not excluded from assessment by the Norfolk Police. This was because the Norfolk Police have a policy to exclude only those applicants in respect of whom the recommendation stated the applicant was not supported. The appellant's response did not say this, so the respondent's application proceeded, but it was unsuccessful.

6. The respondent was not prejudiced by the conduct on which he based his claim for victimisation in relation to his application because, if a reference had been given it would in all probability have been adverse and, this being so, the respondent's application would not have been considered by the Norfolk Police. The ET dismissed the respondent's claim in respect of direct discrimination but his claim for victimisation succeeded. The appeal only concerns this decision and the award. The ET concluded that the respondent had not been caused any economic loss by the victimisation but that he had been caused an injury to his feelings. It was for this reason that the award of £1,500 was made. The EAT dismissed the appellant's appeal on broadly the same grounds as those of the ET. The decision of the ET as to damages was challenged on the grounds that the respondent gave no evidence as to injury to his feelings. The EAT held that such evidence had been given at the liability hearing.

7. In his Notice of Appeal, the appellant contends that:

> i. The ET and the EAT chose the wrong comparator in considering the issue of victimisation. In particular by rejecting a comparator who had brought proceedings against the employer other than under the RRA 1976, the tribunals had misdirected themselves in law.
>
> ii. The ET and the EAT had also misdirected themselves in coming to the conclusion that the appellant had acted "by reason" that the respondent had brought proceedings under the RRA 1976.
>
> iii. The ET and the EAT had erred in ruling that the evidence of injured feelings given at the liability hearing was sufficient to justify the award.
>
> iv. The award was excessive.

The Statutory Provisions

8. Turning to the statutory provisions, the starting point is the definition of racial discrimination contained in Part I, s.1 RRA 1976. This section is in the following terms:

"1. Racial discrimination

(1) A person discriminates against another in any circumstances relevant for the purposes of any provision of this Act if—

(a) on racial grounds he treats that other less favourably than he treats or would treat other persons; or

(b) he applies to that other a requirement or condition which he applies or would apply equally to persons not of the same racial group as that other but—

> (i) which is such that the proportion of persons of the same racial group as that other who can comply with it is considerably smaller than the proportion of persons not of that racial group who can comply with it; and

> (ii) which he cannot show to be justifiable irrespective of the colour, race, nationality or ethnic or national origins of the person to whom it is applied; and

> (iii) which is to the detriment of that other because he cannot comply with it."

9. The following section, s.2, contains a description of what constitutes victimisation. We are here only concerned with victimisation under s.2(1)(a). The relevant part of the section reads as follows:

"2. Discrimination by way of victimisation

(1) A person ("the discriminator") discriminates against another person ("the person victimised") in any circumstances relevant for the purposes of any provision of this Act if he treats the person victimised less favourably than in those circumstances he treats or would treat other persons, and does so by reason that the person victimisied has—

(a) brought proceedings against the discriminator or any other person under this Act; or

(b) given evidence or information in connection with proceedings brought by any person against the discriminator or any other person under this Act; or

(c) otherwise done anything under or by reference to this Act in relation to the discriminator or any other person; or

(d) alleged that the discriminator or any other person has committed an act which (whether or not the allegation so states) would amount to a contravention of this Act,

or by reason that the discriminator knows that the person victimised intends to do any of those things, or suspects that the person victimised has done, or intends to do, any of them.

(2) Subsection (1) does not apply to treatment of a person by reason of any allegation made by him if the allegation was false and not made in good faith."

10. The next section to which it is necessary to refer is s.3. Here the relevant provisions are:

"3. Meaning of "racial grounds", "racial group" etc.

(1) In this Act, unless the context otherwise requires—

"racial grounds" means any of the following grounds, namely colour, race, nationality or ethnic or national origins;

"racial group" means a group of persons defined by reference to colour, race, nationality or ethnic or national origins, and references to a person's racial group refer to any racial group into which he falls . . .

(3) In this Act—

(a) references to discrimination refer to any discrimination falling within section 1 or 2; and

(b) references to racial discrimination refer to any discrimination falling within section 1,

and related expressions shall be construed accordingly.

(4) A comparison of the case of a person of a particular racial group with that of a person not of that group under section 1(1) must be such that the relevant circumstances in the one case are the same, or not materially different, in the other."

11. A distinction is drawn in s.3(3) between "discrimination" which is common to both ss.1 and 2 and "racial discrimination" which is only apparently relevant in relation to s.1. This is at least an indication that racial discrimination is not involved in discrimination by way of victimisation.

12. The Act, having set out what is meant by racial discrimination and discrimination by way of victimisation, deals in the succeeding Parts with the different categories of discrimination. Part II deals with discrimination in the employment field. We are concerned with discrimination against applicants and employees under s.4. s.4 so far as relevant provides:

"(2) It is unlawful for a person, in the case of a person employed by him at an establishment in Great Britain, to discriminate against that employee—

(a) in the terms of employment which he affords him; or

(b) in the way he affords him access to opportunities for promotion, transfer or training, or to any other benefits, facilities or services, or by refusing or deliberately omitting to afford him access to them; or

(c) by dismissing him, or subjecting him to any other detriment."

13. This case involves discrimination by way of victimisation under s.4(2)(b) or (c).

The Interpretation of s.2

14. Although it is important to read the relevant provisions of the Act as a whole, what is in issue on this appeal is the proper interpretation of s.2. As to this, my initial reaction was that as the legislation is concerned with racial discrimination, victimisation which has nothing to do with race is unlikely to be intended to be unlawful under s.4. If this were not the position, there would be a danger of this Act not achieving the intention which is reflected in its long title, namely to make "fresh provision with respect to discrimination on racial grounds and relations between people of different racial groups". To regard a person as acting unlawfully when he had not been motivated either consciously or unconsciously by any discriminatory motive is hardly likely to assist the

objective of promoting harmonious racial relations. However, as the able arguments advanced by Mr Bean QC on behalf of the appellant and Mr Hand QC on behalf of the respondent made clear, the position is not as straightforward as that.

15. Mr Hand submits, rightly in my judgment, that to interpret s.2 properly it is necessary to give effect to three features of the section. First, there is a requirement that the section is to be looked at in its statutory context. This arises because of the presence of the words "in any circumstances relevant for the purposes of any provision of this Act". This feature is supported by the sentence in the second paragraph of the speech of Lord Nicholls of Birkenhead in Nagarajan v London Regional Transport [1999] ICR 877 where at p. 884D where he states: "[s]ection 2 should be read in the context of section 1". Mr Hand contends here that this involves recognising that s.2 is designed to prevent those who have taken steps to resist racial discrimination from being victimised in consequence of doing so.

16. In this case, the general objective was to protect those who brought proceedings under *"this Act"*. I agree with this general approach which is supported by the very wide language with which s.2(2) concludes.

17. The second feature of s.2 to which Mr Hand draws attention is the requirement that for a person to be victimised he must be treated "less favourably than in those circumstances the person alleged to be guilty of victimisation would treat other persons". This is the feature on which Mr Hand accepts the outcome of this appeal depends. He submits correctly that this feature requires a comparison between the manner in which the person victimised is treated and the way in which the appropriate comparator would be treated. The question is: who is the appropriate comparator? This is the rub to which it will be necessary for me to return. Mr Bean submits that the appropriate comparator is some other employee who has brought proceedings but not under the Act. Such an employee, Mr Bean with reason contends, would not have been treated any differently from the way in which the respondent was treated.

18. The third feature which Mr Hand identifies is that the complainant must have been victimised "by reason that [he] has" done the protected act. Here that is set out in s.2(1)(a). Again I accept that Mr Hand has correctly identified a feature of the section. In the application of this third feature, Mr Hand submits all that is required is the proper application of what has become known as a "but for" test. This is a test which is derived from the comparable provisions of the SDA 1975 but is equally applicable to the RRA 1976. It is a test which has been considered by the House of Lords in three decisions to which it is necessary for me to refer. However, before I do so I should explain that it depends on approaching the interpretation of the relevant sections of the SDA 1975 and of the RRA 1976 in the same manner.

19. S.1(1)(a) RRA 1976 requires the discrimination to have been "on racial grounds". S.2(1) RDA 1976 requires the victimisation must be "by reason that . . .". The equivalent provision to s.1 of the RRA 1976 is s.1 of the SDA 1975. That section requires the discrimination to be "on the ground of her sex" (s.1(1)(a)). S.4 of the SDA 1975, which is the equivalent of s.2 of the RRA 1976, requires the victimisation to be "by reason that the person victimised has" done the protected act. In R v The Birmingham City council, ex parte Equal Opportunities Commission [1989] AC 1155 and James v The Eastleigh Borough Council [1990] ICR 554 the House of Lords confirmed earlier authorities which had held that it was not correct to construe the phrase "on the ground of her sex" as referring to the alleged discriminator's reason for taking the action of which complaint is made. The question is objective and not subjective. As Lord Goff said in the *Birmingham* case (at pp. 1194A–C):

> "There is discrimination under the statute if there is less favourable treatment on the ground of sex, in other words if the relevant girl or girls would have received the same treatment as the boys but for their sex. The intention or motive of the defendant to discriminate, though it may be relevant so far as remedies are concerned, . . . is not a necessary condition of liability; it is perfectly possible to envisage cases where the defendant had no such motive, and yet did in fact discriminate on the ground of sex. Indeed, as Mr Lester pointed out in the course of his argument, if the council's submission were correct it would be a good defence

for an employer to show that he discriminated against the woman not because he intended to do so but (for example) because of customer preference, or to save money, or even to avoid controversy."

20. In the James case, which turned on the fact that the retirement age for men was 65 and that for women was 61, with the consequence that a 61 year old man was treated less favourably than his wife who was of the same age, Lord Bridge (at p. 568A) identified the question and the answer as being "[w]ould the plaintiff, a man of 61, have received the same treatment as his wife but for his sex?' An affirmative answer is inescapable."

21. In the same case (at p. 576C–F) Lord Goff said:

> "I incline to the opinion that, if it were necessary to identify the requisite intention of the defendant, that intention is simply an intention to perform the relevant act of less favourable treatment. Whether or not the treatment is less favourable in the relevant sense, *i.e.* on the ground of sex, may derive either from the application of a gender-based criterion to the complainant, or from selection by the defendant of the complainant because of his or her sex; but, in either event, it is not saved from constituting unlawful discrimination by the fact that the defendant acted from benign motive. However, in the majority of cases, I doubt if it is necessary to focus upon the intention or motive of the defendant in this way. This is because, as I see it, cases of direct discrimination under section 1(1)(a) can be considered by asking the simple question: would the complainant have received the same treatment from the defendant but for his or her sex? This simple text possesses the double virtue that, on the one hand, it embraces both the case where the treatment derives from the application of a gender-based criterion, and the case where it derives from the selection of the complainant because of his or her sex; and on the other hand it avoids, in most cases at least, complicated questions relating to concepts such as intention, motive, reason or purpose, and the danger of confusion arising from the misuse of those elusive terms. I have to stress, however, that the "but for" test is not appropriate for cases of indirect discrimination under section 1(1)(b), because there may be indirect discrimination against persons of one sex under that subsection, although a (proportionately smaller) group of persons of the opposite sex is adversely affected in the same way."

22. The third House of Lords decision is that in Nagarajan v London Regional Transport [1999] ICR 877. This case involved the RRA 1976 and s.2(1) of the Act. The House of Lords held, as appears from the headnote of that case, that a finding of direct discrimination on racial grounds under s.1(a) of the RRA 1976 did not require that the discriminator was consciously motivated in treating the complainant less favourably. It was sufficient if it could properly be inferred from the evidence that, regardless of the discriminator's motive or intention, a significant cause of his decision to treat that complainant less favourably was that person's race. This was because no proper distinction could be drawn between the terms "on racial grounds" in s.1(1)(a) and "by reason that" in s.2(1) of the Act of 1976. The discriminator need not have realised that he had in fact been motivated by his knowledge of the complainant having previously sought to enforce her rights under the Act. In his speech, Lord Nicholls first of all considered the position under s.1(1)(a) under the RRA 1976 and then turned to s.2. He said (at p. 886A–D):

> "'On racial grounds' in section 1(1)(a) and 'by reason that' in section 2(1) are interchangeable expressions in this context. The key question under section 2 is the same as under section 1(1)(a): why did the complainant receive less favourable treatment? The considerations mentioned above regarding direct discrimination under section 1(1)(a) are correspondingly appropriate under section 2. If the answer to this question is that the discriminator treated the person victimised less favourably by reason of his having done one of the acts listed in section 2(1) ("protected acts"), the case falls within the section. It does so, even if the discriminator did not consciously realise that for example, he was prejudiced because the job applicant had previously brought claims against his under the Act. In so far as the dictum in Aziz v Trinity Street Taxis Limited [1988] ICR 534, 548.

("a motive which is consciously connected with the race relations legislation") suggests otherwise, it cannot be taken as a correct statement of the law. ... Although victimisation has a ring of conscious targeting, this is an insufficient basis for excluding cases of unrecognised prejudice from the scope of section 2. Such an exclusion would partially undermine the protection section 2 seeks to give to those who have sought to rely on the Act or been involved in the operation of the Act in other ways."

23. In view of the combined fact of the three decisions of the House of Lords to which I have referred, the tribunals in this case were correct to take the view that if the respondent was treated less favourably contrary to s.2 that was by reason of a circumstance referred to in s.2(1)(a) RRA 1976. If it had not been for the proceedings brought under the Act a reference would have been provided.

24. It is now necessary to return to the question as to who is the correct comparator. Here I would like to look favourably upon Mr Bean's submission that you should ask whether the respondent was treated any differently from anyone else who brought proceedings. However, both on authority and on my construction of the Act, I feel driven to conclude that this is not the correct approach. The correct approach to the application of s.2 in this context is to identify the appropriate comparator, not by looking at the reason why the reference was not provided, but by considering what was requested. Here what was requested was a reference and it is necessary to compare the manner in which other employees in relation to whom a reference was requested would normally be treated and compare the way they would normally be treated with the way in which the respondent was treated. It is the request for a reference which is the circumstance which is relevant in finding the comparator under s.2 of the Act. The reason why the respondent was treated less favourably with regard to a reference was because he had brought proceedings. It would not, however, be correct to compare him only with those persons in order to ascertain whether he has been treated less favourably.

25. Turning to the authorities there are two cases which have to be considered here. The earlier case is Cornelius v UC Swansea [1987] IRLR 141 and the later case is Aziz v Trinity Street Taxis Limited [1988] ICR 534. The latter contains the dicta which Lord Nicholls criticised in his speech in Nagarajan. Both cases are decisions of this court. Mr Bean submits the Cornelius case requires us to find in his favour on the question of whether there has been less favourable treatment. Mr Hand contends that the Aziz case means that we are compelled to come to the opposite conclusion.

26. The Cornelius case involved a lady who brought various applications against the University by which she had been employed. One of the applications was in respect of victimisation under s.2 of the SDA 1975. The judgment with which the other members of the court agreed was given by Bingham LJ. I should set out the relevant paragraphs of the judgment in full (paras. 31–33). (It will be remembered that s.4 of the SDA 1975 is materially the same as s.2 of the RRA 1976.)

"In all these sections discrimination has as its primary meaning that which is given by s.1 (as extended to men by s.2). But the Act would be very defective if it stopped there, because those seeking to enforce the Act by the machinery provided or to promote the operation of the Act by word or deed could be subjected to penalties (or less favourable treatment) by persons who could say with some plausibility that they were not discriminating on grounds of sex by simply penalising troublemakers. If, therefore, the objects of the Act were to be achieved, there had to be protection for those who sought to rely on it or to promote its operation. That is the purpose of s.4, which has an obvious although partial analogy to the law of contempt. Two conclusions follow. The first is that in all the relevant substantive sections in Parts II and III of the Act 'discriminate' is to be understood as bearing both its s.1 meaning and its s.4 meaning. The second is that discrimination under s.4 is not discrimination on the ground of sex but discrimination on the ground of conduct of the type there described. I think the language of s.4 makes that clear, but if there were doubt, s.5(1) would resolve it.

In this appeal the crucial provision is s.4(1)(a). For the appellant's complaint to succeed here it would have to appear,

(i) that in refusing or omitting to afford the appellant access for opportunities for transfer or by subjecting her to the detriment of denying her access to the grievance procedure the College treated the applicant less favourably than it would in the same circumstances have treated other persons; and

(ii) that it did so because the appellant had brought proceedings against the College under the Act. That is the effect, on the facts here, of reading s.4(1)(a) into s.6(2)(a) and (b).

There is no finding here that (i) is made out, and it would certainly not be safe to infer that conclusion from the findings which have been made. The same is, in my judgment, true of (ii). There is no reason whatever to suppose that the decisions of the Registrar and his senior assistant on the applicant's requests for a transfer and a hearing under the grievance procedure were influenced in any way by the facts that the appellant had brought proceedings or that those proceedings were under the Act. The existence of proceedings plainly did influence their decisions. No doubt, like most experienced administrators, they recognised the risk of acting in a way which might embarrass the handling or be inconsistent with the outcome of current proceedings. They accordingly wished to defer action until the proceedings were over. But that had, so far as the evidence shows, nothing whatever to do with the appellant's conduct in bringing proceedings under the Act. There is no reason to think that their decision would have been different whoever had brought the proceedings or whatever their nature, if the subject matter was allied. If the appellant was victimised, it is not shown to have been because of her reliance on the Act. I differ from the EAT's view that a breach of s.4 was established."

27. Mr Bean relies on the final paragraph as indicating that it did not matter who brought the proceedings.

28. I do not regard this as being the correct way in which to understand what Bingham LJ was saying. The position is complicated by the fact that Bingham LJ was dealing in the paragraph with both the requirement for less favourable treatment and the requirement that the less favourable treatment had to be by reason of the prohibited act. What I understand Bingham LJ to have been saying was that it had been found that the fact that Mrs Cornelius had brought proceedings under the Act had nothing to do with her being deprived of the opportunity for a transfer or denied access to the grievance procedure. This was therefore a situation where she fell down on what Bingham LJ identified as feature (ii). This is a different question from that raised by the requirement of less favourable treatment, namely feature (i), and it would be a mistake to regard Bingham LJ in the second half of the paragraph as indicating who is a comparator. I do not therefore regard the Cornelius case as requiring this court to adopt a construction of s.2 which is contrary to my opinion. Before leaving Cornelius it is right to draw attention to the fact that two paragraphs earlier Bingham LJ adopts an approach to the Act which is very much in accord with the general approach to the Act's construction which I believe is required.

29. Turning therefore to the case of Aziz. This case also involved the RRA 1976. Mr Aziz had brought a complaint of discrimination against the Association of Taxi Cabs because he thought he had been treated unfairly. His complaint was for discrimination. To support his case he made secret recordings. He was expelled from the Association on the grounds that his doing so was a serious breach of the trust which had to exist between members of the Association. He then complained that his expulsion was victimisation for the purposes of s.2(1)(c) of the RRA 1976. In the case of Mr Aziz, the Association would probably have treated anyone who made the recordings in the same way. It was argued therefore that their conduct was not less favourable treatment. However, this approach was rejected by this court. Slade LJ on this point stated (at pp. 545H–546B)

"A complaint made in reliance on section 2 necessarily presupposes that the complainant has done a protected act. If the doing of such an act itself constituted part of the relevant circumstances, a complainant would necessarily fail to establish discrimination if the alleged discriminator could show that he treated or would treat all other persons who did the like protected act with equal intolerance. This would be an absurd result and in view of the separate, second limb of section 2(1), directed to the questions of causation to which we are about to come, such a construction is not, in our judgment, required for the protection of persons who might otherwise be found to have discriminated unlawfully by virtue of the sub-section. In our judgment, for the purpose of the comparison which section 2(1) makes requisite, the relevant circumstances do not include the fact that the complainant has done a protected act."

30. This part of the judgment of Slade LJ was not criticised by Lord Nicholls, although it is not informed by the three subsequent decisions of the House of Lords to which I have already referred. Slade LJ adopts an approach to s.2 which is consistent with the approach which I regard as being correct. It is therefore in favour of Mr Hand's approach.

Conclusions

31. If the statutory provisions are construed in this way, then it means that the decision of both tribunals were correct. The respondent was treated less favourably and the reason was that he had done a protected act.

32. As to the award of damages, it must be remembered the appeal to this court (and to the EAT) was confined to a point of law. The ET was entitled to take into account the evidence which it received at the earlier hearing as to the effect on the respondent of his being denied a reference. Although, as Mr Bean argued, in the event the respondent may not have been prejudiced by the failure to provide a reference, at the time the respondent would not be aware of this. He could naturally be distressed to think that he might not obtain a job which he wanted because of the refusal of his employer to provide a reference. In these circumstances an award was appropriate. The amount of the award is surprising. In comparison to what is awarded for non-pecuniary loss in relation to personal injury, the award seems high. However, Mr Bean recognises that unless he can show that there should have been no award, this court would not interfere with the decision of the ET. I do not consider Mr Bean has succeeded in establishing that there should be no award.

33. Accordingly I would dismiss this appeal.

Lady Justice Hale:

I agree.

Lord Mustill:

I also agree.

The following questions relate to the law report reproduced above the for the case of *Chief Constable of West Yorkshire Police & others v Khan*. When noting your answers to the questions, you should include reference(s) to the appropriate points in the judgment from which you have drawn your information.

Section A

1. Who brought the initial complaint in the case of *Chief Constable of West Yorkshire Police & others v. Khan*?

2. Give a short statement of the issue raised by the *Khan* case before the Court of Appeal.

3.   (a) In which courts or tribunals was the case of *Chief Constable of West Yorkshire Police & others v. Khan* heard?
    (b) Were these criminal or civil proceedings?
    (c) What were the decisions in each of the hearings?
    (d) Was the decision in the hearing of the case at first instance overturned on appeal?

4. What were the grounds upon which the appeal was brought before the Court of Appeal?

Section B

5. Discover whether the case of *Chief Constable of West Yorkshire Police & others v. Khan* has been reported in any of the published series of law reports.

6. Has the case of *Chief Constable of West Yorkshire Police & others v. Khan* been appealed beyond the Court of Appeal?

7. Are there any other reported cases on section 2 of the Race Relations Act 1976?

8. What did Lord Woolf M.R. make of the case of *Nagarajan v. London Regional Transport*?

9. What view does the Court of Appeal express in relation to the proposition by counsel (Mr Bean) which is referred to in paragraph 27 of the decision?

10. What opinion did Lord Woolf M.R. express about the amount of the damages award made by the Employment Tribunal in this case?

EXERCISE 4

CASE 2

[COURT OF APPEAL]

PICKFORD V. IMPERIAL CHEMICAL INDUSTRIES PLC.

1996 June 25, 26, 27;   Stuart-Smith, Waite and Swinton Thomas L.JJ.   F
July 18

*Negligence—Duty of care to whom?—Employee—Secretary typing for
more than half of working time developing repetitive strain injury—
Employers instructing typists but not secretaries to take rest
breaks—Whether employers owing duty of care—Whether negligent*

    G

    The plaintiff worked as a full-time secretary for the defendants
from January 1984 and for the first three to four years spent
about half her time typing on a word processor and the rest of the
time on general secretarial duties. She claimed that throughout
1987 the typing load increased and by the end of 1988 took up as
much as three quarters of her time, causing her to experience
tightness in the back of her hands and abnormal movements of her   H
fingers by the end of each week. She experienced a brief
incomplete remission in early 1989 but by June 1990 she was so
unable to work that the defendants, unable to offer her suitable
alternative employment, gave her notice terminating her

567

A

employment in September 1990. The plaintiff brought a claim against the defendants in negligence contending that she had contracted prescribed disease A4, namely, cramp of the hand due to repetitive movements, because the defendants caused or permitted her to undertake excessive amounts of typing for long periods without breaks or rest periods. She contended that she should have been given the same instructions to take rest breaks as the typists employed in the defendants' accounts department.

B

The trial judge found that the plaintiff had failed to establish that the cause of her condition was organic, rather than pyschogenic, and rejected her claim.

On the plaintiff's appeal:—

Held, allowing the appeal (Swinton Thomas L.J. dissenting), that the judge, having accepted that the plaintiff had the pre-scribed disease, had wrongly place on her the onus of satisfying him that it had an organic cause; that, further, the judge's

C

conclusion that the plaintiff's condition was psychogenic was unsupportable on the medical evidence and it was insufficient to rely on evidence that for many years the condition had been thought to have a psychogenic origin, since the explanation had to relate to the particular patient; that, once one concluded that the cause of the plaintiff's condition was organic, that supported the plaintiff's contention that she was typing for prolonged

D

stretches during the periods in question and there was no evidence to displace the natural inference that it was the plain-tiff's typing activities that were the cause of her complaint; that, whatever the precise aetiology of the condition, it had been known at least since 1948 that it was caused by prolonged periods of typing or other repetitive movements and it was that which had to be avoided, and, if it was not avoided, it was foreseeable

E

that some people might succumb to the condition; that the defendants knew or ought to have known that the plaintiff spent more than half her time typing and were not entitled to assume that she knew or understood the importance of taking rest pauses from typing; and that, accordingly, the defendants were in breach of their duty to the plaintiff in failing to give instructions to her to take rest breaks (post, pp. 574D, 575G–576A, 578C–D, 580B–C, 583C–E, 585A–B, D, 593B–F, 594A–C, E–G).

F

Decision of Judge Eifion Roberts Q.C. sitting as a deputy judge of the Queen's Bench Division, reversed.

The following case is referred to in the judgments:
Wilsher v. Essex Area Health Authority [1988] A.C. 1074; [1988] 2 W.L.R. 557; [1988] 1 All E.R. 871, H.L.(E.)

No additional cases were cited in argument.

G

APPEAL from Judge Eifion Roberts Q.C. sitting as a deputy High Court judge.

By a statement of claim served on 21 November 1991 and re-served as amended on 11 February 1994, the plaintiff, Ann Margaret Pickford, brought a claim in negligence against the defendants, Imperial Chemical Industries Plc., for damages for personal injury. By a defence served on

H

17 December 1991 and re-served as amended on 14 September 1994, the defendants denied the claim. On 4 November 1994 Judge Eifion Roberts Q.C. sitting as a deputy High Court judge in Mould dismissed the plaintiff's claim.

568

Stuart-Smith L.J.   **Pickford v. I.C.I. Plc. (C.A.)**   **[1997]**

By a notice of appeal dated 26 January 1995 and subsequently   A
amended, the plaintiff appealed. The grounds of appeal were, *inter alia*,
that (1) the judged erred in adopting the defendant's analysis of the
plaintiff's condition; (2) the judge ought to have found that the plaintiff
ought to have been given the same instructions as those engaged on
keyboard work in the defendants' accounts department; (3) the judge
erred in finding that the plaintiff had the discretion, experience and
knowledge to plan her work so as to avoid excessive periods of   B
prolonged typing; and (4) the judge failed to pay any regard to the fact
that there were no physical signs in prescribed disease A4.

The facts are stated in the judgment of Stuart-Smith L.J.

Michael Redfern Q.C. and *Guy Vickers* for the plaintiff.
Benet Hytner Q.C. and *Stephen P. Stewart* for the defendants.   C

Cur. adv. vult.

18 July. The following judgments were handed down.

STUART-SMITH L.J. This is an appeal from a judgment of Judge Eifion
Roberts Q.C. sitting as a deputy High Court judge at Mould on 4   D
November 1994 in which he dismissed the plaintiff's claim for damages
for personal injury against the defendants.

In 1948 the Department of Health and Social Security included as a
prescribed disease for the purpose of industrial injury benefit under the
relevant legislation "PDA4," namely: "Cramp of the hand or forearm
due to repetitive movements, *e.g.* writer's cramp." Under the heading
"type of occupation—any occupation involving" it is said: "prolonged   E
periods of handwriting, typing or other repetitive movements of the
fingers, hand or arm: *e.g.* typists, clerks and routine assemblers."

The plaintiff's case was that she had contracted the condition of her
hands in the course of her employment with the defendants as a secretary
at the premises of their pharmaceutical section at Macclesfield. The
trouble developed in late 1988 and after brief incomplete remission in   F
early 1989 it came to a head in late April and May of that year. It is her
case that it has been caused by excessive typing for prolonged periods
without proper breaks or rest pauses. The result has been that she has had
to cease work as a secretary; although she tried work as a filing clerk for
the defendants in 1990 her hands again became sore and painful after
three days and she could not continue. The defendants were unable to   G
offer her alternative employment and she was given formal notice on 25
June 1990 terminating her employment on 14 September 1990. Since then
she tried unsuccessfully to obtain other work; she eventually retrained as a
photographer and at the time of trial she had started in business on her
own account as such, but as yet she has not had a great deal of work and
the business was not thriving.

Essentially her case is that the defendants caused or permitted her to   H
undertake a very large amount of typing, which she carried out on a word
processor, which she did for long periods of time without breaks or rest
periods; this came about because the defendants did not give her the same

A   instructions as they gave their typists working in the accounts department, who were carrying out typing work for most of the day. If she had been told of the need for rest breaks, she would have taken them and would have interspersed her other secretarial duties between the typing, or left some of the typing undone. It is said that she was not properly supervised. The judge rejected her claim; he held that she did not have an organically based condition and that the defendants were not negligent in failing to

B   give her any instruction.

The plaintiff is now 47; she is unmarried. She began her secretarial career in 1971 and for many years worked as a temporary typist for a local secretarial agency. She spent eight months in that capacity with the defendants until in January 1984 they engaged her as a section secretary on a full-time basis, but doing the same work as she had before. She

C   worked in three sections: technical service, computer applications and laboratory control, managed respectively by Mr. Mason, Mr. Marriot and Mr. Hamilton but overall by Dr. Priaulx within the quality assurance department of which he was the head. The plaintiff worked on her own in an office in the technical services section and responded to Mr. Mason. But she was under the supervision of Dr. Priaulx's secretary who until 1987 was Mrs. Owen and thereafter Mrs. Woodward. Dr. Priaulx's

D   predecessor, Mr. Holbrook worked as a consultant for two days a week following his retirement in 1983. The plaintiff also acted as his secretary; so far as his typing was concerned this involved two or three letters a week and a 20-page report every two or three months. In all this involved about $1\frac{1}{2}$ hours' typing a week.

The plaintiff worked a seven and a half hour day from 10 a.m. to

E   6 p.m. having half-an-hour off for lunch. There were facilities for tea and coffee which the plaintiff consumed as she worked.

She prepared a job assessment report dated 15 November 1986 for the purpose of upgrading her post from grade 3 to grade 4 (which it had previously been when she worked as a temporary secretary). In it she said that she sptnt 50 per cent. of her time typing and the remaining 50 per cent. in general secretarial duties, such as answering the telephone,

F   arranging travel and meetings for those for whom she acted as secretary. This work from time to time involved her leaving the office to make contact with others in the quality assurance section. In addition to Mr. Mason, Mr. Marriott, Mr. Hamilton and Mr. Holbrook she was available to do typing for some 30 to 40 others and from time to time, albeit rarely, for the 100 or so others in the section. The typing consisted of letters,

G   memoranda, minutes, reports and standard operating procedures. In the review she stated that she planned and organised her workload; it was necessary to be flexible to deal with conflicting demands of the various sections she worked for. She was able to give priority to various types of work; but the priorities could change hour by hour as new work came in and she would give priority to an urgent piece of typing. Mr. Mason agreed with the plaintiff's assessment and the job was upgraded.

H   It was the plaintiff's case that, if her job had continued as it had been in 1986 and described in the report, there would have been no problem. But her evidence was that the typing load gradually increased throughout 1987 and 1988 so that by November or December of that year it took up

570

as much as 75 per cent. of her time. There was at that time an upsurge of   A
typing work arising out of the launch of a new drug, Solidex. This had an
effect on her hands so that she experienced strange feelings in her hands
by Friday of each week. It was tightness in the back of each hand and a
feeling that her fingers were not moving normally. But they recovered
with rest over the weekend and she did not think there was anything
seriously wrong.

In a performance review for 1988, discussed with Mr. Mason on 13   B
January 1989 and signed by him on 2 February 1989, it is stated:

> "At times the typing workload is excessive and [the plaintiff] has
> coped well with the pressure. She acknowledges there would be clear
> benefit in the secretarial force within [quality assurance] being
> welded together as a team to spread the workload and help provide
> a more efficient cover during sickness and holidays. Although this   C
> was an objective in 1988 not much progress has been achieved. This
> clearly needs to be developed at a departmental level."

Mr. Mason added that the plaintiff "had worked extremely hard and
conscientiously during the year." Indeed it is a feature of this case that
almost everyone who gave evidence for the defendants and who knew
the plaintiff and her work described her in such terms; her work was of   D
excellent quality and Mrs. Woodward had never received a complaint
about it; she had very high standards and was a perfectionist.

It is convenient to mention at this point two matters touched on in the
1988 performance review. The lack of cover for sickness and holidays; this
was something that troubled the plaintiff because she was required to
deputise for Mrs. Woodward when she was away. In theory her own typing   E
was to be covered by a temporary typist; but sometimes such typists did
not materialise and if they did they were unable to cope, either through
inexperience or lack of the same dedication and persistence as the
plaintiff, with the volume of work, so that when the plaintiff returned to
her normal job she had to cope with a backlog of work.

The second matter relates to the wordplex group. This consisted of four
part-time typists doing the work of two full-time ones. The wordplex group   F
was available to the section amongst others for typing work and from time
to time the plaintiff asked for their help through Mrs. Woodward. But she
was reluctant to use them partly because she was critical of their standards
which were not up to her own and partly because on occasions when she
sent work to them it was returned because they were too busy to do it.
Following the 1988 review in February 1989 it was arranged that the   G
wordplex group would type the plaintiff's standard operating procedures;
and this obviously provided some relief.

In 1987 when the plaintiff went to live on her own in a flat she started
to keep a diary. From about the middle of 1988 there was an increasing
number of entries in this diary, which if they are accurate support the
plaintiff's evidence as to the build up of typing work. Such expressions as   H
"still snowed under at work," "a large pile of typing waiting," "still very
busy" abound. [His Lordship set out entries from the diary, including on
23 May 1989:]

> "I've had to make a doctor's appointment about my hands, which
> are almost seizing up when I do a lot of typing. It started late last

A   year when I noticed that by Friday, my hands were tight and sore (I'd been typing flat out all summer to keep up with the mounds of work, as well as my other jobs). I slowed down to a more reasonable speed and hoped it would clear up. I'd asked for help several times, but been refused. The wordplex group took some eventually and in February took over my [standard operating procedures], but it's never cleared up and recently has got much worse. Afer last week

B   my hands were burning all weekend and this week I can't type normally at all without getting pains."

On 25 May 1989 she visited her general practitioner, Dr. Baker. He tes that she complained of pain in both hands, more in the right than left, that she had first noticed it seven months previously when she was busy typing at work and that it was intermittent at first. On examination

C   he found no abnormality. He diagnosed synovitis and signed off work for 13 days. It is common ground that she did not have synovitis (or tenosynovitis), though the judge accepted that general practitioners often use the term as a working diagnosis, presumably to describe a condition which fits the patient's symptom and history. She appears to have been referred to the defendants' physiotherapist who gave her

D   megapulse treatment; but it did not help and the plaintiff said it made her hands worse.

On 31 May 1989 she was seen by Dr. Lamb, the defendants' works' doctor. She gave him the same history. He could find no physical signs on examination. She returned to work on 12 June and did less typing. But on 19 June she had only been back at work a week when she went back to her general practitioner who noted that her hands were in status

E   quo and he arranged for her to see a consultant, Mr. Auchincloss; but this appointment with him was not until 14 September 1989. On 19 June she took a fortnight's pre-booked holiday to take a Spanish "A" level exam. She returned to work on 3 July; she said that the wordplex group were too busy to do as much typing for her as they had done. On 7 July her general practitioner noted that her hands were still painful and he

F   signed her off for a month. On 10 July she saw Dr. Lamb. It is important to note what Dr. Lamb wrote on 12 July to Mr. Mason, because it shows in my judgment that, whatever Dr. Lamb may have thought subsequently, it was Dr. Lamb's then opinion that the plaintiff's complaints and symptoms were caused by an excessive volume of typing:

> "This young lady came to see me in May complaining of
> symptoms in her hands related to the volume of typing, the greater
G   > the volume the more trouble she was getting. I referred her to our
> physiotherapist, this has not been of any help and as you know she is
> now absent from work with the same problem. She is expecting to
> see a consultant in hospital some time towards the end of August, it
> is my opinion that he is unlikely to find a medical cause for this
> problem and that it relates entirely to the volume of typing that she
H   > has to do.
> "[The plaintiff] has been a typist since she was 18 years old and
> this is only a recent problem for her. It does improve when she rest
> her hands and the volume of typing seems to be the cause of the

572

problem. I think it is very unlikely that we can do anything to change
the circumstances from a medical point of view and that it would be
best if we were to consider some sort of redeployment or change in
work duties for her. She tells me that she will be temping for Dr.
Priaulx during his secretary's absence in August, the amount of
typing that she has to do there will be less than in her current job
and this will give us a good indication of the volume of work which
she is able to do without developing symptoms.

"I suggest that both [the plaintiff] and yourself consider the
redeployment question and start looking for ways to reduce the
amount of typing that she has to do, otherwise I imagine the
problem will continue, whereby she works for a period of time,
eventually develops her symptoms and then has to have a number of
weeks off work on a periodic basis. I shall be reviewing [the plaintiff]
again at the end of August."

She returned to work on 7 August 1989 deputising for Mrs. Woodward
while she was away. But unfortunately, since there was no temporary typist
to do the plaintiff's work, she had to do the urgent typing that her own job
entailed. On 11 August there is an entry in the diary which reads:

"My hands feel as though they are on fire. I'll go in next week but
I am not typing. I could be doing permanent damage. Dr. Baker
would not say anything. If I went to him he would have to sign me
off again."

I regard this entry of some significance; it shows a reluctance on the
plaintiff's part to return to her general practitioner because that will have
the effect of signing her off work. It does not seem to fall easily within the
defendants' case that she was assuming a sick role, that she subconsciously
did not want to work at her job with the defendants. She took a week's
pre-booked holiday from 28 August 1989. She saw Mr. Auchincloss on 14
September and gave him the same history. He told her that she could
return and carry on typing or seek alternative work. In a letter to her
general practitioner, a copy of which he sent to Dr. Lamb, he said that on
examination he could find no abnormality of the hands or wrists:

"These work-related symptoms are impossible to treat and are not
capable of accurate pathological diagnosis. There is no real element
of synovitis and repeated working activities are so variable in
causation of these symptoms that one wonders whether there is a
non-organic component in patients seeking change of occupation or
financial remuneration."

I have quoted this letter because, although Mr. Auchincloss was not called
to give evidence, he is the only one of the many doctors whom the plaintiff
has seen, other than Dr. Lucire, to whose evidence I shall have to refer
later in this judgment. who has speculated or suggested that the plaintiff's
condition is other than organically based or related to or caused by her
typing.

In June 1989 the plaintiff had been given by someone at work who
was familiar with her problem a publication by the Repetitive Strain
Injury Association. She did not get in touch with the association until

573

A after she had seen Mr. Auchincloss and received what she regarded as unhelpful advice and no treatment from him. I should say at this stage that all the doctors who gave evidence in the present case avoided use of the term "repetitive strain injury" as being unhelpful in diagnosis. Dr. Hay likened it to the expression "sports injury," which is virtually meaningless from a diagnostic point of view and is merely an umbrella term covering a number of different conditions. These probably include PDA4 and

B PDA8—tenosynovitis occurring in manual workers where there are frequent or repeated movements of the hand or wrist. This is something that typists can suffer from, but is distinguishable from PDA4 because the former has, but the latter does not have, objective signs which are apparent on examination. It also includes carpel tunnel syndrome, which has recently been added to the list of prescribed diseases as PDA12.

C   The plaintiff signed off sick for a month on 25 September 1989. When she returned to work on 23 October she declined to do any typing because the problem was now affecting everything she did with her hands.

    The Repetitive Strain Injury Association recommended two specialists; one was Mr. Holt, whom she saw on 30 October 1989. He thought that she had the features of occupational cramp and referred her to Dr. Bird, who has greater experience in the field. Between 22 and 24

D November 1989 she attended a career workshop, to see if she could change her career. On 27 November she was signed off long term sick. She saw Dr. Bird on 8 January 1990. He found her to be rather anxious; he could find no abnormal objective findings. He said in a letter written the same day:

    "I felt she was genuine and, although understandably anxious, has

E   given a classical history of overuse syndrome as described by musicians and other individuals with occupations that render them susceptible to this, without any obvious prompting from the Repetitive Strain Injury Association. Whatever the pathology of this condition, previous sufferers have described a point when the symptoms are intermittent and convincingly relieved by rest (which she proved in early 1989) followed by more refractory symptoms

F   which require much longer periods off work for resolution."

    He recommended three months off typing and then a return to typing limited to five minutes per day. The plaintiff was offered two jobs by the defendants. One involved filing, the other photocopying. She did not think she could do the latter because it involved much standing and she had varicose veins. She tried filing for three days in May 1990 but she

G found that her hands were so badly affected that the job caused them to be painful in the morning and they became progressively worse. As I have indicated, her employment terminated in September 1990 and the next month she consulted her solicitors.

    The judge addressed himself to a number of issues. First, does PDA4 have an organic or psychogenic cause? He expressed his conclusion on

H these issues as follows:

    "The most that I can find on the whole of the medical evidence before me is that the condition of cramp of the hand due to repetitive movements may have an organic cause of a psychogenic

574

combination of both causes, or the one cause to begin with and the
other supervening. It is a matter which the court has to consider on
the evidence before it in each case."

That conclusion is entirely unexceptional and is in accordance with the
evidence of Mr. Stanley and Dr. Hay, who gave evidence on behalf of
the plaintiff, though Dr. Hay considered that cases of conversion
hysteria, *i.e.*, psychogenic cases, were rare. Dr. Lucire, a psychiatrist who
gave evidence for the defendants, considered that all cases of PDA4
were non-organic and due to conversion hysteria. [His Lordship set out
the history of the dispute in medical circles and continued:]

The second issue which the judge addressed was whether the plaintiff
had PDA4. Although I have not found it altogether easy to determine
the judge's answer, since he does not express a clear affirmative, I think
he did so conclude. He accepted Dr. Lucire's view that she had had a
prolonged bout of cramp. He said:

"I am disposed to find that she had a cramp of the hand, but I am
not satisfied that it was due to the repetitive movements of typing in
the sense that such movements were an effective cause of the cramp,
as opposed to being merely the causa sine qua non."

The third issue which the judge addressed was: has the plaintiff satisfied
me that the cramp of the hand(s) had an organic cause? He said that the
onus was on the plaintiff. In my judgment this was not the correct
approach and amounted to a misdirection. Having established that she
had PDA4 there were two alternative explanations for it advanced by the
medical experts, one—supported by the evidence of Mr. Stanley and Dr.
Hay—was that it was organic; the other—supported by Dr. Lucire—that
it was psychogenic being a conversion hysteria. No other hysterical or
psychogenic explanation was advanced. It seems to me that what the
judge had to do was simply to decide upon the evidence which of those
two explanations was the most likely. In the result the judge said that he
was not satisfied that it was organic; therefore by inference it must be
psychogenic; but he did not accept Dr. Lucire's explanation that it was
conversion hysteria.

Having read the cross-examination of Dr. Lucire, I do not find it in the
least surprising that the judge did not accept the conversion hysteria
diagnosis. The theory is that the patient is subconsciously undergoing a
conflict, in this case a desire to give up typing on the one hand and a need
to earn a living on the other or obtain financial support or gain. The
result of this conflict is to set up symptoms related to her work or cramp
in her hands. Dr. Lucire said it is essential to the theory that the plaintiff
had knowledge of the symptoms of repetitive strain injury in May 1989;
yet it is plain that she had no knowledge of repetitive strain injury until
she was given some information about it in June and she did not contact
the association till September 1989. Mr. Redfern put various matters to
her which one might have supposed had some bearing on the conflict
theory, none of which she considered of any relevance until finally this
exchange took place: Question—"I can only conclude really that in this
case nothing has a bearing on your diagnosis?" Answer—"very little." Dr.
Lucire's theory was in my view effectively disposed of by Dr. Hay,

A honorary consultant psychiatrist at University Hospital South Manchester. I do not need to refer to his evidence in any detail. He pointed out that conversion hysteria was a very rare condition; it should only be diagnosed when it is established that there is no underlying physical cause and then only after great caution, and such diagnoses had frequently turned out later to be wrong. He found no signs of an hysterical or neurotic personality in the plaintiff and pointed out that her

B work history, which was remarkably good, was inconsistent with this. Conversion hysteria tends to occur in younger people usually with an hysterical temperament. He said he found it difficult to accept the concept expounded in Dr. Lucire's report in these terms: "the option of converting her conflict into a symptom of being deemed sick was unavailable to her until the construction repetitive strain injury was

C introduced." Dr. Hay said:

> "Now to me this means that, if we accept that she was a person who had conflicts in her life situation beforehand, she then comes across the construct of repetitive strain injury so she's consciously aware of the construct, then subconsciously she converts that into a symptom regarding her hands, the argument being that this is

D fulfilling a purpose that she needs. I simply personally can't follow such an argument. It would fit a model simulation but not of conversion hysteria."

I have to say that I found Dr. Hay's reasoning compelling. Mr. Hytner submitted that the judge was wrong to reject Dr. Lucire's diagnosis. Compared with the robustness with which most of Mr. Hytner's submis-

E sions were advanced, I can only say that this one was at best half-hearted and I have no hesitation in rejecting it.

How was it then that the judge reached the conclusion, by inference from his rejection of the plaintiff's case that her condition was organic, that it was psychogenic? I do not know and the judge does not explain. In my judgment it was not open to him simply to make his own diagnosis of hysteria or psychogenic origin in the absence of an arguable psychi-

F atric theory. There must be some reason or explanation why the mind has such a powerful effect on the body as to cause pain and disfunction in the plaintiff's hands such that it prevents her from doing her typing. Conversion hysteria was the only such explanation proposed by the defendants and in my view it did not bear examination. No other case of psychogenic or hysterical mechanism was put to Dr. Hay in cross-

G examination.

It is not good enough in my judgment to say, as Mr. Hytner does, that for many years PDA4 was thought to have a psychogenic origin. The explanation must relate to the particular patient. Conversion hysteria may be an acceptable explanation in some cases. I suppose it is also possible that some significant trauma or shock may be responsible in other individual cases, though there is no evidence about this. We are all

H familiar with the concept of traumatic neurosis following physical injury. But there was no evidence that the plaintiff had sustained any such injury or shock.

Even if the judge's approach was correct, and, even if it was open to him, having rejected conversion hysteria, to find that the plaintiff's

576

A

condition was psychogenic, such a judgment was in my judgment wholly contrary to the weight of the medical evidence. Apart from Mr. Auchincloss, whose somewhat speculative reservations I have referred to, none of the doctors who had seen the plaintiff, including Dr. Lamb, Dr. Baker her general practitioner, Mr. Holt and Dr. Bird ever suggested that her condition was hysterical or psychogenic and this included Dr. Emlyn Williams a rheumatologist called on behalf of the defendants.

B

This doctor had not previously heard of PDA4 until the defendants' solicitor sent him the relevant information and the reports of Mr. Stanley and Dr. Hay; in his report dated 6 August 1994 he said:

> "[The plaintiff] is essentially well rather than ill. She is slim in build and somewhat obsessional by nature. She describes a pain in hands and forearms, precipitated by manual activity—especially typing. Despite pain being present over a five-year period, clinical and laboratory examination has revealed no abnormality. The discomforts which she describes do indeed fit within the criteria accepted for prescribed disease A4. Cramp of the hand or forearm due to repetitive movements. Those criteria include a statement as to causation worthy of inclusion in its entirety.

C

> *"Prescribed Disease A4:*

D

> "The causative factors in this condition are unknown. No structural change in the central nervous system, peripheral nerves or muscles has been demonstrated and electrical reactions are not disturbed. The cause is probably a combination of physical fatigue of muscles and nerves and an underlying psychoneurosis. I have no difficulty in accepting that [the plaintiff], with her paucity of muscle bulk, her asthenic build and her obsessional traits, would be at risk of developing such a disorder."

E

He sought in the course of his evidence to some extent to resile from this, advancing the possible alternative organic diagnosis that a problem at the plaintiff's sixth cervical vertebra might be causing the symptoms. This was never put to Mr. Stanley and was at best advanced as a possibility. What is important is that Dr. Emlyn Williams never suggested anything other than an organic cause.

F

I must also refer briefly to the evidence of Mr. Stanley, he is a consultant orthopaedic surgeon of very great distinction in this field since he specialises in hand and upper limb surgery, very often cases being referred to him by other consultants. He said:

G

> "My experience of occupational cramps is in reality with musicians, in whom it is quite common, and it is estimated that 60 per cent. of musicians during their working career will have a significant upper limb problem during their playing career; sometimes sufficient to stop them playing, mostly fortunately not. Sportsmen I see who have specific difficulties of dystonia and I see people who do work in industry who have repetitive tasks. Mostly I see people who work on [visual display units] . . . a woman who is doing repetitious work has unusual feelings and her hands seize up; the diagnosis of occupational cramp is absolutely spot on; the absence of

H

577

A physical signs which was noted by Dr. Lamb and by Mr. Auchinloss is absolutely correct."

He said that the symptoms were pain and spasm; the spasm being the cramp which the plaintiff experienced when she described the feeling of her hands seizing up. He could find no other cause for her condition. He said:

B   "The problem with word processing is that there is no break on each line and therefore as the typist types there is no natural break for carriage return, as used to exist in the old manual typewriters. It is possible to type for considerable time and speed without a break and it is particularly true of people with an obsessional and highly perfectionist nature."

C He said that once the symptoms had become chronic, as they had by 1990, she could not do photocopying or filing since it involved use of similar muscles.

I must now turn to certain findings of fact which the judge made, which Mr. Hytner submits are sacrosanct and Mr. Redfern submits, in relation to some at least, that the judge was in error:

D   "Essentially she is a dutiful, conscientious and responsible person and the defendants do not suggest that she is or has at any time been malingering. In evidence, she is at times prone to exaggeration and some inconsistency, but not in the sense or to the extent of deliberately misleading the court. . . .

"My findings as to the typing done by the plaintiff in the period November 1988 to May 1989 are these: firstly, considering the range

E   and variety of her non-typing secretarial duties and the absence of any criticism of her discharge of them, it is highly unlikely that as a general rule she spent more than three and three quarter hours per day—50 per cent. of her working time—typing. I accept that from time to time in order to type an urgent letter or document, she may have typed for up to five hours—75 per cent. of her working time.

F   But even then she had ample scope to intersperse it with two and a half hours non-typing secretarial work. Secondly, in the light of the evidence, which I accept, of Mr. Pearce, Mrs. Owen and Mrs. Woodward, I do not think that the plaintiff exceeded her natural optimum speed of about 60 words per minute on the word processor for any sustained period of time, but only exceptionally and briefly to type the odd letter or document. Thirdly, while I accept that there

G   were peaks and troughs and that at times the peaks may have seemed excessive in the plaintiff's perception, she had the necessary discretion, experience and knowledge, as she was well aware, to plan, organise, prioritise and negotiate the work and, if necessary, to seek help so as to enable her to cope reasonably with it."

H Mr. Redfern criticises the first of these findings. First he points out that 75 per cent. of her time is 5 hours and 40 minutes and not five hours. Since it was the plaintiff's case that at the time of the onset of the symptoms in November 1988 and late April 1989 she was on most days spending this amount of time typing, it is perhaps difficult to describe this

578

Stuart-Smith L.J.   Pickford v. I.C.I. Plc. (C.A.)   [1997]

as exaggeration. The judge's finding seems to me more consistent with
dishonesty, which he has negatived. The plaintiff said that after she
ceased her employment her job was done by two people. This was never
controverted in evidence. [His Lordship referred to evidence from Mr.
Holbrook, Mrs. Osmond, and Miss Wilthew and, in particular Mrs.
Woodward, and continued:] I agree with Mr. Redfern that this is
powerful evidence which tends to support the plaintiff's own account
which the judge does not advert to or analyse. It certainly does not
afford any ground for saying that she was significantly exaggerating her
workload of typing, still less that she was dishonest about it.

    This finding of the judge is interrelated to the judge's conclusion that
the plaintiff's condition is non-organic. Clearly the less typing the plaintiff
does, the less likely the condition is to be organic; if like most of the
secretaries in her section she spent about only 20 per cent. of her time
typing, it would be very unlikely that this could involve sufficient
uninterrupted typing to cause the symptoms of an organic condition
conversion hysteria becomes more probable. If one is driven to the
conclusion that the judge was in error on this point, both because he
rightly rejected the only psychogenic explanation advanced and also
because the overwhelming weight of the medical evidence before him was
that it was organic, this finding also in my view will support the plaintiff's
account as to the amount of typing she was doing, since it is only in such
circumstances that the condition will develop. Moreover, until the condition became chronic it responded to rest and less typing, which is what one
would expect of an organic condition. I leave the judge's third finding
under this head until I come to consider the question of negligence.

    The third important finding is that the judge said that he was not
satisfied that the diary entry of 23 May 1989 was accurate; the plaintiff had
not satisfied him that she had had the subjective symptoms alleged before
23 May. Although this is a primary finding of fact, Mr. Redfern challenges
it. The judge gave three reasons in coming to this conclusion. (1) It was
"surprising" that she made no mention of it in her diary, although she
recorded others of trifling significance in her diary such as her symptoms
when she had flu in January 1989. (2) It was "surprising" that she had not
mentioned it when she was discussing the excessive workload in January
1989 with Mr. Mason. (3) It was "noteworthy" that on 25 May 1989, two
days after seeing her general practitioner, she noted in her diary: "if it
doesn't clear up I am in an awkward position, I think it's [the defendants']
fault."

    I am well aware of the inhibitions laid upon this court in interfering
with and reversing the trial judge's findings of fact, especially primary
findings. The law is succinctly summarised in the *The Supreme Court
Practice 1995* at paragraph 59/1/55 and is very familiar to any member this
of court. I do not propose to set it out in extenso. We were also referred
by Mr. Hytner to a passage in the speech of Lord Bridge of Harwich in
Wilsher v. Essex Area Health Authority [1988] A.C. 1074, 1091, where he
reminded the court that similar principles apply in relation to the
evaluation of disputed medical evidence. But it is our duty to reconsider
the matter, paying great weight to the opinion of the trial judge, especially
where there is a conflict of evidence and the demeanour and bearing of

I.C.R. Pickford v. I.C.I. Plc. (C.A.) **Stuart-Smith L.J.**

A the witness plays a significant part in the judge's decision. But in this case there was no conflict of evidence. No one said that the plaintiff had told them in November/December 1988 or late April and before 23 May 1989 that there was nothing wrong with her hands; nor did she so state in her diary. The plaintiff was asked about the fact that there was no reference in the diary and she said that she did not record every ache and pain and that she had hoped it would pass off. Mr. Hytner submitted

B to us that the plaintiff did record every trivial ache and pain and this is the judge's first reason for rejecting her evidence.

Mr. Hytner described this as a cataclysmic conflict between the evidence of the plaintiff and her diary entries. I have to say that I do not think Mr. Hytner's submission bears examination notwithstanding the hyperbole with which it was advanced. He was invited to direct the

C court's attention to the recording of such matters. All that could be pointed to was a reference to a headache on 14 and 15 November 1988, when the plaintiff said she had migraine in one of her language classes, which lasted to some extent into the second day. The second was over a period of about a week in January 1989 when she had flu. She records her symptoms of cough and sore throat. But she only appears to have been off work for a period of five days. She returned to work on Monday

D 23 January although she was not fully recovered.

Moreover in my judgment this finding of the judge, although expressed in terms that he was not satisfied, must be a finding that the plaintiff lied about this entry and that it was a dishonest entry. There cannot be two ways about it; it can neither be mistake nor exaggeration. That being so, it is quite inconsistent with the judge's finding that she

E had not deliberately misled the court. This was a very important part of the plaintiff's evidence and was entirely consistent with the history that the plaintiff always gave to the doctors. I cannot accept that in a reserved judgment, if the judge proposed to make such an important reservation on her honesty, he can do it by implication. In my judgment the truth is that the judge never properly considered the implications of this finding. Firstly it must mean that the plaintiff experienced no problem whatever

F with her hands until 23 May 1989 when she made the appointment with her doctor. Indeed Mr. Hytner so submitted. In my view this is patently absurd. It is perfectly obvious that she must have experienced the problem at least on the day before, and I would also suppose in the week before. Yet there is no mention in the diary on these days. This fact alone completely undermines the judge's first reason.

G In my view the judge's second reason, namely, that she did not tell Mr. Mason in January 1989, is equally tenuous. By then her hands had improved; by all accounts she was a very reserved person. It does not strike me in the least surprising that she did not mention the trouble she had earlier experienced.

The third matter which the judge regards as noteworthy, whatever

H significance we are to give to that, seems to me equally unpersuasive. Every single doctor who ever examined the plaintiff, including Dr. Lucire, considered that her complaints were genuine; there was no suggestion that she was malingering. Yet the judge seems to be suggesting that she was here manufacturing a false case so that she could ultimately sue the

580

defendants. Yet the defendants' case is and was that this was a sudden
onset of an hysterical or psychogenic condition. I cannot understand why
she should make up the antecedent history; she would have no way of
knowing that it fitted precisely into what Mr. Stanley considered was a
classic description of PDA4. To my mind the judge's reasoning on this
point makes no sense. It is certainly not sufficient to found the inference
that she was lying in the face of her evidence and the remarkable
testimonials as to her integrity and conscientiousness that so many
witnesses gave her.

I have come to the clear conclusion that the judge's finding that the
plaintiff's condition was psychogenic cannot be supported, likewise his
rejection of her evidence and diary entry as to the onset of symptoms.
Once it is concluded, as in my view it must be, that her condition was
organic, this casts a flood of light upon and in support of her evidence
that she was typing during the periods in question for prolonged
stretches and for about 75 per cent. of her working day. It was submitted
by Mr. Hytner that this was not possible because she had to do other
secretarial work, such as filing, entering complaints on the database,
arranging meetings etc., and no one complained that she fell down on
these duties. But the plaintiff was relieved of the need to enter
complaints on the database and she said in evidence:

> "When I became very busy I had to let the filing pile up. I just didn't
> have time to do it. Quite often there was urgent work and someone.
> had an urgent report in that they wanted doing. I was unable to
> obtain help elsewhere with it and I would just keep at it until I'd
> done it. . . . Obviously I couldn't type without respite the whole day.
> I had my lunch break and you'd answer the telephone occasionally
> but there were some days, when I got some urgent typing in, when I
> certainly did seem to just be typing flat out for most of the day and
> not managing to get much else done."

I turn then to the final issue, namely, whether the plaintiff established
a breach of the defendants' duty of care to her and whether the judge's
conclusion that she had not should be reversed. PDA4 is rare in typists;
but they also suffer from PDA8, tenosynovitis, from the same cause,
namely, prolonged repetitive movements of the fingers without rest
pauses. The judge concluded:

> "I conclude from the evidence that, while it was theoretically
> foreseeable that a typist might suffer the alleged condition of PDA4,
> it was not reasonably foreseeable that it would happen."

I find some difficulty with this conclusion. It was plainly reasonably
foreseeable that typists might suffer from the condition if they typed for
prolonged periods without break. Not only was this the effect of the
Department of health and Social Security prescribed disease to which I
have referred at the beginning of this judgment and which has been in
existence since 1948, but the defendants, through Dr. Lamb, must in fact
have foreseen this, at least in relation to the typists in the accounts
department.

In November 1987 a memorandum was sent to Dr. Lamb from the
defendants' chemicals and polymer group, dealing with the problems in

A increasing complaints from users of visual display units. Five conditions were identified: (1) backache; (2) eyestrain and headache (under which is the head "work pattern" avoid prolonged usage); (3) effective lighting; (4) radiation/pregnancy; and (5) repetitive strain injury, of which it said:

B "This complaint is most often associated with a combination of poor hand position and typing too fast. It results in pain, swelling and discomfort in the fingers and wrist. Any suspected cases should be referred to medical department (Sister S. Mackenzie)."—Sister Mackenzie was not at the Macclesfield premises—"Again it was stressed that the main interest was with intensive users *e.g.* clerical, secretarial, accountancy personnel who use a visual display terminal for several hours per day."

C   This document from the defendants was in line with a Health and Safety Executive paper published in 1983, which the defendants had. The booklet contained guidance and recommendations about the use of visual display units as they relate to the health and well being of their users. It was said that:

D "Several health risks arising from the utilisation of [visual display units] have been suggested more or less widely discussed including . . . symptoms related to postural and visual fatigue. . . . Individual skills, capabilities and attitudes differ widely. Training needs should ideally, therefore, be tailored to individual needs and requirements. . . .

E "In most tasks, natural breaks or pauses occur as a consequence of the inherent organisation of the work. These informal breaks help to maintain performance by preventing the onset of fatigue. In some [visual display unit] work, for example, those data entry tasks requiring continuous and sustained attention and concentration, together with high data entry rates, such naturally occurring breaks are less frequent. In situations where this type of task cannot be organised in any other way, and where natural breaks in work do not occur, the introduction of rest pauses should help attention and concentration to be maintained. It is difficult to be specific about

F guidance on rest pauses, since it is likely that if strictly laid down rest pauses are adhered to they will often be found to be unnecessarily prolonged and frustrating for some, and, under other circumstances, too short to prevent the onset of fatigue. The most satisfactory length of pause can only be determined by consideration of the invidual operator's job, but three general statements can be made:

G "(a) Some of the symptoms reported by operators are often the result of the effort expended in order to maintain performance in the face of accumulating fatigue. Rest pauses should therefore be arranged so that they are taken prior to the onset of fatigue; not as a recuperative period from it. (b) Short, frequently occurring pauses appear to be more satisfactory than longer ones taken occasionally.

H (c) Ideally the break should be taken away from the visual display unit. However, it should be reiterated that, wherever practicable, the job should be designed to permit natural breaks, or changes in patterns of activity, as an integral part of the tasks to be performed.

582

This may involve, for example, a mix of [visual display unit]-based
and non-[visual display unit]-based work." A

[His Lordship set out evidence from Dr. Lamb relating to those
documents and continued:] The judge expressed his conclusion on
negligence in two important passages. First, he said:

> "Dr. Lamb's evidence, which I accept, was that a formal system of
> instruction, warning and advice was adopted and implemented for
> the typing staff in the accounts department and difficulties in B
> changing posture could arise. But such a system was not considered
> necessary for secretaries as they carried out many non-typing duties
> in the course of the working day. The expert evidence on both sides
> demonstrates the low incidence of occupational cramp right across
> the various occupations. Mr. Stanley said it was quite low."

The judge then noted that there were 4,000 people with the condition in C
1993, which does not seem to me all that small, and continued:

> "Occupational cramp, as I accept, is a condition which, in most
> cases, disappears in weeks or months. It is uncommon and in typists
> its incidence, on the evidence, is very rare. Having weighed up the
> remoteness of the risk of a typist contracting the condition and the D
> consequences in that event, I do not consider that the defendants
> could reasonably have been required to take steps to avoid the risk.
> Let me, however, deal with the steps which it is alleged the defendants
> ought to have taken but did not take. What Mr. Redfern submitted
> was that the defendants, by requiring the plaintiff to carry out
> excessive typing and increase her optimum typing speed in order to
> cope with it, had forced her into the same category as the typists in E
> the accounts department and accordingly ought to have ensured that
> she had the same instructions, the same warnings and the same advice
> as they had. I cannot accept the premise that the defendants required
> the plaintiff to carry out excessive typing and increase her optimum
> speed. As I have found, she had the necessary discretion, experience
> and knowledge to plan, organise, prioritise and negotiate the work, as F
> she herself wrote in the job description. There is no evidence that she
> was urged to increase her speed or quicken her output. There were no
> complaints or criticisms which might have induced her to do so.
> Moreover, even when occasionally she may have typed for up to five
> hours in a working day, she had about two and half hours' non-typing
> work with which to intersperse it. Some of the non-typing work would
> have broken it up in any event, as it involved attending to callers and G
> answering the telephone over such matters as travel arrangements,
> holiday entitlements and mileage allowances, to mention but a few of
> the matters affecting a significant workforce."

In my judgment it is crucial to this finding that the plaintiff had the
necessary knowledge to plan, organise, prioritise and negotiate her work.
In my view this can only mean that she has the requisite knowledge that H
it is necessary for her to take breaks from prolonged spells of typing for
her own health. There is simply no evidence that she did know this and
she said that she did not. It was common ground that she had not been

A given the same instruction and warning as those in the accounts department. This was because the defendants through Dr. Lamb did not appreciate that she was doing anything like the amount of typing she was in fact doing. The majority of secretaries only spent about 20 per cent. of their time typing and quite clearly such people were not at risk.

Mr. Redfern submits that there was a lack of supervision here and a lack of liaison between Mrs. Woodward and Dr. Lamb. I think there is

B much force in Mr. Redfern's submission. Mrs. Woodward knew, or certainly ought to have known, that the plaintiff was at times under great pressure so far as typing was concerned and was spending a great deal of her day doing it. But she knew nothing about PDA4 or the need to take rest pauses in prolonged bouts of typing, because she had not received any instruction to that effect. But even so, she said she would have been

C alarmed if she had known she was working for Mr. Holbrook. Dr. Lamb did not appreciate that secretaries did anything like as much typing as the plaintiff did.

I agree with Mr. Redfern that the important thing is that those who are liable to do a great deal of typing on a visual display unit should be told that they must take breaks and rest pauses. I think it advisable to explain why this is necessary, especially if the employee asks or there is

D any risk that the instruction will not be obeyed. This instruction was given to the typists in the accounts department; in my opinion it should have been given to the plaintiff.

I must deal with a number of the submissions made by Mr. Hytner.

(1) Since the prevailing medical view in 1988 was that PDA4 was psychogenic in origin, the defendants could not reasonably foresee organic

E cramp and were not therefore negligent in failing to instruct the plaintiff. I do not accept this submission. It is quite plain that whatever the precise aetiology of the condition was thought to be it had been known at least since 1948 that it was caused by "prolonged periods of typing or other repetitive movements." It was that which had to be avoided and, if it was not, it was foreseeable that some people might succumb to the condition.

F (2) The employers were then and are now in an impossible position. Since there are two schools of medical thought, one organic, one psychogenic, they cannot know what to do. If it is organic then a warning that excessive prolonged use without break might damage health was required; if it is psychogenic a warning in such terms might be counter productive. He painted a pathetic picture of employers frenetically running between the Mr. Stanleys and the Dr. Lucires of this world,

G getting conflicting advice. I confess I am not moved by his terrible vision. All employers have to do is to give the very sensible instruction, advice and warning which the defendants themselves gave those they considered at risk of doing excessive typing.

(3) At one stage Mr. Hytner appeared to be submitting that, because the Health and Safety Executive documents related primarily to eye strain and neck or back problems due to fixed posture, that somehow meant that

H no instruction was necessary if what eventuated was PDA4. I do not accept this. The fact that there are other conditions which are liable to afflict those who engage in prolonged and excessive use is an additional reason why proper instruction should be given, if PDA4 is a foreseeable

584

risk as well, which in my view it plainly is. Mr. Hytner made the following concession:

A

> "If the Health and Safety Executive documents relate to muscular-skeletal injuries but do not specifically relate to PDA4, and if the employer fails to heed the advice given in the leaflet (in relation to rest pauses) aimed at muscular-skeletal injuries, if the plaintiff sustains a muscular-skeletal injury broadly of the same type as those aimed at in the Health and Safety Executive document and it can be demonstrated that such injury would not have occurred if the precaution recommended in this document had been carried out, then it would not help the defendants that PDA4 was not referred to specifically in this document."

B

In my opinion this document is plainly directed at muscular-skeletal injuries and it is not confined to those in the back and neck. Cramp of the hand is also plainly a muscular injury, since the muscles of the hand do not work properly. I see no reason to doubt the plaintiff's evidence that, if she had appreciated the need to take rest pauses before her hands became fatigued, she would have taken them. And no doubt she would have been able to arrange her other work in such a way that she could intersperse it between stints of typing, although the amount of typing she did might have suffered.

C

D

(4) There was no evidence that it was the practice in 1988 in industry or commerce to give the instructions suggested. It is true that Mr. Pearce said so. Mr. Stanley said that he knew of a number of companies that did give a warning or instruction, but he did not know whether they did so in 1988. But in the light of the fact that the condition is a prescribed disease and the advice from the Health and Safety Executive I cannot accept the submission. Moreover, the defendants themselves gave such instruction and advice. In their chemical and polymer section they gave it to those who used a visual display unit for several hours a day. At Macclesfield they gave it to typists in the accounts department.

E

(5) PDA4 in typists is rare and in most cases it clears up in weeks or months. Therefore, the risk of injury is small and the injury is not usually serious. This risk has to be balanced against the cost to the employer of implementing the advice and instruction. The judge referred to the rarity of the condition and the fact that most cases are not very serious. He did not seek to balance this against the cost. Mr. Stanley said that, where the condition became chronic, disability could last for years. Even to be disabled for a few months is not something that can be ignored. Mr. Hytner painted a heart-rending picture of employers throughout the land having to take on large numbers of extra typists, thereby adding greatly to the costs of industry and commerce, if they were to give this advice. I think this picture was greatly exaggerated and was totally unsupported by any evidence from the defendants. There was no evidence that it had caused any or any significant extra expense in the accounts department. In the plaintiff's case, as I have said, she could probably have alleviated the position by interspersing her other work in long spells of typing. Even if further typing help would have been needed, it looks very much as though it was needed in any event.

F

G

H

A
(6) Finally, it is said that the defendants could not reasonably foresee that the plaintiff would suffer injury because they were entitled to suppose that she could and would break up periods of typing with her other work. So long as her typing did not exceed 50 per cent. of her time, I would accept this. But the defendants owed a duty of care specifically to the plaintiff. In my opinion they knew or ought to have known that in the periods in question the level of typing greatly exceeded this. They

B
were not entitled to assume that the plaintiff knew or understood the importance of taking rest pauses or breaks in her typing. They knew that she was highly conscientious and hard working; she was just the sort of person who would spend herself to get through the work.

There is one further matter to which I should refer. That is the judge's finding, to which I earlier referred, that the plaintiff only exceptionally and briefly increased her typing speed beyond her optimum speed of 60

C
words a minute. There was evidence that the judge was entitled to accept that a typist could not type faster than her optimum speed for sustained periods. The judge was entitled to find that the plaintiff exaggerated in this respect. But in my view it does not affect the position. On any showing all the evidence was to the effect that the plaintiff was a fast typist. It is prolonged unbroken spells of typing that are the trouble.

D
For these reasons I have come to the conclusion that the defendants were in breach of their duty to the plaintiff. They should have given her the same advice, instruction and warning as they gave to typists in the accounts department.

At the trial Mr. Redfern criticised the defendants for permitting the plaintiff to do typing after her first return to work in June 1989. The

E
judge rejected these allegations of negligence; I think he was right to do so. Mr. Redfern did not press the appeal on this point. It seems to me that by then the condition had become chronic. The plaintiff clearly cannot be criticised for doing such typing work as she did before she left the defendants' employ. There is therefore no break in the chain of causation between the defendants' negligence up to 23 May 1989 and the subsequent condition from which she suffered.

F
I would allow the appeal.

SWINTON THOMAS L.J. I have read the judgment of Stuart-Smith L.J. in which he sets out the history which is relevant to this appeal. Judge Eifion Roberts Q.C. heard this case over a period of 11 days, in the course of which he heard the evidence of a substantial number of witnesses, lay and

G
expert. He gave a full, reasoned judgment in which he made a number of findings, each one based on his assessment of the evidence that he had heard.

The important findings from the point of view of this appeal were these: (1) That the judge could not resolve the dispute between the two schools of medicine in this field as to whether as a matter of generality prescribed disease A4, cramp of the hand or forearm due to repetitive

H
movements, has an organic or a psychogenic root, or is based on a combination of organic and psychogenic factors. (2) That in May 1989 the plaintiff had symptoms of cramp which could be characterised as PDA4. (3) That he was not satisfied that the cramp suffered by the

586

plaintiff had an organic cause, or that the cramp was caused by repetitive A
movements giving rise to an organic lesion, as opposed to repetitive
movements on the keyboard of the word processor allied to a psychogenic disorder. The judge expressed his findings by saying:

> "I am not satisfied that [the cramp] was due to the repetitive
> movements of the typing in the sense that such movements were an
> effective cause of the cramp as opposed to being merely the sine qua B
> non."

(4) That he did not accept the plaintiff's evidence that she had suffered
cramp in her hands as early as November and December of 1988 as
recorded by her in a diary entry of 23 May 1989. (5) That at the relevant
time in 1988 or 1989 the plaintiff as a general rule did not spend more
than three and three quarter hours per day—one half of her working C
day—typing, although on some occasions she might spend as much as
five hours typing, that her work was interspersed with other secretarial
duties, and that in the course of her typing work she had ample time to,
and was likely to, intersperse that work with other non-typing secretarial
work. (6) That it was not reasonably foreseeable to the defendants,
certainly in the state of knowledge in 1988 and 1989, that the plaintiff's
work would result in her contracting PDA4, typist's cramp. (7) That the D
plaintiff had failed to establish that the defendants were negligent.

The plaintiff, through Mr. Redfern, on this appeal has carried out a
root and branch attack on the judge's findings of fact. Indeed in order to
succeed she has to do so. Mr. Redfern submits that the judge's findings
(3), (4), (5), (6) and (7) were wrong and cannot be supported by the
evidence. He has, accordingly, undertaken a formidable task, namely, to E
show that after an 11-day hearing an experienced judge has erred in
respect of most of his important findings of fact. In my judgment,
although certain of the findings may have relevance to other findings,
they are not interdependent in the sense of one following on the other,
but are independent findings, and if the plaintiff fails to reverse any of
those findings, then the appeal must fail. I turn, then, to look at each of
those issues individually. F

(1) *The general medical issue*

It is necessary to refer briefly to this issue to set the scene for and
place in context the judge's findings in relation to the plaintiff herself.
[His Lordship referred to the history of medical opinion as to the
aetiology of cramp of the hand or forearm due to repetitive movements, G
noted that in 1970 and 1985 a leading textbook expressed the view that it
was primarily psychogenic, and continued:] In his judgment the judge
reviewed the expert evidence that he had heard in some detail and said:

> "The most that I can find on the whole of the medical evidence
> before me is that the condition of cramp of the hand due to
> repetitive movements may have an organic cause or psychogenic H
> cause or a combination of both causes, or the one cause to begin
> with and the other supervening. It is a matter which the court has to
> consider on the evidence before it in each case."

I.C.R.   Pickford v. I.C.I. Plc. (C.A.)   **Swinton Thomas L.J.**

A   On the basis of the evidence before him that finding cannot be faulted and, indeed, was the only finding at which a judge could arrive on this issue.

(2) This finding was not challenged.

(3) *Causation*

B   The plaintiff's case was that her symptoms were organically based. The defendants' case was that they were psychogenic. [His Lordship referred to the views of the medical witnesses, the conflict between the two opposing theories, the fact that PDA4 was very uncommon and there had to be some predisposing cause for PDA4 in addition to repetitive movements, the evidence as to the plaintiff's personality and medical reports; noted the absence of any theory as to a non-

C   psychogenic predisposing factor in the plaintiff's case; concluded that the bulk of medical research pointed to a psychogenic basis; set out specific findings of the judge on the issue; and continued:] It was central to the plaintiff's case to establish that the cramp had an organic basis. Accordingly, although it may not be of importance, the burden of so proving lay on her. The judge found that she had failed to satisfy him

D   that there was an organic cause but that, on a balance of probability, it had a psychogenic cause. On the totality of the evidence, that was a finding that the judge was entitled to reach and, furthermore, in my judgment it accorded with the common sense of the case.

(4) *The diary entry for 23 May 1989*

E   The judge said in relation to the plaintiff:

> "Essentially she is a dutiful, conscientious and responsible person and the defendants do not suggest that she is or has at any time been malingering. In evidence, she is at times prone to exaggeration and some inconsistency, but not in the sense or to the extent of deliberately misleading the court."

F   Mr. Redfern submits that, having made that finding, it was not open to the judge to disbelieve her evidence in relation to the diary of 23 May 1989. A judge trying a case such as this is perfectly entitled to find that as a matter of generality a plaintiff is not deliberately misleading the court but in relation to a particular matter is not telling the truth.

I do accept Mr. Redfern's submission that there is no room for error in relation to that entry. Either it is true or it is not. I also accept that

G   there were indications that it was truthful. There were also strong indications that it was not. If it was true that she suffered pain in her hands in November and December 1988, one would certainly expect, bearing in mind the nature of the diaries, that she would have made entries to that effect. She made complaints in relation to other matters in her diaries and to fellow employees, including Mr. Mason with whom

H   she had a good relationship, but made no mention of cramp or pain in her hands. She carried out activities which were inconsistent with such complaints. Reading the totality of her evidence, particularly her cross–examination, it is self-evident that she was not a satisfactory witness. The

588
Swinton Thomas L.J.   Pickford v. I.C.I. Plc. (C.A.)   [1997]

judge having heard the evidence, particularly her evidence, had to come
to a conclusion on this issue of fact and he was entitled to come to the
conclusion that he did. In my judgment it would be quite impossible for
a Court of Appeal to substitute its own finding of fact on this issue for
that of the judge. At best, the plaintiff would be entitled to a retrial but,
for the reasons that I have given, that is not an appropriate course in this
case.

A

(5) *The extent of the typing done by the plaintiff*

B

This was an important finding of fact, because, unless the plaintiff can
succeed in setting it aside, she cannot show, as Mr. Redfern conceded,
that her injury was foreseeable or that the defendants were negligent.
The judge's primary finding was:

> "My findings as to the typing done by the plaintiff in the period
> November 1988 to May 1989 are these: firstly, considering the range
> and variety of her non-typing secretarial duties and the absence of
> any criticism of her discharge of them, it is highly unlikely that as a
> general rule she spent more than three and three quarter hours per
> day—50 per cent. of her working time—typing. I accept that from
> time to time in order to type an urgent letter or document, she may
> have typed up to five hours—75 per cent. of her working time. But
> even then she had ample scope to intersperse it with two and a half
> hours' non-typing secretarial work."

C

D

The judge also found, which is of relevance on this issue, that the
plaintiff was at times prone to exaggeration and some inconsistency.

The plaintiff completed a lengthy job description in relation to her
work in 1986. She said that the typing load was "fairly heavy," and
described the many other secretarial duties which she performed,
including answering "the many calls which come in from both inside and
outside the company," and "arranging meetings, and letters, memos,
minutes." She referred to leaving the office to see people, delivering
work and obtaining information from diaries. She referred to the need to
be flexible to deal with the conflicting demands of the various sections.
She said that she apportioned her work at the ratio of approximately 50
per cent. typing and 50 per cent. for other work.

E

F

It was the plaintiff's case that between 1986 and 1988/89 there was a
substantial increase in her typing work so that possibly as much as 75 per
cent. of her time was spent on typing in November and December 1988.
Things then improved but in April and May 1989 the typing workload
increased again. There were some complaints of overwork in her diary and
there was some support for this in the evidence of Mr. Mason and Mrs.
Woodward, her immediate superiors. If there was more typing than she
could reasonably cope with then she could send the excess to the typing
pool, known as the wordplex centre. There was no backlog on the
plaintiff's work and no complaints about the work that she was doing. She
did not do overtime which was available to her. Throughout this period
she was carrying out the manifold secretarial duties to which she had
referred in her job appraisal. Inevitably this involved regular and frequent
changes from typing. The evidence which the judge accepted was

G

H

A that the plaintiff's workload was no greater than any other secretary at the defendants' premises where she worked.

The judge heard a body of evidence on this issue. Some of it gave some limited support to the plaintiff's contention that she was over-worked but there was also much evidence that she did not do excessive typing. There was no evidence which vitiated the judge's finding that the plaintiff's normal workload consisted of about 50 per cent. typing rising

B exceptionally for a short period to 75 per cent. at peak times. There is, of course, no mischief in itself in a person spending 75 per cent. of the working day or more on typing provided that the work is interspersed with periods either of rest or on other work. Indeed, those who worked in the wordplex centre and the accounts department spent the bulk of their working time typing. The judge found that the plaintiff could and

C did intersperse typing work with other tasks and breaks. This was wholly in accord with the evidence from the plaintiff herself and other witnesses that she had numerous other secretarial duties to perform. Even on the plaintiff's own account, which the judge did not accept, she spent at least 25 per cent. of her working time on other tasks or having a break which meant that she was not typing during those periods.

The judge had to consider not only the plaintiff's job appraisal, but

D the evidence in relation to the tasks other than typing which she carried out. He considered her evidence and her diary entries and the evidence from the other lay witnesses. In my judgment, the judge having heard that body of evidence on the point was certainly entitled to come to the conclusion that as a normal rule the plaintiff spent 50 per cent. of her time typing and, exceptionally, on occasions as much as 75 per cent. As

E to his finding that this was interspersed with other secretarial duties and tasks, this crucial finding was entirely in accord with the whole of the evidence, including the plaintiff's own evidence, and cannot be faulted. In my judgment the plaintiff has wholly failed to show that the judge was not entitled to make these important findings.

(6) *Foreseeability*

F It was common ground between the witnesses that PDA4 was a rare phenomenon. Even Dr. Stanley agreed that this was so. In the transcript of his evidence this appears:

"Q. Nevertheless you find that even in your experience occupa-tional cramp of the hand is a comparatively rare condition?
A. Uncommon certainly."

G The defendants, employers of a very large workforce, had never experienced this condition as a result of typing. None of the witnesses, many of great experience, had any knowledge of a secretary suffering from it. Dr. Teesdale, a doctor employed by the International Safety, Health and Environment Department of Zeneca Pharmaceuticals, had never in his career seen a case of writer's cramp or come across that condition in a

H typist. Dr. Thompson, the ergonomist called on behalf of the plaintiff, knew of no case where industrial benefits had been awarded as a result of PDA4. Dr. Williams, the rheumatologist called by the defendants, knew of no case where a person had contracted PDA4. Dr. Pierce, the

590

ergonomist called by the defendants, had never come across a case of
PDA4 as a result of typing. Dr. Lamb had never experienced a case of
writer's cramp or typist's cramp. Many employees, including those in the
wordplex centre and the accounts department, type for far longer
periods than the plaintiff without difficulty.

A

Nevertheless, despite proposals that PDA4 should be removed from
the list, it remained a prescribed disease with the result that employers
were required to take such steps as were reasonably necessary to
counteract it if it was reasonably foreseeable that the plaintiff would
contract PDA4. The question is whether it was foreseeable and the
evidence which I have set out, and which was much more fully explored
at the trial, is very relevant to that issue.

B

As I have said, the predominant view in the 1980s was that PDA4 had
a psychogenic root. The defendants had no reason to suspect that the
plaintiff had any defect, either genetic or psychological which made her
more susceptible to contract it. There was no evidence before the judge
that employers could reasonably foresee that this plaintiff would be
struck by this rare condition. There was no evidence as to the typing
threshold which would put this plaintiff at risk from PDA4.

C

However the most important factor on this aspect of the case is the
actual nature of the plaintiff's work. I have set this out under paragraph
(5) above.

D

The Health and Safety Executive pamphlet issued in 1983 in relation
to visual display units contains this paragraph:

"*Rest pauses.*
  "35. In most tasks, natural breaks or pauses occur as a consequence of the inherent organisation of the work. These informal
breaks help to maintain performance by preventing the onset of
fatigue. In some [visual display unit] work, for example, those data
entry tasks requiring continuous and sustained attention and concentration, together with high data entry rates, such naturally
occurring breaks are less frequent. In situations where this type of
task cannot be organised in any other way and where natural breaks
in work do not occur, the introduction of rest pauses should help
attention and concentration to be maintained. It is difficult to be
specific about guidance on rest pauses, since it is likely if strictly laid
down rest pauses are adhered to they will often be found to be
unnecessarily prolonged and frustrating for some and, under other
circumstances, too short to prevent the onset of fatigue. The most
satisfactory length of pause can only be determined by consideration
of the individual operator's job . . ."

E

F

G

In the plaintiff's case there can be no doubt that natural breaks or
pauses did occur as a consequence of the inherent organisation of her
work. On any basis, even taking the plaintiff's case at its highest, and
that case was not accepted by the judge, she did have natural breaks and
pauses in the course of her work. She was a busy secretary, doing her
secretarial work which involved carrying out a good deal of typing
interspersed with her other tasks. As I have said she did substantially less
typing than other employees and she had natural breaks in that work.

H

A   The judge found that an employer could not reasonably foresee that employee doing the plaintiff's work was at risk to suffer PDA4. Not only on the evidence was the judge entitled to come to that conclusion but, in my judgment, he was right to do so.

(7) Negligence

B   It was conceded by Mr. Redfern that, if the defendants were negligent, then that negligence must have occurred prior to May of 1989 when the plaintiff first raised the question of cramp in her hands. Mr. Redfern submitted that employers should warn employees of the risk that they will contract PDA4 if they do excessive typing, that they should give instructions to employees not to engage in excessive typing, and instruct

C   them to take regular rest periods.

Dr. Thompson, the plaintiff's ergonomic expert, agreed that it was not the practice in 1988/89 to warn employees of the risk of the danger of contracting PDA4. Dr. Pearce, for the defendants, gave evidence to the same effect. Dr. Stanley said that in 1994 some companies gave such a warrning but he had no idea whether such warnings were given in 1988. There was in my judgment no evidence which could justify a judge

D   making a finding that in 1988/89 it was a practice within industry to give employees any such warning.

The judge found that the defendants did not require the plaintiff to try out excessive typing at her optimum speed. She had, he said, the necessary discretion, expertise and knowledge to plan, organise, prioritise and negotiate her work. Furthermore, the plaintiff's work was by

E   its nature varied. As the judge said, putting the plaintiff's case at its highest, she had in excess of two hours every day when she was not doing typing work, and the work lent itself naturally to rotation and interspersement. In those circumstances, there was abundant evidence to justify the judge's findings that there was no duty on the defendants to warn this plaintiff, doing her job, not to engage in excessive typing and to break up the pattern of her work and, in my judgment, it is not open to

F   this court to reverse those findings.

Mr. Hytner reminded us of the passage in the speech of Lord Bridge Wilsher v. Essex Area Health Authority [1988] A.C. 1074, 1091:

G   "Where expert witnesses are radically at issue about complex technical questions within their own field and examined and cross-examined at length about their conflicting theories, I believe that the judge's advantage in seeing them and hearing them is scarcely less important than when he has to resolve some conflict of primary fact between lay witnesses in purely mundane matters."

Both the limbs referred to by Lord Bridge are relevant to this appeal. The passage is apt to cover a number of the issues that have arisen on

H   this appeal. I do not believe that it is open to the court to reverse the various findings of fact made by the judge who had the advantage of seeing and hearing the witnesses.

I would, accordingly, dismiss this appeal.

592

WAITE L.J. The judge asked himself five questions which he stated at
the outset of his judgment in these terms:
A

> "This is a case in which a mass of medical, ergonomic and other
> evidence has been called on both sides. In the light of the helpful
> submissions made by both counsel, I am content to accept that the
> ultimate issues in the case can be identified in this way: firstly, whether
> PDA4, cramp of the hand due to repetitive movements, has an
> organic cause; secondly, whether the plaintiff has had PDA4; thirdly,
> if she has had it, whether her PDA4 has an organic cause; fourthly,
> whether her PDA4 was caused by her work as opposed to being work-
> associated; and, fifthly, whether the defendants were negligent."

B

He answered the first two questions affirmatively, holding in regard to
question one:

C

> "The most that I can find on the whole of the medical evidence before
> me is that the condition of cramp of the hand due to repetitive
> movements may have an organic cause or a psychogenic cause or a
> combination of both causes, or the one cause to begin with and the
> other supervening. It is a matter which the court has to consider on
> the evidence before it in each case."

D

and in regard to question two:

> "On the basis of the plaintiff's subjective account of what she felt on
> 23 May 1989, coupled with Dr. Lucire's opinion"—that she had a
> prolonged bout of cramp—"I am disposed to find that she had a
> cramp of the hand . . ."

E

Neither side has criticised those findings, and there has been no cross-
appeal against the judge's conclusion (on question two) that the plaintiff
contracted PDA4 during the course of her employment with the defendants. He answered the third question (did the plaintiff's PDA4 have an
organic cause?) by saying: "She has failed to satisfy me that the cramp of
the hand had an organic cause." and the fourth (causation) by holding:
"The plaintiff has failed to satisfy me that her typing work caused the
cramp of the hand in the legal sense, albeit it set the stage for it."
F

In the light of those answers, and on the general ground that he did
not consider the risk of contracting PDA4 to have been a risk in the
plaintiff's case that should either have been foreseen by the defendants
or made the subject of a warning, the judge answered the fifth and final
question (were the defendants negligent?) in the negative.

G

The principal criticisms of the judge's reasoning raised by this appeal
relate to the third and fourth of the judge's questions, and I will deal
with them separately.

The finding of no organic cause for the PDA4

The judgments of Stuart-Smith and Swinton Thomas L.JJ. (which I have
had an opportunity of reading in draft) have dealt with the background of
developing medical opinion on the question whether PDA4 is attributable
to organic, as opposed to psychogenic, causes. It was the defendants'
case at the hearing that the plaintiff's injuries had a specific
H

A psychogenic cause—namely, the condition known as conversion hysteria. The only expert relied on by the defendants to support that theory was Dr. Lucire, and her evidence (in this respect) was not accepted by the judge, who found that the plaintiff was not suffering from conversion hysteria. The direction which the judge, against the background of that finding, gave himself in regard to the third question was this: "The defendants do not have to satisfy me that the cause"—of the PDA4—"is

B psychogenic: the onus is on the plaintiff to establish that it is organic."

That represents, to my mind, a plain misdirection in law. Why should a plaintiff who has established a condition of PDA4, and who has satisfied the court that the only psychogenic condition relied on against her does not apply in her case, be under any duty to prove a negative and demonstrate that her complaint had no psychiatric origin? Given the

C intricacies of the human mind, and the breadth of emotional range to which everyone is subject from mere stress at one extreme to hysteria at the other, it seems to me to be illogical, as well as unjust, to lay upon an individual complaining of industrial injury the burden, in the absence of any specific psychiatric diagnosis established by his opponent, of proving a non-psychogenic origin for physical symptoms that arc accepted to be genuine.

D
Causation

The plaintiff's case was a straightforward one depending upon natural inference. She was suffering from PDA4—a complaint suffered by, among others, musicians and typists. It is indisputably a rare complaint, but sufficiently significant to justify statutory classification as a prescribed disease. It was significant enough, moreover, for the defendants to draw

E attention to it in the memorandum prepared by their chemicals and polymer group; and for them to include in the training programme for their general typing staff advice to take rest pauses from typing work. No equivalent advice was given to the plaintiff who (as was undisputed) did on occasions type without a break, sometimes for long periods. That gave rise to an obvious inference that the plaintiff was one of the rare

F victims who develop PDA4 through typing.

In the section of his judgment dealing with this topic the material relied on by the judge to support his conclusion that the plaintiff's typing work had nevertheless not caused the cramp in her hand consisted of: (a) An article in the *Medical Journal of Australia* in 1987 by Dr. Hocking, an occupational health adviser, stating that his studies had not supported the view "that the keystroke rate is a major factor in the aetiology of

G repetitive strain injury." (b) The ergonomists called on each side—Dr. Thompson and Mr. Pearce—were agreed that repetitive movements were unlikely to cause injury unless accompanied by other factors. (c) The judge's own findings (which are fully quoted in the judgment of Stuart-Smith L.J.) as to the hours worked by the plaintiff at typing and other tasks, concluding with the finding:

H   "she had the necessary discretion, experience and knowledge. as she was well aware, to plan, organise, prioritise and negotiate the work and, if necessary, to seek help so as to enable herself to cope reasonably with it."

594

(d) A further finding that the muscular fatigue felt by the plaintiff at the end of the working day did not amount to an illness or an injury or a lesion or a disease.

This material was in my judgment wholly inadequate to deal with the central causative link on which the plaintiff's case depended; namely that she was a secretary with typing duties who at times typed continuously without a rest. If the judge thought that his finding as to the nature of her duties—permitting her to devise her own rest programme if she chose to do so and/or introducing involuntary breaks as a necessary incident of the variety in her duties—was sufficient, alone or in conjunction with the other material, to resolve the issue, he was in my judgment mistaken. It does not matter very much to my mind whether his finding in this respect is to be treated as misdirected or against the weight of the evidence; it cannot on either basis—be sustained.

Conclusion

Those two deficiencies in the judgment are sufficient to just the intervention of this court. I would add, however, in agreement with Stuart-Smith L.J. that the judge's finding that the plaintiff had in effect fabricated her diary entry of 23 May 1989 is so manifestly inconsistent with his findings as to her general integrity, and so inadequately explained, that this court would be justified, exceptionally, in treating it as a finding that was reached per incuriam through failure to accord it due consideration or as unsustainable on the evidence.

We are therefore required in this court to decide for ourselves, on the body of evidence presented to the judge, what findings he ought to ought to have made on his last three questions. As to psychogenic influence, there is no evidence, once conversion hysteria is rejected, to justify a finding that the origin of the plaintiff's PDA4 was anything other than organic. As to causation, there is no positive evidence to displace the natural inference that the plaintiff's typing activities were the cause of that complaint. As to negligence, it is sufficient to say that the defendants, who enjoy a deservedly high reputation for staff management and safe working, have themselves set what is clearly a reasonable standard of care by the instructions given to their general typing staff that they should take rest periods routinely during typing work on visual display units. It is easy to understand how the duty to give a similar warning to the plaintiff, as one whose tasks included typing and who would therefore be similarly at risk of PDA4, came to be overlooked. But the duty was there all the same. They were in breach of it and she is entitled to damages.

For those reasons, in agreement with Stuart-Smith L.J., whose reasoning I fully support in all respects, I would allow the appeal.

Appeal allowed with costs.
Leave to appeal refused.

Solicitors: William Hood & Co., Macclesfield: Halliwell Landau, Manchester.

G.F.

Pickford v. Imperial Chemical Industries plc.   a

HOUSE OF LORDS
LORD GOFF OF CHIEVELEY, LORD JAUNCEY OF TULLICHETTLE, LORD SLYNN OF
HADLEY, LORD STEYN AND LORD HOPE OF CRAIGHEAD
23–26 MARCH, 25 JUNE 1998   b

*Negligence—Duty to take care—Employer—Employee developing symptoms of
repetitive strain injury—Employee claiming damages for negligence in respect of
injury allegedly caused by amount of typing work—Employee failing to satisfy judge
that her condition was organic in origin—Judge also holding that her employer was
not under a duty to instruct her to take rest breaks and dismissing claim—Whether* c
Court of Appeal entitled to reverse judge on burden of proof and findings of fact.

The plaintiff was employed by the defendants, ICI, as a full-time secretary,
working a seven and a half hour day from 10 am to 6 pm with a half hour lunch
break. In May 1989 the plaintiff went to see her general practitioner complaining
of pain in both hands, which she had first noticed some seven months previously. d
Although her general practitioner could find no abnormality on examination, he
signed her off work for a short period. Thereafter, she consulted a number of
doctors, who were unable to find any physical explanation for the pain. In
September 1990 ICI terminated the plaintiff's employment as there was no work
available for her for which she accepted she was fit. Thereafter, the plaintiff
commenced proceedings against ICI for damages, claiming that by reason of e
their negligence she had contracted a prescribed disease, PDA4, in the course of
her employment; that it was organic in origin; that it had been caused by the very
large amount of typing which she had carried out on her word processor at speed
for long periods of time without breaks or rest periods; and that ICI were
negligent because they had failed to warn her of the foreseeable risk of f
contracting the disease and of the need to take rest breaks. At the trial the judge
heard conflicting medical evidence about the cause of the plaintiff's PDA4: in
particular, whether it was an organic condition due to trauma or physical injury,
as the plaintiff submitted, or whether its basis was psychogenic. The judge
dismissed the plaintiff's action, holding that she had failed to establish that her
condition was organic in origin or that it was caused by her typing work, as g
opposed to being merely associated with it. He also held that it was not
reasonably foreseeable, in the state of knowledge about the condition in 1988
and 1989, that her work as a secretary would be likely to cause her to contract
PDA4, nor were ICI required to specify rest pauses during the plaintiff's typing
work, even though they had advised typists working in the accounts department
to take regular breaks, since she had ample scope to intersose and rotate her h
typing with her non-typing work and it could reasonably be expected that she
would do so without being told. The plaintiff's appeal was allowed by a majority
of the Court of Appeal, which reversed the trial judge both as to where the
burden of proof lay and on his primary findings of fact on the issues of causation,
foreseeability and negligence. ICI appealed to the House of Lords.

                                                                      j

Held—(Lord Steyn dissenting) In order to succeed, the onus was on the plaintiff to
prove that her condition had been caused by repetitive movements while typing.
Although it was open to her employers to lead evidence in rebuttal to the effect that
its cause was psychogenic and not organic, they did not have to prove that it was due
to conversion hysteria. While failure to prove that alternative explanation was

a a factor to be taken into account in deciding whether the plaintiff had established
an organic cause, it was no more than that, since it still left open the question, in
the light of the wider dispute revealed by the medical evidence, whether an
organic cause had been established for the cramp so that it could be said to have
been due to the plaintiff's typing at work. It followed that the majority in the
Court of Appeal had erred, since they had inverted the onus of proof on the
b issue of causation. Moreover, the court should not have interfered with the
judge's decision that the plaintiff was not entitled to damages, since his findings
that the condition was not reasonably foreseeable in her case and that ICI were
not negligent in the respects alleged by her were soundly based on the evidence.
The appeal would therefore be allowed (see p. 463h, j, p. 464d to f, p. 470b, c,
p. 471j to p. 472a, g, h, p. 473j to p. 474g, p.475a to e, p. 477c, d, j to p. 478f and
c p. 479c, j to p. 480c, post).

Notes

For general duty of employers to their employees, see 20 *Halsbury's Laws* (4th
edn reissue), para 554.

d **Cases referred to in opinions**

Watt (or Thomas) v Thomas [1947] 1 All ER 582, [1947] AC 484, HL.
Wilsher v. Essex Area Health Authority [1988] 1 All ER 471, [1988] AC 1074,
[1988] 2 WLR 557, HL.

Appeal

e Imperial Chemical Industries plc appealed with leave of the Appeal Committee
of the House of Lords given on 18 December 1997 from the decision of the
Court of Appeal (Stuart-Smith and Waite LJJ; Swinton Thomas LJ dissenting)
([1997] ICR 566) on 18 July 1996 allowing an appeal by Ann Margaret Pickford
from a decision by Judge Eifion Roberts QC, sitting as a deputy judge of the
f Queen's Bench Division of the High Court, on 4 November 1994, whereby he
dismissed her action for damages for negligence against the appellants. The facts
are set out in the opinion of Lord Hope.

Benet Hytner QC and *Stephen Stewart QC* (instructed by *Halliwell Landau*,
Manchester) for the appellants.
g *Michael Redfern QC* and *Guy Vickers* (instructed by *Heather Jobling & Co*,
Macclesfield) for the respondent.

Their Lordships took time for consideration.

25 June 1998. The following opinions were delivered.

h **LORD GOFF OF CHIEVELEY.** My Lords, I have had the advantage of reading
in draft the speech prepared by my noble and learned friend Lord Hope of
Craighead. For the reasons he has given, I would also allow this appeal.

LORD JAUNCEY OF TULLICHETTLE. My Lord, I have had the advantage of
reading in draft the speech prepared by my noble and learned friend Lord Hope
j of Craighead. For the reasons he has given, I would also allow this appeal.

LORD SLYNN OF HADLEY. My Lords, I have had the advantage of reading in
draft the speeches prepared by my noble and learned friends Lord Steyn and Lord
Hope of Craighead. They have set out the facts and the competing views so fully
that it is not necessary to repeat them. I therefore summarise my conclusions.

I accept that at the relevant time it was foreseeable to the employers that if employees typed for excessively long hours this might produce not only backache and eye strain but also a risk of cramp of the hand or repetitive strain injury. The fact that the present employers gave a warning and took special precautions in relation to their accounts department supports this.

It seems to me, however, that on the evidence the trial judge was entitled to find that the plaintiff was not in the same position as staff in the accounts department. She was employed not just for typing but also for general secretarial work. True it is that she did sometimes type for 75% of the working hours particularly in April and May 1989 but she often typed for not more than 50% of the day, her other activities intervening. Some of those other activities she could, as I see it, arrange so as to break up her periods of typing and some of them would of themselves interrupt her typing. The plaintiff was clearly efficient and experienced and, albeit highly conscientious, was capable of avoiding and able to avoid excessively long periods of typing. I am not satisfied therefore that the employers were negligent in failing to give her warnings similar to those given to the accounts department which it is claimed should have been given to her or to so control her activities that she did not type for long consecutive periods.

I differ with considerable hesitation from the majority in the Court of Appeal because of their great experience in cases of this kind and because of the complex interplay of medical evidence in the case. I am however satisfied for the reasons given by Swinton Thomas LJ and by my noble and learned friend Lord Hope of Craighead that the trial judge was entitled to find that the plaintiff had not discharged the onus of proving, as it was necessary to prove, that the pain she suffered was organic in origin.

It is obvious that the trial judge found this a difficult case, as it was, and I have considerable sympathy with the plaintiff as a conscientious and loyal employee. But at the end of the day I do not consider that it was open to the Court of Appeal to reject the judge's findings.

I would therefore allow the appeal.

LORD STEYN. My Lords, a deputy judge of the High Court decided that a secretary's claim against her employers for what is commonly called repetitive stress injuries failed on the facts as he found them. It was not an easy case to try. And there is a presumption that a trial judge's conclusions on issues of fact are correct. But in agreement with the majority in the Court of Appeal ([1997] ICR 566) my view is that the trial judge's assessment of the evidence was fundamentally flawed. Moreover, on balance I am satisfied for the reasons so lucidly and trenchantly given by Stuart-Smith LJ (with whom Waite LJ expressed agreement in a separate judgment) that the employee was entitled to succeed on liability.

Since 1948 cramp of the hand or forearm due to repetitive movements such as typing has been classified as a prescribed disease for the purpose of industrial benefit. It is described as PDA4. The causative agent is still uncertain but the DSS Notes of 1983 (leaflet NI 2) state that it is 'probably due to a combination of physical fatigue of muscles and an underlying psychoneurosis'. It rarely occurs among typists. But the risk is known. Thus Imperial Chemical Industries plc (ICI), the employer in the present case, had in place a system of warning and supervising intensive users of word processors in their accounts department at Macclesfield. But no warnings were given to the plaintiff, Miss Pickford, and the *a* extent of her typing was not supervised. The employers assumed that she was not an intensive user of a word processor.

By all accounts given those who worked with her Miss Pickford was a diligent and conscientious employee. She was also an excellent and fast typist. In 1986 the typing content of her job was apparently about 50%. But it was her case at trial that by November or December of 1988 typing was taking up as much as 75% of

b her time. It was then that she began to experience strange feelings in her hands by the weekend. That was her oral testimony. Her diary entries reflected the constant pressure of her typing load. Her entry of Tuesday, 23 May 1989, recorded that her hands 'are almost seizing up when I do a lot of typing'. It stated that 'it started late last year when I noticed that by Friday, my hands were tight and sore (I'd been typing flat out all summer to keep up with mounds of

c word, as well as my other jobs)'. Her case was therefore based on the link between a sharply increased typing workload and the manifestation of those symptoms between November 1988 and May 1989 when she first took medical advice. What then followed is common ground. Miss Pickford was advised to stop typing. She was therefore compelled to stop working as a secretary. And ICI

d did not offer her satisfactory alternative employment. In September 1990 ICI terminated her employment.

Miss Pickford had an excellent work record. She was a conscientious and indeed dedicated employee. The judge found that she was not a malingerer. He also found that she was an honest and truthful witness. Yet he rejected the account given in her diary entry of 23 May 1989 to the effect that her symptoms

e had started in late 1988. He therefore also rejected her oral evidence, which expanded on the diary entry but was to the same general effect. No matter how one strives to find a plausible explanation, which may support the reasoning of the deputy judge of the High Court, I must confess that this particular decision confounds common sense. In her diary entry and oral evidence, Miss Pickford

f could not possibly have made an honest mistake about the pressure of typing work and her symptoms over a period of six months immediately preceding her seeking medical advice. The judge came into a conclusion which lacks intellectual coherence. Plainly her diary entry of 23 May, made at a time when it is acknowledged she knew nothing about PDA4, was broadly speaking accurate and so was her oral evidence expanding on it.

g It follows that the judge misdirected himself in the assessment of Miss Pickford's evidence. A misdirection on one point does not necessarily justify a complete disregard of all the judge's findings of fact. Everything depends on the nature of the misdirection and the circumstances of the particular case. In the present case the misdirection was not on an isolated point of evidence. It related to the essence of Miss Pickford's case: if the evidence of Miss Pickford about

h mounting pressure of typing in late 1988 and early 1989, and the emergence of symptoms over six months, is rejected her case failed at the first hurdle. Moreover, the judge's finding had a domino effect: if the pressure of her typing did not increase as and to the extent that Miss Pickford testified, the emergence and continuance of her symptoms became more questionable. The judge's error

j led him to treat Miss Pickford as honest but inclined to exaggerate. It caused the judge to give inadequate effect to the picture of mounting typing pressure emerging from Miss Pickford's diary entries. Critically, it led him to accept only that Miss Pickford 'from time to time may have typed up to the five hours'. Leaving aside the fact that 75% of her working day was 5 hours and 40 minutes, the judge's finding materially understated the effect of Miss Pickford's oral evidence. In short the judge's error dragged down the whole of his conclusions of fact. His error disabled him from fairly assessing Miss Pickford's evidence.

    a

    Much of the argument on the present appeal centred on the natural breaks from typing caused, for example, by Miss Pickford answering the telephone. This was a relevant matter. But this is how the judge approached the matter:

> '. . . while I accept that there were peaks and troughs and that at times the peaks may have seemed excessive in the plaintiff's perception, she had the necessary discretion, experience and knowledge, as she was well aware, to plan, organise, prioritise and negotiate the work and, if necessary, to seek help so as to enable herself to cope reasonably with it.'

    b

Again the judge fell into error. It was established at the trial that Miss Pickford was unaware of the risk posed by prolonged repetitive movements: she only became aware of that months after she first sought medical advice. It is therefore wrong to say that she had the necessary knowledge to prioritise her work. In any event, the alleviating effect of natural breaks was a matter of fact and degree upon which Miss Pickford's evidence was not accepted by the judge. And his relevant findings are directly linked with his earlier rejection of the diary entry of 23 May and oral evidence in support of it.

    c

    d

    ICI relied on an Australian expert, Dr Lucire, who put forward the theory that Miss Pickford suffered from conversion hysteria. Miss Pickford's excellent work record was inconsistent with this theory. But more importantly it was proved at the trial that this medical phenomenon only arises where the individual has knowledge of the risks of repetitive strain injury. Miss Pickford had no such knowledge at the relevant time. Admittedly, the judge did not accept the conversion hysteria theory. On the other hand, he did not, as the evidence compellingly required, find that it could be eliminated as a possibility. Had he done so, the judge would have been bound to accept the opinion of Mr Stanley (an orthopaedic consultant) and Dr Hay (a consultant psychiatrist) that Miss Pickford's symptoms were largely (but not exclusively) due to an organic cause, *i.e.* excessive typing. The argument of the appellants that the Court of Appeal reversed the burden of proof is wrong: the march of commonsense reasoning, closely tied to the facts of the case, led to the Court of Appeal's conclusion.

    e

    f

    The judge found that Miss Pickford had PDA4. The contrary was not argued in the Court of Appeal or, after some hesitation, not before the House. That immediately raises the point that there must be an explanation for the fact that she contracted PDA4. What was the cause of her PDA4? There really was no alternative on the evidence to concluding that this condition was caused by Miss Pickford's typing work. No doubt there was also an underlying psychoneurotic cause but that does not affect the legal position. Unfortunately, the judge encountered conceptual difficulties. He said:

    g

    h

> '. . . I am disposed to find that she had a cramp of the hand, but I am not satisfied that it was due to the repetitive movements of typing in the sense that such movements were an effective cause of the cramp, as opposed to being merely the causa sine qua non . . .'

    j

The judge concluded that the cramp in Miss Pickford's hand was associated with her work but not caused by it. He said that the typing was 'only a causa sine qua non'. This is not the first time that a judge has been led astray by a Latin tag. Plainly the judge thought that the typing contributed to Miss Pickford's cramp a and it was therefore even on his own findings in causative terms a sufficient contributory cause.

The judge was persuaded that Miss Pickford did not sustain 'an illness or an injury or a lesion or a disease'. This was a misconception. If Miss Pickford's oral testimony is substantially rejected as the judge did, her claim had to fail. But if the thrust of her case is accepted, viz that she sustained continuing symptoms

b which disabled her from continuing to type, then she plainly sustained a disability. Since at least 1948 the argument that PDA4 cannot ever be an injury can be dismissed as wholly unmeritorious.

That leaves the issue of negligence to be considered. I must approach this aspect on the basis that there are compelling reasons for departing from the findings of fact of the trial judge and accepting the evidence of Miss Pickford as

c well as that of her expert witnesses. Nevertheless I have found this the most difficult issue in the case. On balance I am persuaded that, although ICI had an excellent employment record, they culpably failed in this case to appreciate that Miss Pickford was carrying an enormous typing load and that she had in fact become an intensive user of the word processors. Her immediate supervisor

d failed to supervise the extent of her typing. Significantly, Dr Lamb, the defendant's medical officer, did not know that secretaries did anything like as much typing as Miss Pickford did. She sought to have been given the warnings to take breaks and rest pauses like the typists in the accounts department. And, it seems to me that she should have been told why it was necessary and there should have been supervision of the extent of her typing.

e My Lords, amid all the tangled words and imperfect scientific insights afforded by the evidence in this case, the cumulative effect of the central proved facts establish that Miss Pickford's work caused her disability and that her employer could, by the exercise of reasonable care, have avoided the occurrence of her disability.

For these reasons I would dismiss the appeal.

f

LORD HOPE OF CRAIGHEAD. My Lords, the respondent was employed by the appellants as a secretary at the premises of ICI Pharmaceuticals (ICI) at Macclesfield. She had worked as a secretary and typist elsewhere since 1970. She went to ICI in 1983 at first as a temporary secretary. In January 1984 she

g obtained employment there full time as the secretary to three section managers in the quality control department. She worked a seven and a half hour day from 10 am to 6 pm, with half an hour off for lunch. Among the various duties which she was expected to perform was typing work. At first she used an electric typewriter, but during 1984 she was provided with a word processor. In November 1986, when preparing a job assessment, she estimated that her typing

h work took up 50% of her working time. Her other secretarial duties took up the remaining 50%. Towards the end of 1988 and again in April and May 1989 there was an increase in the amount of her typing work. But she continued nevertheless to perform all her other duties as a secretary.

On 25 May 1989 she went to see her general practitioner, Dr. Baker. She

j complained of pain in both hands, more in the right than the left. She told him that she had first noticed this about seven months previously. Dr Baker could find no abnormality on examination, but he signed her off work for a short period. She was then seen by the works doctor, Dr Lamb. He noted that the volume of typing seemed to be the problem, but he was unable to find any physical explanation for the pain in her hands. After further visits to Dr Baker

she was referred to a consultant orthopaedic surgeon, Mr Auchincloss. He saw
her on 14 September 1989. In his opinion the symptoms were work related, but
they were impossible to treat and were not capable of pathological diagnosis.

a

The respondent was not satisfied with the advice which she received from Mr
Auchincloss. He had told her that she could carry on typing and put up with it, or
else seek alternative work. He said that he would not be seeing her again, as he
had nothing to offer her. In September 1989 she wrote to the Repetitive Strain
Injury Association, one of whose publications had been given to her by a work
colleague. She asked them for information on repetitive strain and for the name
of someone whom she might contact as an expert on this condition. On their
recommendation she was seen thereafter by a number of specialists. Meantime in
November 1989 she was signed off work as long-term sick. She returned to work
in May 1990, but after three days' work including filing she left again due to pain
in her hands. The appellants terminated her employment with them on 14
September 1990, as there was no work available for her for which she accepted
she was fit.

b

c

On 20 November 1991 she commenced proceedings against the appellants for
damages. She claimed that by their negligence they had caused her to sustain
repetitive strain injury. On 11 February 1994 her statement of claim was
amended to allege that she suffered not from repetitive strain injury but from
Prescribed Disease A4 (PDA4). Repetitive strain injury is a familiar expression,
but medical experts agree that as a medical term it is unhelpful. It covers so
many conditions that it is of no diagnostic value as a disease. PDA4 on the other
hand does have a recognised place in the list. It was included in 1948 as a
prescrived disease by the Department of Health and Social Security for the
purpose of industrial injury benefit. It was described in the list of prescribed
diseases in leaflet NI 2 which was issued by the Department of Health and Social
Security in October 1983 in these terms:

d

e

'Cramp of the hand or forearm due to repetitive movements *e.g.* writer's
cramp. Type of occupation—any occupation involving prolonged periods of
hand writing, typing or other repetitive movement of the fingers, hand or
arm: *e.g.* typists, clerks and routine assemblers.'

f

The respondent's case was that she had contracted the condition in the course
of her employment with the appellants as a secretary. She maintained that it was
PDA4, that it was organic in origin and that it was due to repetitive movements
of her hands while typing. She said that it had been caused by the very large
amount of typing which she had carried out on her word processor at speed for
long periods of time without breaks or rest periods; that was reasonably
foreseeable that typing at speed for long periods without breaks or rest periods
might give rise to it; and that the appellants were negligent because they had
failed to warn her of the risk of contracting the disease and of the need to take
rest breaks.

g

h

The trial was heard in the High Court by Judge Eifion Roberts QC. He heard
evidence over a period of ten days from a substantial number of expert and lay
witnesses. Much of the medical evidence was directed to the question whether the
condition was PDA4 and, if so, whether it was organic in origin. The medical issues
were controversial, as the condition is such a mysterious one. There is a strong
body of medical opinions to the effect that it is an organic condition, due to some
kind of trauma or physical injury. There is another strong body of medical opinion
that the basis of it is psychogenic, as the product of a somatisation—that

j

a it is all in the mind, in layman's terms. It was admitted that the condition is rare in typists. The appellants said that it had never occurred among typists on their premises. The ergonomic experts on each side were agreed that repetitive movements alone were unlikely to cause injury. And no pathology for the condition has yet been demonstrated. So the medical experts differed as to the basis of the condition generally and as to the cause of it in the respondent's case

b in particular. Much of the evidence from the lay witnesses was directed to the work which the respondent was doing in the performance of her duties as a secretary. The amount of the typing in comparison with her other duties was an important issue, especially in regad to the opportunity which this gave for natural breaks in her typing work.

c The deputy judge held, after analysing the evidence, that the respondent had failed to establish that she was entitled to damages. In the course of a long and careful judgment he said that the most that he could find on the whole of the medical evidence was that the condition of cramp of the hand due to repetitive movements (PDA4) might have an organic cause or a psychogenic cause, or a combination of both causes or one cause to begin with and the other superven-

d ing. He was disposed to hold that the respondent had a cramp of the hand, but she had failed to satisfy him that its cause was an organic one. She had also failed to satisfy him that it was caused by her typing work, as opposed to being merely associated with it.

He then asked himself whether it was reasonably foreseeable that a secretary who was typing to the extent which he had found established by the evidence

e would be likely to suffer from PDA4. He held that, while this was theoretically possible, it was not reasonably foreseeable. As for the breaches of duty which had been alleged, he did not think that it was incumbent on the appellants to specify rest pauses during the respondent's typing work. This was because she had ample scope to interpose her typing with her non-typing secretarial work.

f The work lent itself naturally to rotation and interspersment. It could reasonably have been expected that a person of her intelligence and experience would break it up without being told. He rejected the allegation that a warning should have been given of the risk of contracting PDA4. It was not the practice in the industry to give such a warning. This could be counterproductive, because it might precipitate the condition which it was intended to avoid.

g It will be clear from this summary that the issues which the judge had to decide were all issues of fact. The answers which he gave to them were the result of his assessment of all the evidence, after seeing and hearing all the witnesses. He had to resolve an acute conflict in the expert medical evidence. Another disputed question which he had to resolve was what to make of the respondent's evidence. This was important because of the account which she gave as to the

h development of her condition and as to the nature and amount of her typing work. His impression of her was that she was a dutiful, conscientious and responsible person, and it had not been suggested that she was malingering. But he thought that in her evidence she was at times prone to exaggeration and some inconsistency, although she was not trying to deliberately mislead the court. In

j this sicuation he had to examine her evidence on these matters very carefully. He had to test it against the evidence of the other witnesses whose evidence seemed to him to be reliable.

The respondent appealed against the order made by the trial judge. The Court of Appeal ([1997] ICR 566) allowed her appeal, but this was a decision by a majority. Stuart-Smith LJ and Waite LJ were satisfied that there were sufficient

deficiencies in the judgment to justify their intervention on the facts. Having
examined the evidence, they reversed his findings on causation, foreseeability
and negligence. Swinton Thomas LJ dissented. He said that he did not believe
that it was open to the court to reverse the various findings of fact made by the
judge who had had the advantage of seeing and hearing the witnesses.

I have come to the view, with the greatest of respect to the very experienced
judges who constituted the majority, that the Court of Appeal ought not to have
disturbed the findings which were made by the trial judge. I am unable to accept
the criticisms which were made of his judgment by the majority. It seems to me
that he came to a decision on all the main issues which he was fully entitled to
reach on the evidence. I have also found it hard to reconcile some of the
criticisms of the judgment which were made by the majority with the state of the
evidence. This has intended to strengthen my view that the trial judge reached a
decision which he was entitled to reach and that it ought not to have been
reversed on appeal.

It will be necessary for me to examine in some detail the reasons which the
majority gave for reversing the trial judge. It was to these reasons that Mr Hytner
directed the main part of his argument. He said that the Court of Appeal had
been wrong to reverse the trial judge both as to where the burden of proof lay in
this case and also on various primary findings of fact by the trial judge which
went to the root of the issue of causation, foreseeability and negligence. Mr
Redfern, in seeking to support the decision of the majority, maintained that the
decision by the trial judge was vitiated by errors which he had made, especially
with regard to the medical evidence. I shall deal with these arguments stage by
stage as I examine the state of the evidence.

The medical issues

The judge described the three issues which fall under this heading in this way:
firstly, whether PDA4, cramp of the hand due to repetitive movements, has an
organic cause; secondly, whether the respondent has had PDA4; and thirdly, if
she has had it, whether her PDA4 has an organic cause. I have placed them all
under the heading of medical issues. But is it clear from his judgment that the
judge was unable to resolve all of them without taking account of a substantial
body of evidence from the lay witnesses about the work which the respondent
was doing during the critical period.

As to the first issue, the judge said that the most that he could find on the
whole of the medical evidence was that the condition of cramp of the hand due
to repetitive movements may have an organic cause or a psychogenic cause or a
combination of both causes, and that this was a matter for the court to consider
on the evidence before it in each case. In the Court of Appeal Stuart-Smith LJ
described this conclusion as entirely unexceptional. But he then went on to make
some comments about the state of the controversy which reveal that his
approach to it was very different from the position of neutrality which the judge
had decided to adopt at this stage in his exmaination of the evidence.

The judge's conclusion was, as Stuart-Smith LJ noted, in accordance with the
evidence of the respondent's witnesses Mr Stanley, an orthopaedic surgeon, and
Dr Hay, a psychiatrist. The appellants' witness Dr Lucire, who was also a
psychiatrist, said in her evidence that she had found that, where an organic cause
was present, it was not related to repetitive movements but to some other
organic disorder such as gout. Her explanation for the condition was that in her
experience it was due invariably to a somatisation syndrome. Stuart-Smith LJ

a said that her evidence was that all cases of PDA4 are due to conversion hysteria. But that was to oversimplify the effect of her evidence. It is true that her diagnosis was that, in the respondent's case, the cramp was the product of conversion hysteria—that is to say, that her mind was using her body to escape from a situation at her work which she had found to be objectionable. But her evidence, when speaking about the condition generally, was not so confined. She

b talked in quite general terms about somatisation and the phenomenon of hysteria. She said that one had to be careful in ascribing either an organic cause or a psychogenic cause. In this respect she agreed with Dr Hay, although there was an important difference between them as to the proper starting point. Dr Hay's position was that a diagnosis that there was a psychogenic cause had to be made with great caution, and then only when there was an absence of a physical

c cause. He said that conversion hysteria was a rare condition and that it was a diagnosis which had frequently been shown to be wrong. But Dr Lucire's experience was to the contrary.

As to the state of the controversy, Mr Stanley was a strong supporter of the organic school. Yet he accepted that it was an impossible task for a judge to

d decide which school was right and which school was wrong. In the light of his evidence there can be no doubts that the trial judge was right not to attempt to resolve this dispute. He was right also to describe the possible causes on either side in quite general terms within which a range of diagnoses might be acceptable. But it seems to me that Stuart-Smith LJ was unwilling to accept that the question as to which school was right was still an open one. Having, as I

e think, oversimplified the effect of Dr Lucire's evidence, he said that with advances in medical knowledge and improved medical technology the psychogenic approach had to a large extent been discredited. That however was not the judge's view of the medical evidence which was before him in this case. Whatever may have been the case where other conditions have been said wrongly to have

f had a psychogenic origin, the evidence in this case was that the pathology for PDA4 is uncertain as it has yet to be demonstrated. I do not think that general knowledge about the improvements in medical science and technology, which were not the subject of any evidence, provided a sufficient basis for differing from the judge's view that a neutral position had to be adopted in this case as to the present state of the controversy.

g This difference of view between the majority in the Court of Appeal and the judge on this initial question has an important hearing on the way in which, from different starting points, they approached the other issues in the light of the medical evidence. I do not think that I am being unfair to the majority when I say that it seems to me that they were, from the outset, sceptical about the suggestion that the condition was anything other than organic in origin. The judge, on the

h other hand, was much more circumspect. As to the second issue, he was careful to say that, while he was disposal to find that the respondent had a cramp of the hand, he was not satisfied that it was due to the repetitive movements of typing in the sense that such movements were an effective cause of it. His choice of words were important, because PDA4 has been defined as 'cramp of the hand due to

j repetitive movements'. To accept without qualification that her cramp was PDA4 might be taken as resolving the next issue, as to whether there was an organic cause in this case. That, the most controversial medical issue in the case, the judge wished to examine separately. The majority in the Court of Appeal said that the judge had concluded, without saying so, that the respondent had PDA4. They omitted to add the qualification which the judge had made. By implication

they were criticising his finding as lacking in clarity. I think that they were wrong
to do so, as the judge made it clear that the question whether this was cramp due
to repetitive movements was one which, at this stage, was still unresolved. Their
difference of view from the judge on this point provides the explanation for the
further and more fundamental difference between them about the proper
approach to be taken to the third issue.

The judge said, in regard to the third issue as to the cause of the cramp, that
the appellants did not have to satisfy him that the cause was psychogenic: the
onus was on the respondent to establish that the cause was organic. Stuart-Smith
LJ said that this was a misdirection ([1997] ICR 566 at 574):

'Having established that she had PDA4 there were two alternative
explanations for it advanced by the medical experts one—supported by the
evidence of Mr. Stanley and Dr Hay—was that it was organic; the other—
supported by Dr Lucire—that it was psychogenic being a conversion
hysteria. No other hysterical or psychogenic explanation was advanced. It
seems to me that what the judge had to do was simply to decide upon the
evidence which of these two explanations was the most likely. In the result
the judge said that he was not satisfied that it was organic; therefore by
inference it must be psychogenic; but he did not accept Dr Lucire's
explanation that it was conversion hysteria.'

Waite LJ (at 593) was equally critical of the approach which the judge took as to
where the onus lay on this issue:

'That represents, to my mind, a plain midsdirection in law. Why should a
plaintiff who has established a condition of PDA4, and who has satisfied the
court that the only psychogenic condition relied on against her does not
apply in her case, be under any duty to prove a negative and demonstrate
that her complaint had no psychiatric origin? Given the intricacies of the
human mind, and the breadth of emotional range to which everyone is
subject from mere stress at one extreme to hysteria at the other, it seems to
me to be illogical, as well as unjust, to lay upon an individual complaining of
industrial injury the burden, in the absence of any specific psychiatric
diagnosis established by his opponent, of proving a non-psychogenic origin
for physical symptoms that are accepted to be genuine.'

In my opinion the judge was right to insist that it was for the respondent to satisfy
him that her cramp had an organic cause. This was the basis of her case that her
condition was foreseeable and that, in failing to take precautions against it, the
appellants had been negligent. Unless an organic cause for it was established, her
claim for damages was without any foundation in the evidence.

There is no doubt that in most cases the question of onus ceases to be of any
importance once all the evidence is out and before the court. But in this case it was
not so simple. As Lord Thankerton observed in *Watt (or Thomas) v Thomas* [1947]
1 All ER 582 at 586, [1947] AC 484 at 487, the question of burden of proof as a
determining factor does not arise at the end of the case except in so far as the
court is ultimately unable to come to a definite conclusion on the evidence, or
some part of it, and the question arises as to which party has to suffer from this.
From time to time cases arise which are of that exceptional character. They include
cases which depend on the assessment of complex and disputed medical evidence,
where the court finds itself in difficulty in reaching a decision as to which side of
the argument is the more acceptable. I think that this was such a

a   case, and that the judge was justified in reminding himself where the onus lay as he exmained the evidence.

    There were two competing explanations for the condition which had been advanced by the medical experts. Neither of them was wholly satisfactory. Mr Stanley's explanation that the cramp had an organic cause was open to some criticism. He did not see the respondent until more than three years after May

b   1989, so he could not say whether the symptoms which formed part of his diagnosis were present on that date. He said that he found three manifestations of functional distonia when he saw her in 1993: a significant weakness of grip, poor function of the hands and loss of muscle bulk. But her grip was tested by Mr Holt, a rheumatologist recommended by the Repetitive Strain Injury Association, in October 1989. He reported that she had a very good grip, and

c   that he was rather doubtful whether her condition was repetitive strain injury. Dr Williams, another rheumatologist, examined her in October 1992. He found that her grip was scale four on a scale of five, and that this was normal for a person of her build. The judge said that he found the results of these tests difficult to reconcile with the test which Mr Stanley had carried out, and he noted Mr

d   Stanley's acceptance that disuse atrophy is common where the hand is not used. He also noted that none of the doctors who had seen the respondent in 1989 and 1990 had seen any spasm or tremor which, although they are not always present, are two of the symptoms of PDA4 described in the guidance notes. As for Dr Lucire's diagnosis of conversion hysteria, the judge noted that this explanation also was a difficult one to accept in the light of Dr Hay's evidence.

e   The position which the judge reached after reviewing the medical evidence was that he was unable to decide on that evidence alone whether the organic explanation was the more probable. That was why, after saying what he did about onus, he proceeded to examine the other evidence in order to see whether the onus had been satisfied. This included the respondent's evidence, some of which

f   he thought was exaggerated, and the evidence of two ergonomists. They were agreed that repetitive movements were unlikely to cause injury unless accompanied by other factors, none of which were found by the judge to have been present in this case. He also took into account the findings which he had made about the speed, duration and amount fo the respondent's typing work after testing her evidence against that of other witnesses for whom she worked during

g   the critical period. It was only after completing this review and making his findings in the light of all this other evidence that he reached his decision that the respondent had failed to satisfy him that her cramp had been caused by the typing work.

    The majority in the Court of Appeal appear to have thought that the whole matter ought to have been disposed of by looking solely at the medical evidence.

h   On their approach it was enough that the judge was unwilling to accept Dr Lucire's explanation that the respondent's condition was conversion hysteria. That being so, as there was no other explanation, the conclusion was in their view inevitable that this was a condition which was organic in origin. I have already observed that in my opinion they were approaching the matter from the

j   wrong starting point. But their disposal of this issue is open to objection on more fundamental grounds.

    In the first place what they were doing was to invert the onus of proof. The respondent's whole case was that her cramp had an organic cause. It was essential to her success that it was proved to have been caused by repetitive movements while typing. So, according to the ordinary rule, the onus was on her

to prove that the cause which she had alleged was the right one. It was open to
the appellants to lead evidence in rebuttal to the effect that its cause was a
psychogenic one. But they did not have to prove that it was due to a conversion
hysteria. Failure to prove this alternative explanation was a factor to be taken
into account in the decision as to whether the respondent had established an
organic cause, but it was no more than that. It still left open the question, in the
light of the wider dispute revealed by the medical evidence, whether an organic
cause had been established for the cramp so that it could be said to have been
due to the respondent's typing work. It was precisely because he was unable to
answer this question in her favour on the medical evidence that the judge turned
for such assistance as it might offer to the other evidence.

In the second place, the judge had the advantage of seeing and hearing all the
medical evidence. The majority of the Court of Appeal said that they were well
aware of the rules which define the approach which an appellate court should
adopt in these circumstances. But they did not apply them as they should have
done in the circumstances. As Lord Bridge of Harwich said in *Wilsher v Essex
Area Health Authority* [1988] 1 All ER 871 at 883, [1988] AC 1074 at 1091, the
advantage which the trial judge enjoys is not confined to conflicts of primary fact
on purely mundane matters between lay witnesses. In this case, the medical
experts were at odds with each other about complex issues which were
particularly difficult to resolve as no pathology for the condition known as PDA4
has yet been demonstrated. They were examined and cross-examined on these
issues over several days. Their demeanour and the manner which they gave their
evidence was before the judge, who saw and heard them while they were in the
witness box. All the Court of Appeal had before them was the printed evidence.
The view of the judge that he was unable to come to a conclusion about the
effect of this evidence without taking into account the evidence of the lay
witnesses was entitled to much greater weight than the majority were willing to
give to it. For my part, I think that this approach to this matter was entirely
justified in the light of the difficult issues which were presented to him by the
medical evidence. In the light of the evidence about the nature and duration of
the respondent's typing work, I regard the view of the majority that the judge
had no alternative but to accept that there was an organic cause for the crmap as
a wholly mistaken one. I think that it was due to an imcomplete understanding of
the effect of the evidence.

There is one other criticism of the judge's findings with which I must deal
before I leave the issues covered by the medical evidence. It relates to the judge's
treatment of the respondent's entry in her diary for 23 May 1989. This was the
first entry in the diary, which she had been keeping since 1987, in which she
mentioned any trouble in her hands. She recorded in this entry that it had started
late in the previous year when she noticed by Friday that her hands were tight
and sore, and that she had been typing flat out all that summer to keep up with
her typing work. The judge said that he had difficulty in accepting her
explanation for not mentioning the problem in earlier entries at the time when
the pain was afflicting her and for doing so on 23 May 1989 retrospectively. In
expressing this view he said that he had regard also to the opportunities which
she had had to mention her trouble on other occasions at or about that time.
These included occasions when she could have mentioned it both to her general
practitioner and to Mr Mason, one of the managers, where she was discussing
her work appraisal with him. He had already noted in his judgment that she was
at time prone to exaggerate during her evidence and to some inconsistency,
although not to the extent of deliberately misleading the court.

a   The majority in the Court of Appeal were particularly criticial of his assessment of her evidence. They said that his reasons for not accepting her diary entry made no sense. He could only have meant that she had lied about this entry, which was quite inconsistent with his finding that she had not deliberately misled the court. They made much of this point, as it was their view that the judge had not taken proper advantage of the fact that he had seen and heard her

b   while she was giving her evidence. Having rejected his treatment of her evidence, they went on to rely upon her evidence without subjecting it to the same critical analysis as the judge had given to it. But I think that they made too much of the point, and that they misunderstood the nature of the difficulty. There was no reason to think that the diary entry was a lie. There was no suggestion that she had made up the entry deliberately in order to mislead the court. She had made

c   it in her own private diary, to record her own thoughts at the time when she was writing it. The point which concerned the judge was not whether it was a dishonest entry—was it really to be thought that she would lie to herself—but rather whether, as an accurate record of the history of her condition, it was reliable. I think that the judge was fully entitled to express his concern on this point, and to insist that before he accepted the entry as a reliable one it should

d   be tested against the rest of the evidence. On this matter also the majority ought to have acknowledged that the judge had the advantage over them of hearing the respondent's explanation while she was giving her evidence. As Swinton Thomas LJ said in his dissenting judgment, the judge was entitled to come to the conclusion that he did on this issue of fact, and it was quite impossible for a Court of Appeal to substitute its own finding of fact on it.

e

Causation

The fourth issue which was identified by the judge was whether the respondent's PDA4 was caused by her work as opposed to being work related. Although

f   she had failed to satisfy him that her cramp had an organic cause, it was still necessary for him to examine this issue in order to decide whether the disease might nevertheless have been caused by the prolonged typing work which the respondent said she had to do while employed by the appellants as a secretary.

The majority in the Court of Appeal had no difficulty with this issue. Stuart-Smith LJ said that once it was concluded, as in his view it had to be, that her

g   condition was an organic one, this cast a flood of light upon and in support of her evidence that she was working—that is to say, typing—during the critical periods for prolonged stretches and for about 75% of her working day. This however was the evidence of a witness whom the trial judge, who had the opportunity of observing her in the witness box, described as at time prone to

h   exaggeration and some inconsistency. One of her complaints had been that the pressure of work had been such that during most days she had to type not only for long hours but also at high speed. Her normal typing speed was 60 words per minutes, but she estimated that the was getting up to 80 words per minute on her word processor. The judge heard evidence from other witnesses to the effect that a typist could not exceed her natural optimum speed of about 60 words per

j   minute on the word processor for any sustained period, but only exceptionally and briefly to type the odd letter or document. Stuart-Smith LJ said that the judge was entitled to find that the respondent had exaggerated in this respect, but that in his view that did not affect the position as on any showing all the evidence showed that she was a fast typist and it was prolonged unbroken spells of typing that were the trouble. Speed however was not the only matter about

which the judge held that the respondent was prone to exaggerate. This
assessment of the reliability of her evidence applied also to the question whether
she was typing for prolonged periods—a very loose expression, which in this case
meant very little unles it was related to the opportunities which arose naturally
during the course of that work for breaks and othe rest periods.

    What the judge found on this issue was that at the relevant times in 1988 and
1989 the respondent did not as a general rule spend more than three and three
quarter hours per day—50% of her working time—on typing. He accepted that
from time to time during these periods, in order to type an urgent letter or
document, she might have typed for up to five hours per day—75% of her
working time, leaving aside her half an hour lunch period. But he also found that
during these periods she had ample scope to intersperse her typing with the
remaining two and a half hours of non-typing secretarial work. While there were
peaks and troughs, and while the peaks may have seemed excessive in the
respondent's perception, she had the necessary discretion, knowledge and
experience to plan, organise, prioritise and negotiate the work and, if necessary,
to seek help to enable herself to cope reasonably with it. As there was no
evidence to show that she was not coping with her other non-secretarial work,
the implication was that the periods of typing were not being undertaken for
prolonged periods without interruption as she had claimed. The majority in the
Court of Appeal were critical of these findings. But much of their discussion of
this issue seems to have been influenced by the view which they had already
formed that her condition was organic and that, as it was only in circumstances of
excessive typing that this condition would develop, her account of what she was
doing was supported by the nature of her condition as being accurate. They were
also of the view that the difference between the respondent's account of her
work and what the judge was prepared to accept about this was so great that he
must have been saying that she was being dishonest about it—something which
in his assessment of her evidence was expressly negatived. There were some
other details which they used to support their view that the judge ought to have
accepted the respondent's account of the time which she had had to spend on
her typing work. For example, Stuart-Smith LJ said that she had said that her job
was done by two people after she ceased her employment with ICI.

    The judge had however heard a good deal of evidence on this issue. Some of
this evidence gave some limited support to the respondent's contention that she
was from time to time being overworked. But there was also much evidence,
other than her own assessment, to show that she was not working without any
interruption for prolonged periods on typing work. On the only occasion when
she was asked to put a figure on this, the respondent said that the time which she
spent on typing during the critical periods amounted to 'possibly around 75 per
cent' of her working time. Strictly speaking, after allowing for her lunch break,
the judge's finding that this could be expressed as five hours of her working time
was a slight underestimate. But the important point which emerged clearly from
the evidence of the other witnesses was that throughout her working time,
despite several complaints in her diary of overworking, the respondent was able
to satisfy all the other demands which were made on her in the performance of
her other duties as secretary to three section managers. There were no
complaints by those for whom she was working of poor service or of inefficiency.
The nature of those other duties was such that she had to attend to them, as and
when they arose, throughout her working day. They provided frequent natural
breaks from typing as she answered the telephone, left her desk to speak to the

a managers elsewhere when they were not contactable by telephone, arranged
   meetings for them, made diary entries and so on. Her own job description, which
   she had prepared to show the work she was doing in 1986 to provide a secretarial
   service in her department, impressed the judge because of the range and variety of
   her work. As for the suggestion that her job was done by two people when she left
   her employment, the evidence showed that nothing much could be made of this.

b The respondent accepted that there was some readjustment of her work after she
   left ICI. One of the managers, Mr Mason, took on his own secretary and there was
   an increase in the work which had to be done for the other managers.

   Taking the evidence as a whole, the judge was far better placed than the Court
   of Appeal was to assess to what extent, if at all, the respondent was exaggerating
   and which of the other witnesses who tended to contradict her were the more

c reliable. Here indeed were primary findings of fact on mundane matters, to
   adopt Lord Bridge's description in *Wilsher v Essex Area Health Authority* [1988] 1
   All ER 871, [1988] AC 1074, with which the Court of Appeal were not entitled to
   interfere. As for the comment that the organic nature of the respondent's cramp
   cast a flood of light on her claim that she was typing for prolonged periods, this
   proposition may equally well be run round the other way. It may indeed be said

d that the judge's conclusions about the amount and nature of the respondent's
   typing work, based on his assessment of the reliability of the evidence given by
   the various witnesses, cast a great deal of light upon the question whether her
   condition had been proved to have been an organic one.

e *Foreseeability and negligence*

   The judge held that it was not reasonably foreseeable, in the state of
   knowledge about the condition in 1988 and 1989, that the work which the
   respondent was required to do as a secretary would be likely to cause her to
   contract PDA4. As he put it, while it was technically foreseeable that a typist

f might suffer from this condition, it was not reasonably foreseeable that this
   would happen to a secretary who was typing to the extent which he found
   established by the evidence. He also held that the respondent had not established
   the grounds on which she had claimed that the appellants were negligent.

   In her particulars of negligence, the respondent had alleged that the appellants
   were negligent because they had failed to warn her of the risk of developing the

g condition from typing at a fast speed all day without respite apart from her lunch
   break. At the trial the allegation was that they had failed to take steps to ensure
   that she was given the same instruction, warnings and advice as were given to the
   typists in the accounts department. The judge did not think that the appellants
   were under a duty to prescribe for the respondent rest periods from her typing

h work, as she had ample non-typing secretarial work to intersperse with it. He
   said that her work lent itself naturally to rotation and interspersement. He
   pointed out that the respondent herself had rejected the notion that a regime
   might be imposed upon her which, as a secretary and not a typist, she would have
   regarded as unsuitable. This was, he said, a matter of common sense. He rejected
   the allegation that a warning should have been given to her, on the grounds that

j the condition was uncommon and, on the evidence, very rare in the case of
   typists, that it was not the practice in the industry to give such a warning and that
   to do this, in the case of such a vague condition which was not easily identifiable,
   might well be counterproductive.

   The majority in the Court of Appeal held that it was plainly reasonably
   foreseeable that typists might suffer from the condition if they typed for long

periods without break, and that the appellants should have given the same
advice, instructions and warning as they gave to the typists in the accounts
department. It is clear from their reasoning that they were proceeding on the
basis that the amount and nature of the respondent's typing work was not
materially different from that done by the typists in that department. As in their
case, as they understood it, she also was required to type for long periods without
breaks or rest pauses. So she needed to be given the same advice and instructions
as had been given to them so that she would take breaks and rest periods, and
she should have been given a warning in order to ensure that she did what she
was told. Without that warning she would not have had the requisite knowledge
that it was necessary for her own health to take breaks from prolonged spells of
typing work.

There are two flaws in this approach which in my opinion wholly undermine
the conclusions by the majority that in this case the appellants were negligent.
The first is their assumption that the respondent's evidence that she was typing
for prolonged periods and breaks and rest pauses was accurate and reliable. The
second is their failure to appreciate, and to take into account, the fact that the
nature and variety of her other work lent itself naturally to rotation and
interspersement with her typing work. This was not something that had to be laid
down in advance. The breaks and rest pauses from typing, on the judge's
findings, occurred naturally throughout her working day because of the variety of
the duties which she had to perform as a secretary.

In effect, the majority rejected the judge's assessment that the respondent's
evidence was affected from time to time by exaggeration and inconsistency and
that it had to be tested carefully against the other evidence. They left out of
account his detailed analysis of the evidence of the other witnesses whom he
accepted as reliable. Had they accepted that analysis, they would have seen that
her position was quite different from that of the typists in the accounts
department. The typists who worked there had no other work to do other than
typing. In their case steps had to be taken by way of forward planning to ensure
that they took breaks and rest pauses. In her case this was not so. Even when she
was spending up to 75% of her time on typing work she still had 25% of her
time, in addition to her lunch break, to do her other work which was spread
naturally over her working day. Unlike the typists, she had both the experience
and responsibility to organise and plan her own work according to its requirements from day to day. She did not need to be told what to do.

There was also a good deal of evidence to show that the appellants had taken
steps to inquire into, and to provide against, the possibility that the operators of
word processors might suffer from fatigue—in itself not harmful to health—and
possible injury due to poor posture and other undesirable working practices. At a
meeting held in Runcorn in May 1987 five possible health concerns had been
identified by them. These were backache, eyestrain/headache, effective lighting,
radiation/pregnancy and repetitive strain injury. In the case of repetitive strain
injury it was noted that this complaint was most often associated with a
combinationof poor hand position and typing too fast. It was not suggested that
the respondent had been adopting a poor hand position, and her complaint of
typing too fast was rejected by the judge on the evidence. It was noted that the
results of repetitive strain injury were pain, swelling and discomfort in the fingers
and wrist. The respondent's complaint when she went to see the works doctor,
Dr Lamb, on 31 May 1989 was of pain in the back of her hands. He said that he

a   was unable to find any physical sign of the pain, and that he had not seen or heard of similar symptoms.

As for the giving of warnings, the respondent said in her particulars of negligence that she should have been told of the risk of contracting PDA4. The giving of warnings of the risk of disease or injury is a precaution which is familiar in the field of litigation for personal injury. But in the case of conditions such as

b   PDA4, which are not easily identifiable and not well understood, great caution must be exercised as to the content of any such warning and as to whether to give a warning at all is appropriate. To impose a duty which may cause more harm than good would be undesirable. The law does not compel employers to take steps which may bring about the condition which they wish to prevent. Conditions which are associated with functional or psychogenic disorders present

c   particular difficulty. So the judge was right to pay careful attention to the advice of the experts, and to the practice in the industry, as to precise terms of any warning that the appellants might responsibly give to their employees about the risk of contracting PDA4.

Dr Hay said that those who were prone to anxiety might perceive that they had

d   the symptoms of the disease, so a balance had to be struck. On the other hand a balanced warning might simply do no more than accord with the common sense precautions which everyone would take. Mr Stanley said that it would be disgraceful to give a warning which said that if you developed pain you may never work again. The warning which he would have regarded as acceptable was simply to go and see the works doctor if you develop unusual pain or discomfort.

e   But that was not the kind of warning which the respondent was looking for—she went to her general practitioner two days after she had noted in her diary for the first time that she had pain in her hands, and a few days later she was seen by the works doctor. The judge accepted the evidence of Mr Pearce, the appellants' ergonomist, that it was not the practice in industry in 1988 and 1989 to give a

f   warning of any kind about the risk of contracting PDA4, and that of Dr Teasdale, the appellants' chief medical officer, who said that no literature had ever come to his attention advocating such a warning. His evidence was that the appellants were well aware that poor siting of equipment could lead to eye strain and other disorders, and that steps had been taken to ensure suitable workstation design and siting and that appropriate information was given to visual display

g   operatives. But he would have regarded a warning that muscle fatigue might develop into PDA4, a rare disease, to be counterproductive and, in the absence of advice by a suitable expert body such as the Health and Safety Executive to the contrary, he did not consider it necessary or proper to give such warnings. The judge also accepted Dr Lamb's evidence that a formal system of instruction, warning and advice was adopted and implemented for typing staff in the

h   accounts department as the working day was confined to accounts and difficulties in changing postures could arise in their case. But such a system was not considered necessary for secretaries as they carried out many non-typing duties in the course of their working day.

Stuart-Smith LJ said that he was not moved by the suggestion that the giving

j   of warnings might give rise to difficulty. In his opinion all employers had to do was to give the instructions, advice and warning which the appellants gave to those they considered to be at risk of doing excessive typing. It seems that the kind of warning which he had in mind was that described by Dr Lamb, which is not what the respondent was asking for. But the judge had ample evidence before him to justify the decision which he took that in the respondent's case this was unnecessary. I think that he was right to regard her case as entirely different *a* from that of the typists in the accounts department. She was not required, as they were, to work continuously on a word processor, and the appellants had no reason to anticipate that she was exposed to the same risk of contracting PDA4 which, in any event, was miniminal in their case.

The decisive point which emerges from this part of the case is that the respondent's claim that her typing work was comparable with that done by the *b* typists in the accounts department was shown, by a careful analysis of the evidence, to be exaggerated and unsupportable. The findings by the judge that the condition was not reasonably foreseeable in her case and that the appellants were not negligent in the respects alleged by her were, in my opinion, soundly based on the evidence. I do not think that the Court of Appeal should have interfered with his decision that the appellants were not liable to the respondent *c* in damages. I would allow this appeal.

Appeal allowed.

Lawrence Nesbitt Esq   Barrister.

The following questions relate to the law reports reproduced above the for the case of *Pickford v. Imperial Chemical Industries plc*. When noting your answers to the questions, you should include reference(s) to the appropriate points in the judgment(s) from which you have drawn your information.

Section A

1.   (a) Set out a list of all the courts before which this case came.
     (b) Indicate what was the outcome of the hearing at each instance.

2. Where in the law reports can we discover who were the dissenting judges in this case?

3. According to the accounts given by the judges in the Court of Appeal, what were the issues which had been addressed by the trial judge in this case?

4. What was the basis of the appeal brought against the decision of the first instance judge?

5. What were the "2 deficiencies in the judgment" of the High Court which led Lord Justice Waite to his decision?

Section B

6.   (a) In what respect(s) does the judgment of Lord Justice Swinton-Thomas in the Court of Appeal decision in this case differ from the judgments of Stuart-Smith and Waite LL.J.?
     (b) On what point(s) does the opinion of Lord Steyn in the House of Lords differ from the opinions of Lord Hope and the othe Law Lords?

7. Look up the reference in the report of the Court of Appeal decision at page 578G–H to (a) "inhibitions laid upon this court in interfering with and reversing

the trial judge's findings of fact". Having done this, research any subsequent changes (including any made by the Woolf reforms) to this situation.

8. Since Lords Goff and Jauncey merely agreed with and adopted the reasons given by Lord Hope, what purpose, if any, was served by their sitting on the case?

9. Find alternative references to the law reports reproduced here in the case of *Pickford v. Imperial Chemical Industries plc.*

10. Has *Pickford v. Imperial Chemical Industries plc.* been cited in any subsequent case?

11. Write a short statement giving the ratio of the case in relation to *Pickford v. Imperial Chemical Industries plc.*

EXERCISE 5

Reading research material

Reading and understanding research materials does not just involve seeing what conclusion the author has reached. Understanding the evidence the author has for the conclusion drawn is as important as understanding the conclusion itself. This section is intended to improve your critical awareness of the materials that you are reading. Reading something critically means reading it to see what weaknesses there are in it. The fewer the weaknesses, the stronger the conclusion. When reading something remember that there are flaws in all articles and books. As a reader your task is to assess the merit of a particular argument by being aware of its weaknesses as well as its strengths. With practice critical reading will become an unconscious habit which you will bring to all your reading. Start by reading "Arresting Statistics: The Drift to Informal Justice in England and Wales" by Paddy Hillyard and David Gordon, the article reprinted below. When you have read the article once go back and read it again making detailed notes. When doing this, concentrate on trying to identify the strand of argument that Hillyard and Gordon are trying to develop, paying close attention to the evidence that they present for the various points that they make. Your notes should tell you both what the authors have written and what you think the possible objections to the various details of their argument are. When you think you understand the article, and have made your notes, try to answer the questions set out in Section A below. Refer to the original article when your notes give you insufficient information to answer the question. After you have finished the questions in Section A compare your answers with those that we have given at the back of this book. If your answers differ from our you may need to go back and reread the article in order to get a better understanding of it. Once you are sure you understand the answers to Section A go on and complete the questions in Section B.

Arresting Statistics: The Drift to Informal Justice in England and Wales

Paddy Hillyard* and David Gordon**

This paper re-examines some of the current theoretical models and paradigms of criminal justice in England and Wales based on an analysis of national arrest statistics between 1981 and 1997. The data show that there has been a large increase in the number of arrests in the period but the number of people prosecuted has declined. An increasing number of people are being arrested and released without any further action. The principal arguments is that there

* School of Social and Community Sciences, University of Ulster, Newtonabbey BT37 0BQ, Northern Ireland.
** School for Policy Studies, University of Bristol, 8 Priory Road, Bristol, BS8 1TZ, England.
We are very grateful to a number of people who have read earlier drafts of this paper: David Brown, Rod Morgan, Andrew Sanders, Joe Sim, and two anonymous reviewers for this journal. This paper arose from work carried out during the preparation of a successful ESRC research application, No. R00 237879: 'A Spatial Analysis of Crime and Criminal Justice in England and Wales'.

has been a radical shift in power away from the formal open and public system of justice towards a more informal closed system. The paper concludes that while these trends lend support to a number of theoretical perspectives on the criminal justice process, particularly Choongh's social disciplinary model, the radical transformation which has taken place in the form of criminal justice can only be understood within the broader politics and economic structures of modern Britain.

Introduction

Over thirty years ago Packer published his highly influential two models of the criminal justice process: crime control and the process.[1] The former emphasizes the repression of crime while the latter model is concerned with the possibility of error and builds in safeguards and forms of redress to the administration of justice. It has since been used in a number of analyses of policing and the administration of justice[2] and one of the standard legal textbooks draws highly on the models as an organizing framework for a critical and extensive analysis of the British criminal justice system.[3]

More recently. Choongh[4] has drawn attention to the limitations of Packer's models of justice. His main criticism is that neither model explains the experiences of a significant minority of individuals whose cases terminate at the police station, not because of the lack of evidence, but because the police never had any intention of charging the individual in the first place. He distinguishes these 'police cases' from 'criminal cases' and suggests that, in the former, arrest and detention are used to achieve police goals as opposed to the latter where they are used for criminal justice goals. Police goals are primarily focused 'on reproducing social control, maintaining authority by extracting deference and inflicting summary punishments'. He calls this a social disciplinary model.[5] He continues:

> Its initial and primary purpose is to remind an individual or a community that they are under constant surveillance: the objective is to punish or humiliate the individual, or to communicate police contempt for a particular community or family, or to demonstrate that the police have absolute control over those who challenge the right of the police to define and enforce 'normality'.[6]

He then draws on an ethnographic study to support the key characteristics of the social disciplinary model: the imposition of control, extracting deference and summary punishment. He concludes that his data show two intersecting systems of criminal process: one a criminal justice process and the other a 'shadow' system of police punishment, which is disconnected from the former.

---

[1] H.L. Packer, *The Limits of Criminal Sanction* (1968).
[2] See, for example, T. Bunyan and L. Bridges, 'Britain's new urban policing strategy: The Police and Criminal Evidence Bill in context' (1983) 10 *J. of Law and Society* 85, and M. McConville, A, Sanders, R. Leng, *The Case for the Prosecution* (1991).
[3] A. Sanders and R. Young, *Criminal Justice* (1994).
[4] See S. Choongh, *Policing as Social Discipline* (1997) and S. Choongh, "Policing the Dross" (1998) 38 *Brit. J. of Crim.* 623.
[5] A term used by McConville and Mirsky in relation to a study of New York City courts. See M. McConville and C. Mirsky 'Guilty Pleas courts: A social disciplinary model of criminal justice' (1995) 42 *Social Problems* 216.
[6] Choongh, *op. cit.* (1998), n.4, p. 626.

Cohen,[7] drawing on Foucault and taking a broader sociological perspective of developments in the criminal justice system as a whole, has described the emerging patterns of social control. He argued that there was a blurring of the boundaries between different forms of control, a net widening and the thinning of the mesh embracing new populations, a professionalisation of control accompanied by a dispersal of state power to new sites, and an expansion of technology aimed at preventive surveillance.

North American scholars have suggested that similar profound changes are afoot in the criminal justice system and they too draw on the work of Foucault. Feeley and Simon[8] in two very influential papers have argued that a new paradigm of criminal law has emerged which they call "actuarial justice". Instead of a concern with individuals and a preoccupation with guilt, responsibility, and treatment, the new paradigm is concerned with techniques for identifying, classifying, and managing groups assorted by levels of dangerousness. The population itself, in its biological and demographic sense, is taken as the target of power and the central aim is to reduce risk of future offending. This new penology runs counter to the principles of legality in either of Packer's models of justice. There is little concern to establish either that a crime has been committed or that an individual has been responsible.

Ericson and Haggerty[9] have suggested that crime control is being replaced by the efficient production of knowledge useful in the administration of suspect populations. Suspects' rights are increasingly being replaced by the systems' rights to better knowledge. Again, the drive behind such developments is the reduction of risk. Efficiency in punishment has, they have argued, given way to efficiency in the production and distribution of knowledge useful to the management of population. The quest for actuarial justice has meant that some basic principles of criminal law—morality, procedure, and hierarchy—are on the wane. At the heart of the risk society is surveillance. It provides "bio-power",[10] the power to make biographical profiles of human populations.

The motor force for the changes in much of this body of theory is not described. In contrast there are a number of theoretical perspectives which locate developments firmly in the crisis facing advanced capitalist societies, of growing social fragmentation, inequality, and insecurity. For example, there are Hall's arguments on drifting into a law and order society[11] or authoritarian populism,[12] Norrie and Alderman's "consensual authoritariams",[13] Gamble's strong state,[14] and Hillyard and Percy-Smith's coercive state thesis.[15]

The purpose of this paper is to re-examine some of these ideas about criminal justice using macro rather than micro data. Instead of using data from studies on the street or within police stations, a range of national statistics relating to the use of police powers,

---

[7] See S. Cohen, "The Punitive City: notes on the dispersal of social control" (1979) 3 *Contemporary Crises* 339, and S. Cohen, *Visions of Social Control* (1985).

[8] M.M. Feeley and J. Simon "The New Penology: Notes On the Emerging Strategy of Corrections and Its Implications" (1992) 30 *Criminology* 449, and M.M. Feeley and J. Simon, "Actuarial Justice: The Emerging New Criminal Law" in *The Futures of Criminology*, ed. D. Nelken (1994) 173.

[9] R.V. Ericson and K.D. Haggerty, *Policing the Risk Society* (1997).

[10] id. pp. 91–94.

[11] S. Hall, *Drifting into a law and order Society* (1980) and S. Hall, "The Great Moving Right Show" *Marxism Today*, January 1979.

[12] S. Hall, "Authoritarian populism: a reply to Jessop *et al.*" (1985) *New Left Rev.* 119. See, also, P. Scraton (ed.), *Law, Order and the Authoritarian State* (1987).

[13] A. Norrie and S. Alderman "'Consensual Authoritarianism' and Criminal Justice in Thatcher's Britain" in *Thatcher's Law*, eds A. Gamble and C. Wells (1989) 112.

[14] A. Gamble, *The Free Economy and the Strong State* (1988).

[15] P. Hillyard and J. Percy-Smith, *The Coercive State: The Decline of Democracy in Britain* (1987).

cautious, prosecutions and other disposals in England and Wales are analysed. The principal focus is on the use and outcome of arrests. While there are a number of limitations to the macro approach, it provides the only means to understand the changing form of the criminal justice system over time. In order to achieve this, a fairly lengthy discussion and analysis of arrest statistics is necessary before exploring whether the empirical data is consistent with the different theoretical models and paradigms. Thus, whilst giving a detailed picture of the changing form of the criminal justice system in England and Wales over the last 20 years, the paper will argue that the data supports elements of a number of the theories.

Arrest statistics

An arrest involves taking a person into custody, physically detaining him or her, and carrying out a range of detailed procedures. The person loses his or her freedom for a period of time, suffers varying degrees of public and private approbrium, embarrassment, and perhaps significant direct and indirect costs. The Royal Commission on Criminal Procedure in 1981 noted that the police following an arrest fail at times to understand "the sense of alarm and dismay felt by some of those who suffer such treatment" and concluded that arrest "represents a major disruption to the suspect's life".[16]

Until the beginning of the nineteenth century, an arrest was simply a mechanism for bringing an offender to court after sufficient evidence had been collected. Now its function is much broader. It is often used as part of the investigation, not as the culmination of it.[17] Often its purpose is to secure evidence, which in the past was obtained before the arrest took place. It is also used as the main point of entry to the police cautioning scheme aimed at diverting both juveniles and adults away from the courts.

Notwithstanding the "coercive nature" of an arrest, there have been very few studies of the arrest and detention process and there has been even less analysis of the available statistics, which have been routinely collected on arrests by police force areas. Under section 62 of the Criminal Law Act 1977, anyone who had been arrested and held in custody had the right to have someone notified of their arrest. This led police forces to collect information on the number of arrests and the length of time taken to notify the nominated person, and these statistics were published in the annual reports of the Chief Inspector of Constabulary for each force (other than the Metropolitan Police) for the years 1978 to 1985. They noted the total number of arrests and the number not dealt with in under four hours and twenty-four hours. The Police and Criminal Evidence Act 1984 (PACE) repealed this provision and their publication ceased in the Chief Inspector's Annual Reports. However, police forces appear to have continued the practice of recording the data because a series of Parliamentary Questions elicited the total number of arrests for each police force for the years from 1986 to 1995.[18] There is thus a statistical series of arrests for each police force in England and Wales for the period 1978–1995.

Within each force the definition of an arrest was probably consistent over the period, but how far the definition was consistent across police forces is now subject to debate following the attention focused on this stage of the criminal justice process as a result of ethnic monitoring. It was always known that the Metropolitan Police took a more

---

[16] *Report of the Royal Commission Procedure* (1981; Cmnd. 8092; Chair, Sir Cyril Philips) 44.

[17] Sanders and Young, *op. cit.* n.3, p. 70.

[18] For arrest figures of all police forces except the Metropolitan Police see 177 *H. C. Debs.*, col. 265w (25 July 1990); 178 *H. C. Debs.*, col. 256w (1 November 1990); 152 *H. C. Debs.*, cols 560–561w (12 May 1987); 215 *H. C. Debs.*, cols 410–411w (4 December 1992); 245 *H. C. Debs.*, cols 620–621w (29 June 1994).

restrictive definition and recorded arrests for notifiable offences only, a term that broadly covers the more serious offences,[19] but it has recently come to light that these figures are subject to a further limitation: they exclude all cases in which there is no further action and cover only arrests which resulted in a caution or prosecution.[20] It is likely that other inconsistencies in the definition of an arrest within different police forces will emerge over time.

The Criminal Statistics for England and Wales also contain some information on arrests although it is important to note that at no point have they ever routinely been included in statistics on the total number of arrests in each police force area. They show for indictable offences, summary motoring offences and summary offences, the numbers that were summoned, arrested and bailed, and arrested and held in custody. The crucial limitation of these statistics is that the information is collated only at the point at which a person arrives at court and not when they enter the system. The statistics therefore exclude all those people who were arrested and released unconditionally. In addition, they fail to distinguish between those who were initially arrested and charged and those arrested and subsequently summoned. Bottomley and Pease[21] drew attention to the incompleteness of these statistics in the mid eighties and commented that the Home Office appeared to have a "curious reluctance to publish systematic information".

Considerable improvements have been made in recent years to the amount of information that is available on arrests, in part as a direct result of successive Conservative governments' interests in monitoring the efficiency and effectiveness of all public services.[22] In 1983 the government spelt out in a circular which was expected of the police.[23] Weatheritt[24] has described, in detail, subsequent developments in accountable policing and the construction of a set of performance indicators both for the Audit Commission and for Her Majesty's Inspectorate of Constabulary. However, progress towards the implementation of performance indicators on a uniform basis has been much slower and less comprehensive than for other public services. In 1988 the Audit Commission published the first of a number of studies on the police and this work culminated in the publication in April 1995 of the first set of performance indicators for the police.[25] They covered three main areas: 999 calls and emergencies, crime and detection, and police resources. However, there were no performance indicators regarding arrest. Indicators covering this and other areas are collated by Her Majesty's Inspectorate of Constabulary (HMIC) and include a number of indicators relating to the number of persons arrested/reported for offences. The HMIC at the time of writing still has not published any of these figures apparently because of the variability of the data between forces.[26]

The implementation of section 95 of the Criminal Justice Act 1991 led to the collection of further information on arrests. Under this section the Home Secretary has a duty to publish each year information which he or she considers expedient to help those working

---

[19] For all arrests made by the Metropolitan Police for notifiable offences, 1980 to 1993, see 245 *H. C. Debs.*, cols 622w (29 June 1994).

[20] See M. Fitzgerald and R. Sibbitt, *Ethnic Monitoring in Police Forces: A Beginning* Home Office Research Study 173 (1997) 73. It is remarkable that this information was not made explicit in either the Home Office Bulletins or in response to Parliamentary Questions on arrests.

[21] A. Bottomley and K. Pease, *Crime and Punishment: Interpreting the Data* (1986).

[22] *Efficiency and Effectiveness in the Civil Service* (1982; Cmnd. 8616).

[23] *Manpower, efficiency and effectiveness in the police service*, circular 114/1983 (1983).

[24] M. Weatheritt, "Measuring Police Performance: accounting or accountability?" in *Accountable Policing: Effectiveness, Empowerment and Equity*, eds R. Reiner and S. Spencer (1993) 24.

[25] Audit Commission, *Local Authority Performance Indicators, Volume 3, Police and Fire Services* (1995).

[26] See Fitzgerald and Sibbert, *op. cit.*, n.20, p. 69.

in the criminal justice system "to avoid discriminating against any persons on the ground of race or sex or any other improper ground".[27] Following discussions between the Home Office, the Association of Chief Police Offices (ACPO) and HMIC, a letter was sent to all Chief Constables on March 1995, introducing ethnic monitoring in police forces from April 1996. To make it administratively simple it was agreed that it should be based on a police officer's judgment of the ethnic appearance of the suspect or victim.[28] The first figures on arrests broken down by ethnic apperance of the suspect were published for the financial year 1996/97 in December 1997.[29]

Apart from the ethnic appearance, the police were not required to obtain any other information on the social characteristics of those arrested until 1 April 1998 when they agreed on a voluntary basis to collect information on the gender and the age of those arrested. The collection of this information became mandatory on 1 April 1999. The purpose of this is to identify more clearly some of the differences between police forces in the use of arrests.[30]

Trends in arrest

Figure 1 notes the total number of arrests for all police forces in England and Wales from 1981 to 1997.[31] When the data are smoothed[32] it can be seen that the total number of

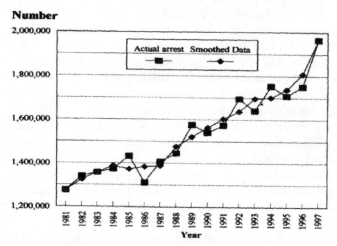

Figure 1: Total number of arrests in England and Wales 1981 to 1997

[27] Criminal Justice Act 1991, s.95 1(b).
[28] Home Office, *Race and Criminal Justice* (1997) 8.
[29] id.
[30] Home Office, *Race and Criminal Justice* (1998).
[31] The figures for 1996 and 1997, in fact, relate to the financial years 1996/97 and 1997/98 because, as noted, the number of arrests are now being compiled for the financial year for all police performance indicators. As most criminal statistics are still compiled for the calendar year, comparisons which use the two sets of figures are subject to some error.
[32] Smoothing is a standard exploratory data analysis (EDA) technique to help identify trends in time series data (data measures over time) Random sampling errors can make trends difficult to see (they add noise to the data and obscure the signal/trend). Statistical smoothing fits a model to the time series data which minimises the obscuring effects of random measurement errors and allows trends to be more clearly identified. See P.F. Velleman and D.C. Hoaglin, *Applications, Basics and Computing of Exploratory Data Analysis* (1981) ch. 6.

arrests has been increasing over the whole period with a more rapid increase since PACE became law in 1986.. While the movement between any two years is likely to be subject to "noise", the sharp decline between 1985 and 1986 was probably due to the preparation and training which was required for the introduction of the Act. The Chief Inspector of Constabulary[33] recorded that "There is evidence that training for and the requirements of PACE have had an adverse effect on the ability of the police to investigate crime'. He went on to point out that "research has shown a reduction, both in the number of arrests and total of 'clear-ups'." In absolute figures the increase in the number of arrests has been considerable. In 1981 there were 1.27 million arrests in England and Wales and in 1997 these had increased to 1.96 million.[34] This represents an increase of well over half a million arrests, or 54 per cent, in seventeen years. To put the figures into some perspective, the police arrested 27 people per 1000 in 1981. By 1997 this has risen to 43 per 1000 of the population.

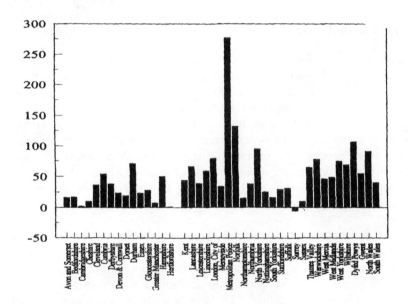

Figure 2: Percentage increase in arrests shown by police force areas, 1981 to 1997

Figure 2 shows the percentage increase or decrease in the number of arrests for each of the 43 police forces between 1981 and 1997. The variation is considerable with an increase of 277 per cent in the Metropolitan Police to a decrease of 6 per cent in Surrey. Two forces—Dyfred Powys and Norfolk—had increases of over 100 per cent in the period. At the other end—Hertfordshire, Cambridgeshire, Humberside, and Greater Manchester—had increases of fewer than 10 per cent. It is impossible without further research to explain these wide changes in the use of arrests.

The data on the ethnic appearance of those arrested, which have now been published for 1996/97 and 1997/98, show that a disproportionate number of the ethnic minority community are arrested. They constitute just under 12 per cent of all arrests, but less than

[33] Her Majesty's Chief Inspector of Constabulary, *Annual Report for 1986* (1986).
[34] If the Metropolitan Police had recorded all its arrests the total would have exceeded 2 million.

6 per cent of the overall population. Black people in particular are more likely to be arrested than either white people or Asians. Similarly stark differences are found within police force areas. A recent analysis suggests that when arrests are represented as a proportion of the respective populations aged ten or over, some 70 per cent of all police forces in England and Wales arrested four or more times as many black people than white people and Avon and Somerset, Cleveland, Merseyside, Sussex, Surrey, and Wiltshire all had black/white arrest ratios of over 8:1.[35]

The interpretation of these differences, however, has been subject to debate. The Home Office, in presenting the figures, drew attention to the work of FitzGerald and Sibbitt, who have stressed the importance of a cautious approach to the analysis of the data particularly when comparing different forces. They point out that the basis of the figures may vary; that offence patterns differ among ethnic groups; and that it is difficult to establish the implications of the ethnic differences in the arrest figures without additional information on the outcome of the arrest.[36]

Standarised arrest rates

The number of arrests, like the number of deaths recorded in any particular area, are likely to be strongly related to the demographic characteristics of the population. In the case of deaths, if an area has a larger proportion than other areas of older women, the number of deaths will be expected to be higher than in those areas with smaller proportions of old women. Similarly, in the case of arrests, those areas with high proportions of young men, will be expected to have higher rates of arrests than those areas with larger proportions of older men. To overcome these variations in the population structure, deaths are normally presented as standardised mortality ratios that allow comparison between areas after controlling for the effects of the different age and sex distributions.[37] The same technique has been used to produce standardised arrest ratios (SARs).

The first stage involved aggregating the local based statistics for the 1991 Census for each of the 43 police force areas. The expected number of arrests was then calculated based on the proportion of age and sex groups in the population and weighted using the proportions of each age and sex group cautioned and prosecuted in 1985. This information was taken from Tarling.[38] The standard arrest ratio was calculated as:

SAR = Expected arrests/Observed arrests* 100

The SARs for each police force in England and Wales are shown in Figure 3. The most important feature is the north/south divide with the highest SARs, that is, those which are in the top quartile, mostly falling above a line drawn from the Merseyside across to Humberside. Only three other police forces south of this line fall into the highest quartile—Nottinghamshire, West Midlands, and South Wales. The lowest SARS are equally clearly distributed and cover the South West and a swathe from Surrey northwards through London to Cambridgeshire and Suffolk.[39] This spatial distribution of arrests is a clear example of what Bromley[40] describes as a "geography of law" in his

[35] 'The Cycle of UK Racism', *Statewatch*, January–February 1999, 1.
[36] Fitzgerald and Sibbitt, *op. cit.*, n.20, chs 4 and 5.
[37] C. Marsh, *Data Analysis* (1987) ch. 14.
[38] R. Tarling, *Analysing Offending: Data, Models and Interpretations* (1993).
[39] The position of London is problematic because of the Metropolitan Police's failure to record all arrests.
[40] N.K. Bromley, *Law, Space and the Geographies of Power* (1994).

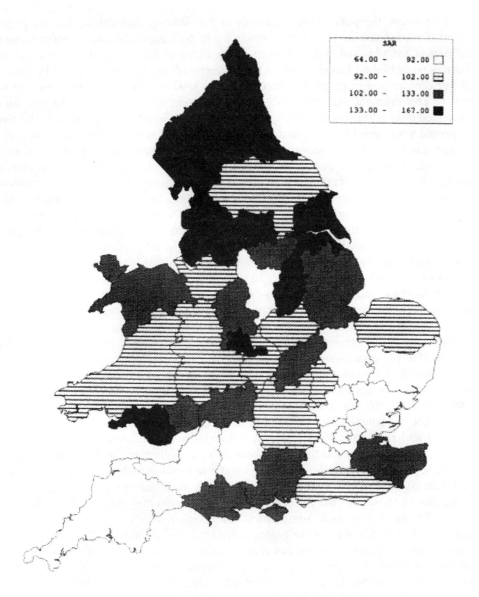

Figure 3: Standardised Arrest Ratios for each Police Force Area, 1991

highly original book that begins to explore the relationship between law and geography. In so far as an arrest is a coercive act depriving people of their liberty and mobility, this distribution is a comment on the geography of coercion and immobility. Significantly, the distribution maps very precisely the distribution of poverty and wealth in England and Wales.[41]

[41] See D. Gordon and R. Forrest, *People and Places, Volume 2: Social and Economic Distinctions in England—A Census Atlas* (1995) and D. Gordon "Census based deprivation indices: their weighing and validation" (1995) 49 *J. of Epidemiology and Community Health* (suppl. 2) s.39.

The outcome of arrests

After an arrest, the police have a number of possibilities, they can charge the person or report them for summons; bail the person for further inquiries; issue a formal caution if the person has admitted guilt; refuse to charge them; or take no further action. Currently, there is no published information on the outcome of any particular arrest. In 1981 some 28 per cent arrived in court after arrests and by 1997 this figure had increased to 45 per cent.[42] The criminal statistics also record the number of people who are formally cautioned after admitting the offence. But what these figures do not tell us is the number of people who have been arrested but drop out of the system before court because the charge may be refused or because no further action is taken following an arrest. In order to provide a composite picture of the different types of disposal following arrests, an attempt has, therefore, been made to provide an estimate of the outcome of arrests where the charge is refused and no further action is taken. Included in these cases will be a number where some other action has been taken, such as being held on a warrant, released pending further inquiries or an informal warning. For convenience this group of cases have been called "NFA cases" although this is not strictly accurate. It must be emphasised that any attempt to make estimates of this sort is fraught with difficulties and is somewhat speculative. However, in the absence of more comprehensive statistics relating to arrest and its disposal, it is essential to use whatever information is available to produce national figures in an attempt to understand what is happening in the criminal justice system as a whole. In addition, national data provide the only source for making comparisons of the criminal justice process over time. As will be seen from the figures presented here, it has changed considerably over the last decade.

The principal difficulty in attempting to make an estimate of the different outcomes of arrests is that the distinction between indictable and summary offences bears no relation to the type of entry into the system of these different types of offences. A proportion of people who are subsequently charged or cautioned with summary offences will have been arrested and then summonsed. Arrest followed by a summons is now, however, rare. Phillips and Brown[43] found that only about two per cent of arrests resulted in a summons and these were mainly motoring offences and a few others such as shoplifting. In order to make an estimate of different arrest disposals it is necessary to make three assumptions. First, that all those who were proceeded against for summary offences were first arrested except for those who were summonsed for revenue, wireless telegraphy, and "other" offences. This is likely to overestimate considerably the numbers that enter the system through arrests because it assumes that offences such as playing in the street, truancy, allowing a chimney to go on fire, and pedal-cycle offences were all dealt with by the suspect being arrested. Secondly, that all those cautioned for both indictable and summary offences were arrested. Again this is likely to overestimate considerably those arrested because most of those cautioned for summary offences would not have been arrested. Lastly, that all prosecutions for drunk driving—a summary motoring offence— were dealt with by arrest.

By adding up the total number of people proceeded against or cautioned for indictable and summary offences, except for revenue, wireless telegraphy and "other" summary offences, and those proceeded gainst for drunk driving, and then subtracting this figure from the total number of arrests, the remainder is assumed to be an estimate of all NFA

[42] Home Office, *Criminal Statistics for England and Wales 1981 and 1997* (1981, 1997).
[43] C. Phillips and D. Brown, *Entry into the criminal justice system: a survey of police arrests and their outcomes*, Home Office Research Study 185 (1998) 83.

cases. It must be emphasised that this is likely to be a very conservative estimate of the numbers as throughout the analysis our assumptions have always overestimated the numbers disposed of by some formal disposal.[44]

Figure 4 shows the total number of arrests for each year between 1981 and 1997 broken down by all the possible dispositions. There are a number of remarkable features. First, the total proceedings for both indictable and summary, non-motoring offences dealt with have declined over the period. Indictable proceedings have dropped by 8.3 per cent, summary proceedings by 35 per cent. Second, the number of cautions for both indictable and summary offences have increased over the period, the former by 109 per cent and the latter by 103 per cent. In recent years, however, the number of cautions has started to decline.[45] Third, the number of NFA cases has been steadily increasing over the period. In 1981 167,099 arrests were disposed in this way and the figure had risen to 838,802 in 1997—a fivefold increase. Put another way, these cases constituted 13.1 per cent of all arrests in 1981. By 1993 the figure had increased to 43 per cent of all arrests.

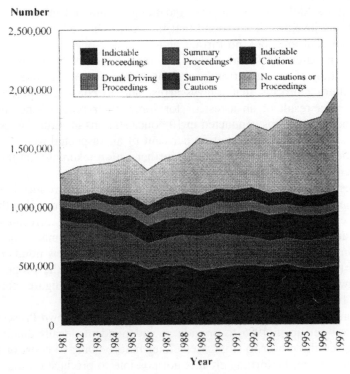

*Excluding Revenue, Wireless Telegraphy
and other Offences

Figure 4: Outcomes of arrests in England and Wales 1981–1997

[44] There are other problems attempting to relate arrest data with disposal data. First, a number of people will be arrested on more than one occasion during the year. Conversely, one defendant may be proceeded against for more than one offence at one appearance and proceedings figures relate to one court appearance not one offence. In addition, an arrest recorded in one year may not be disposed of and recorded until the next year.
[45] The trend in cautioning is relatively easy to explain. For many years the police were encouraged to make more use of cautions but then in 1994 the government introduced a circular restricting its use. See *Cautioning of Offencers*, Home Office circular 18/94 (1985) and C. Wilkinson and R. Evans, "Police Cautioning of Juveniles: The Impact of Home Office Circular 14/1985" (1990) *Crim. Law Rev.* 165.

Various studies lend support to the upward trend in the proportion of NFA cases. Steer[46] looked at the dispositions of a random sample of arrests in Oxford and found that 8.3 per cent of people arrested were released unconditionally. In 1976 Gemmill and Morgan-Giles[47] in another study for the Royal Commission on Criminal Procedure examined disposals for both adults and juveniles in four police divisions and found the unconditional release rate varying between nine per cent and 14 per cent for adults and 0 per cent and 48 per cent for juveniles. The overall rate was 14 per cent. In 1979 a study by Softly[48] found an unconditional release rate of 11 per cent. In a post-PACE study of 5,500 records for prisoners held during March 1987 in thirty-two police stations. Brown[49] found that some 12 per cent of all adults were released unconditionally. A similar study, carried out by Sanders et al.,[50] which examined the custody records in 10 police stations for 15 days in 1988 found that 13.5 per cent were released unconditionally, but neither Brown nor Sanders et al. tracked the eventual dispositions. However, another study conducted between 1986 and 1988 provides a better comparison as each case was tracked through to the eventual disposition.

In the late 1980s McConville, Sanders, and Leng[51] examined just over 1,000 dispositions of adults and juveniles. They found that the police charged 50 per cent of suspects, cautioned 21 per cent and took no further action in over one-quarter of all the cases.[52] Following this, in later 1993 and early 1994 the Home Office conducted the most comprehensive study of arrests currently available.[53] The aim of the study was twofold: to examine the filtering process that follows arrest and to compile a profile of those in custody either as a result of an arrest or for some other reason. The survey, using a variety of methodologies, was conducted in 10 police stations in seven forces and covered 4,250 detainees. The study found that 52 per cent of all suspected were charged, 17 per cent were cautioned and 20 per cent had no further action taken against them. A further 13 per cent were dealt with in various other ways.

These figures are remarkably similar to the national estimates produced in this study as can be seen in Table 1. This compares the outcome of all arrests in the studies by McConville, Leng and Sanders and Phillips and Brown with the corresponding national estimates for similar points in time. It also notes the national estimates for 1997.

At each point in time the national estimates differ by only a few points from the case studies. In particular, there is a very close agreement between the proportion of NFA cases for the two case studies and the national estimates and the figures confirm that the NFA rate has been increasing.

A proportion of all prosecuted cases will be stopped by the Crown Prosecution Service (CPS) which was set up in 1986 to provide an independent, legally qualified review of cases. It was given the power to stop cases either before going to court or to take them out of the court system. Unfortunately it is not possible to produce estimates before and after the setting up of the CPS for the national arrest data on the proportion of prosecutions which are then terminated by the CPS either before or in court. A number

[46] D. Steer, *Uncovering Crime: the Police Role*, RCCP research study No. 7 (1980).

[47] R. Gemmill and R.F. Morgan-Giles, *Arrest, Charge and Summons—Current Practice and Resource Implications*, RCCP research study No. 8 (1980).

[48] P. Softley, *Police Interrogation: An Observational Study in Four Police Stations*, RCCP research study No. 4 (1980).

[49] D. Brown, *Detention at the Police Station under PACE Act, 1984*, Home Office research study No. 104 (1989).

[50] A. Sanders, L. Bridges, A. Mulvaney, and G. Crozier, *Advice and Assistance at Police Stations and the 24 Hour Duty Solicitor Scheme* (1989).

[51] M. McConville, A. Sanders, and R. Leng, *The Case for the Prosecution* (1991).

[52] In 4 per cent of the cases either no information was available or an informal warning was given.

[53] Phillips and Brown, *op. cit.*, n.43, p. 173.

of research studies, however, provide information on this aspect of the criminal justice process. McConville, Sanders, and Leng found that six per cent, and Phillips and Brown seven per cent of their sample of cases were terminated by the CPS. A study by Crisp and Moxon[54] showed that the proportion of cases discontinued increased considerably between 1987 and 1992. The CPS has, therefore, steadily asserted its authority in this area.

Table 1: Comparison of the disposal of arrests between selected case studies and national data

	McConville et al. 1989 %	England and Wales 1989 %	Phillips and Brown 1993 %	England and Wales 1993 %	England and Wales 1997 %
Proceeded against	50	54	52	46	43
Cautioned	21	15	17	17	14
NFAed	25	31	20	37	43
Other disposal	4		12		

The most important finding which emerges from this analysis of the disposals of arrest data for England and Wales over time is the increasing importance of the police station—police territory *"par excellence"*, as Holdaway has put it[55]—as a site for the disposal of cases. This can be shown graphically by adding together all cautions and NFA cases and comparing them with the total number of cases disposal of in the courts. The two sites are very different. One is a closed site controlled by Home Office circulars and its own rules and procedures where justice cannot be seen to be done. The other is open to the public and is subject to the criminal law. One can be best described as a formal system the other as an informal system of justice. It can be argued that it is wrong to describe the police cautioning system as an informal system because it is subject to a very clear set of procedures and the individual has to admit to the offence. This is certainly correct. But "informal" is being used to distinguish this system from the "formal" system. As Lee has pointed out, cautioning, while representing a punitive strategy of dealing with juvenile offenders, "is much less acceptable to the public, much more behind the scene and socially invisible than other forms of punishment."[56] In this sense it is an informal system.

Figure 5 shows the outcome of all arrests between 1981 and 1997 for informal and formal disposals. The major feature is that the formal systems is declining in importance and the police are becoming increasingly significant in the disposal of arrests. In 1981 the courts disposed of 75 per cent of all cases apart from a small proportion which were discontinued prior to the court. By 1993 the figure had declined to 49 per cent and by 1997 to 42 per cent and a proportion of these would have been terminated by the CPS before going to court. As can be seen, the informal disposals exceeded the number of formal disposals for the first time in 1992. Phillips and Brown[57] in their 1993 study looked

[54] D. Crisp and D. Moxon, *Case Screening by the Crown Prosecution Service: how and why Cases are Terminated,* Home Office research study no. 137 (1994).

[55] S. Holdaway, *Inside the British Police* (1983).

[56] M. Lee, "Pre-Court Diversion and Youth Justice" in *Contemporary Criminology,* eds L. Noaks, M. Levi, and M. Maguire (1995) 332.

[57] Phillips and Brown, *op. cit.,* n.43, p. 174.

at the data in a different way. They emphasised that over 60 per cent of suspects who had been arrested were dealt with "officially by the criminal justice system". The distinction we are making, however, is not between official and unofficial disposals but between formal and public, and informal and closed arrest disposals.

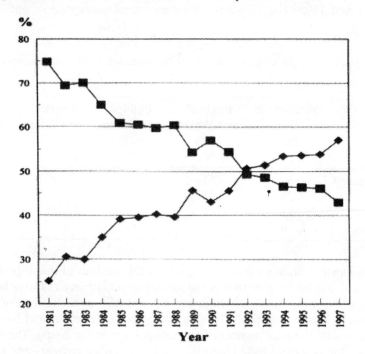

Figure 5: Disposal of arrests in police stations and in Courts 1981 to 1997

There can be little doubt from this macro analysis of the available national statistics on arrests and disposals that fundamental changes have taken place in the criminal justice process in England and Wales over the last 17 years. The number of people arrested has been rapidly increasing, yet the number of people proceeded against in the courts has been declining. At the same time, the police use of caution had doubled by 1992 but has been declining progressively since that date. In addition, both the police and the CPS are deciding not to proceed with an increasing number of cases—the police by releasing more and more unconditionally and the CPS by discontinuing proceedings or withdrawing charges. How can these charges be explained and to what extent do national data support or undermine the current theories and models of the criminal justice process? Without detailed research, and it is important to note that there does not appear to be any current research which is specifically focused on these fundamental changes in the administration of justice, any comments must be speculative.

The increase in arrests may be explained by a variety of legal factors. For example, the police may be using a lower standard of reasonable suspicion than in the past or they may be increasingly using arrest to collect intelligence as forces shift towards more proactive policing methods. Certainly this form of policing is a particularly important element in relation to specific types of crime, for example, drugs,[58] and political violence up to the

---

[58] See, for example, N. Dorn and N. South, "Drug Markets and Law Enforcement" (1990) 30 *Brit. J. of Crim.* 171.

current cease-fire by the IRA.[59] In addition, the expansion in the computer capacity of the police may be changing the way the police operate and the collection of intelligence may be playing a more significant role.

The most likely legal explanation for the increase, however, is that there has been a considerable expansion in the powers of arrest and the police have taken every opportunity to use them. Indeed, PACE not only provided for arrest in relation to summary offences in specific circumstances but also preserved the summary arrest powers provided in 21 existing statutes. It also may have encouraged police forces to rely more on arrests and less on summons as it routinised arrest procedures. Additionally, the Public Order Act 1986 widened the powers of arrest for public order offences.[60] Since then there have been numerous other important pieces of legislation. The Criminal Justice Act 1988 provided the police with more powers in relation to offensive weapons and the Criminal Justice and Public Order Act 1994 substantially increased the range of arrestable offences.[61] The Crime and Disorder Act 1998 adds to this picture expanding the range of behaviour to be criminalised and establishes new relationships between a range of different organisations in the fight against perceived disorder.

These legal developments[62] are fully congruent with Packer's Crime Control model where the central function of the criminal process is the repressing of crime. At the same time, the decline in the number of people prosecuted and the expansion in NFA cases could be explained by factors associated with the due process model. There is little doubt that PACE safeguards have probably had a major influence following arrest by making it more difficult to bring charges. There have been increases in the proportion of those exercising their right to silence[63] and in the number of suspects legally advised at police stations.[64] In addition, PACE controls have probably made it more difficult to "persuade" suspects to confess particularly where the initial evidence is weak—the amount of pressure that can be exerted upon them has been reduced. On the other hand, there are number of recent developments that will make it easier to obtain confessions. In particular, the provisions of the Criminal Justice and Public Order Act 1994 concerning inferences which can be drawn from silence, will probably lead to a reduction in suspects' use of silence in police interviews.

These legal factors associated with the due process model, however, are likely to account for only a proportion of the massive increase in NFA cases. Other factors appear to be at work and Choongh's social disciplinary model offers a more plausible account. The rise in NFA cases support the notion that the police are increasingly pursuing police-defined objectives and have expanded a "shadow" system of police punishment. The key feature is that the police lack interest in legal or factual guilt and are more concerned with imposing control and maintaining order. Although it is impossible to distinguish in the national data between arrests made where there is no evidence ("police cases", in Choongh's words) and arrests where there is evidence but it is insufficient to sustain a charge ("criminal cases"), it is entirely plausible that much of the expansion in the number of NFA cases are the former rather than the latter.

[59] P. Hillyard, *Suspect Community: People's Experiences of the Prevention of Terrorism Acts* (1993).
[60] Sanders and Young, *op. cit.*, n.3, pp. 86–87.
[61] Public order arrests achieve a high prosecution rate because the charges require only police evidence.
[62] Non-legal factors may partly explain the increase in arrests, particularly in recent years. New administrative and bureaucratic demands have been placed on the police to produce more extensive information and they have been subject to more external scrutiny. These factors may have forced police forces to take much more care in the recording of arrests; arrests which in the past would have slipped through the recording procedures, may now be captured. Hence a proportion of the rise may simply reflect changes in recording practices.
[63] Phillips and Brown, *op. cit.*, n.43, pp. 73–4.
[64] id., p. 59.

The national data, as has been emphasised, provide little detail on the characteristics of those arrested but two points emerge which support the idea that policing is about controlling key groups. First, there is a strong correlation of arrests with areas of high deprivation and, second, a disproportionate number of black people are arrested. This suggests that the poor and the dispossessed as well as members of ethnic minorities are particularly likely to be the subject of police attention. Phillips and Brown's study[65] confirms this. Some 54 per cent of those arrested in his sample were unemployed, 14 per cent were school pupils or students, and only 27 per cent were employed. Two per cent were treated by the police as mentally retarded. Some 13 per cent were black and seven per sent were Asian. Phillips and Brown also found that NFA was more likely where the suspect was black or Asian.

Choongh suggests that a key element of the social disciplinary model is the notion of authority: the police see themselves as its embodiment and policing strategies appear to revolve around efforts to neutralise the anti-social elements in society, and their authority as an institution has been challenged. Thus, despite being given significantly expanded powers and considerably increased resources, these policies appear to have had little or no impact on either the prevention or the detection of crime. At the same time, the setting up of the CPS has caused an extra frustration; officers on the beat have seen more and more of their cases thrown out principally because of insufficient evidence. In such a context, it may be suggested that the police have attempted to reassert their authority over the suspect communities by expanding the number of arrests. By releasing people unconditionally they have not risked having the case thrown out and hence avoided further challenges to their authority. From this perspective, an arrest accompanied by unconditional release can be seen as a symbolic statement with the person being formally taken into custody, processed through the rituals of the custody regime, interviewed for intelligence, and then let go. It is questionable how long the police will continue to attempt to assert their authority in this way. Their disillusionment with the practices of the CPS appear to be fairly widespread and it is entirely plausible that the arrest rates will, at some point, decline as the police become more disillusioned.

The trend described in this paper also lend some support to the new paradigms of criminal law suggested by Cohen, Feeley and Simon or Ericson and Haggerty.[66] Thus the downturn in the use of the courts and the rise in the number of NFA cases can be seen as a classic example of the net widening described by Cohen. It can also be interpreted as a shift away from a concern with guilt, responsibility, and treatment towards managing groups. However, it is debatable how far the British police have moved towards any systematic attempts at identifying, classifying, and handling groups with the aim of reducing the risk of future offending. The evidence from Choongh's study and this analysis suggests that the form of management is still very under-developed. Notions of risk and suspects' rights being increasingly displaced by systems' rights to better knowledge with the aim of risk reduction do not appear to pervade police discourses as yet.

Developments in policing in Britain, at least, appear to be less about risk and more about power and authority at both the institutional and political level. The changes in the criminal process have not occurred, as often implied by the theories which draw heavily on Foucault, in some vacuum and without any agency. On the contrary there have been strong political froces at work as Hall, Gamble, Scraton, and Hillyard and Percy-Smith have argued.[67] Successive governments have mobilised their electoral support around law

---

[65] id., p. xii.
[66] Feeley and Simon, op. cit., n.8.
[67] See, for example, Hall, op. cit., nn.11, 12; Gamble, op. cit., n.14; Scraton, op. cit., n.12; and Hillyard and Percy-Smith, op. cit., n.15.

and order. Even when there was a slight downturn in recorded crime at the end of the last Conservative administration, the incoming Labour government continued to criminalise certain types of behaviour and expanded the powers of the police and other agencies in its fight against a perceived breakdown in social order. Target groups and classes of people have been clearly identified by politicians and have included squeegee merchants, immigrants, and the homeless sleeping rough. While the young, black, and working-class have always been subject to discriminatory policing, the political message to those involved in social control has been unambiguous. The problem lies with the marginalised and dispossessed. At the same time, there is no commitment to introduce policies which will confront the growing inequalities based around race, class, and gender. The same groups will continue to be subject to what Scheingold has perceptively called triple victimisation:

> This amounts to—first being excluded from the benefits of advanced capitalism; then being disproportionately victimised by crime; and finally becoming the principal target of crime and social control measures that are indiscriminate, intrusive, and repressive.[68]

Conclusions

This paper has focused on a neglected aspect of criminal justice—the national statistics on arrests and disposals. It has highlighted the substantial rise in the arrest rate over the last 17 years and the substantial decline in the prosecution rate. The control apparatus to deal with those who are perceived to disturb the social order has been reconfigured away from the courts towards a range of decision-making sites. There has been a radical shift in power away from a formal, open, and public system of justice towards an informal and closed system. There has been a significant displacement of the court as the site of decision-making to a range of bureaucratic sites—the police station, the CPS and, in the case of juveniles, committees of social welfare experts. The power of the professional has increased as the power to the magistrate has waned. Ritual and tradition in public have given way to informality in private, legal formalism to professional judgment, and public justice to performance indicators. In short, the criminal justice process in Britain has undergone a metamorphosis: "a day in court" is now a privilege of a minority of those drawn into the system. Although much of the analysis is somewhat speculative because of the absence of comprehensive data, it does support elements of a number of the different theories, paradigms, and models of the criminal justice process. In particular, the data lend strong support to Choongh's social disciplinary model and the expansion of what appears to be a "shadow system" of police punishment. All the changes in the form of the British criminal justice system over the last 20 years, however, need to be located within the broader politics and economic structures of modern Britain.

Section A

1. What issue are the authors intending to discuss?

2. What is the function of an arrest?

[68] S.A. Scheingold, "Constructing the New Political Criminology: Power, Authority, and the Post-Liberal State" (1998) 23 *Law and Social Enquiry* 868.

3. Why do the authors discuss "standardised arrest rates (SARs)" rather than arrest rates?

4. Hillyard and Gordon suggest that "areas of high deprivation" experience much closer policing. Can you suggest any reasons why this should be so?

5. If it is true that the "formal system of justice" is disappearing and an "informal system" is emerging, why is this of significance?

Section B

6. (a) What is the major piece of legislation that concerns powers of arrest within England and Wales?
    (b) What are the possible consequences of an arrest?

7. Hillyard and Gordon criticise the movement from formal to informal justice. You may think their criticisms are accurate but can you think of any advantages to this change?

8. Much of the weight of Hillyard and Gordon's argument rests on an analysis of various kinds of statistics. What limitations are there to this kind of evidence. How else might you look into whether or not there has been the movement that Hillyard and Gordon describe?

EXERCISE 6

Study skills

These exercises have a different format to those which have preceded them.

1. Take brief notes of the first two pages of the case report of *R. v. Jackson* which you will find in Chapter 5 of this book. Before you start, re-read the suggestions about taking notes in the section of Chapter 7 entitled "Lectures, Listening and Notetaking". When you have finished take a break of one hour. After your break assess your notes against the following criteria.

Presentation

Use of paragraphs, headings, underlining.

Clarity

How easy are they to read? Can you remember what your abbreviations mean? Are there any words you are likely to come across frequently, for which you could make up your own standard abbreviation?

Content

Have you included all the important information? Do you have a full reference, so that you could consult the original text at a later date if necessary?

You can do this by yourself, or you can work with another student and compare each other's work.

2. In this exercise, you are asked to evaluate written work. In each case, you are given the plan for an essay, and then the essay which was written, using the plan. In each case you are asked to carry out a number of tasks. Again, you can do this on your own, or with another student.

   (a) Read the plans below. Write down any comments you have on good or bad features of each plan.
   (b) Now read the two essays as if you were the tutor. Decide which one is better, and why. In each case, write down a list of the reasons for your decision.
   (c) Draw up a list of criteria for judging the essays; use your answer to question (b) to help you. Read the two answers again, and decide whether the two students have performed well or badly on each item in your list. If you wish, you can award each essay a mark, in the same way as a tutor would.
   (d) Imagine you are the tutor handing back the essays to the students who wrote the essays. What was good about the answers? How are you going to tell them about the less good points? Make sure you are able to explain clearly how the students might improve their weaker points.

(e) Is there any similarity between these answers and your own, in terms of approach, style, strengths and weaknesses? Imagine you are the student who has written the answer. How would you feel about the comments of the tutor? What are you going to do about them?

Essay evaluation

Essay title:

"Tribunals provide a cheap, effective means of allowing ordinary people to settle disputes without having to use lawyers." Discuss.

Essay Plan 1

Franks Report—purpose of Tribunals
Tribunals—no lawyers so cheap
Tribunals informal—so good for ordinary people
Are they effective—better than nothing, but not really effective without lawyers (see Genn research) and for I.T.s especially, lawyers are vital (see Genn research, also Blankenburg and Dickens); this means not really cheap—because lawyers needed, but no legal aid (see Access to Justice Act 1999).

Essay 1

The Franks Report stated that Tribunals should be readily accessible to ordinary people. This attitude is currently reflected in the way in which litigants can bring proceedings in tribunals. Often, it is only necessary to write a letter, or fill in a very simple form.

Currently, it is not compulsory for litigants at tribunals to be represented by lawyers. This means that people do not have to pay the costs of employing lawyers, which can be very expensive.

Also, the rules of procedure of most tribunals make it clear that the proceedings must be informal, so the lawyers do not wear formal court dress, the hearing room is not set out like a court room, and evidence is not taken on oath. This makes tribunals accessible to ordinary members of the public who are not trained as lawyers, because otherwise they might be easily intimidated by lawyers using legal jargon and wearing formal clothes. Also, it removes the inbuilt advantage which lawyers have in a formal court setting with which they are very familiar, but which other people find intimidating.

Tribunals are also made more informal because the panel is not made up of judges, but of two laypeople and one lawyer. The presence of the laypeople (who have expertise in the area over which the tribunal has jurisdiction) is another factor in increasing informality and making the whole atmosphere less awe-inspiring.

Tribunals do appear on the face of it to be effective in providing ordinary people with a means of settling their disputes without going to a court, but research carried out by

Genn and Genn (Genn and Genn, 1989) found that applicants had a much greater chance of success if they were represented, particularly if they were represented by a barrister. This means that if ordinary people want to win their cases, tribunals are not really cheap, because a lawyer is needed to increase chances of success and since there is no legal aid available to assist with the cost of employing lawyers for tribunal representation, the cost of lawyers must be met by the litigants themselves.

Another reason why tribunals are not as effective in giving ordinary people access to justice as they might seem to be at first is that some tribunals are in fact very formal in nature and this introduces all the disadvantages of a conventional court hearing. The best example of such a tribunal is the Industrial Tribunal, which deals with all kinds of employer/employee disputes and also with cases of discrimination due to sex or race. Research has established that Industrial Tribunals are very formal and that they are adversarial in nature, just like traditional courts (Blankenburg and Rogowski, 1986). Also, many of the legal rules in this area are very complex, and it is unrealistic to expect that an ordinary person will be able to use and understand them as well as a trained lawyer (Dickens *et al*, 1985). Dickens *et al* also found that many litigants did not even understand that they could call witnesses, and many of those who did realise that this was possible did not realise that it would be helpful to do so.

Essay Plan 2

Tribunals intended for ordinary people
Lawyers not necessary
Lots of different kinds of Tribunal
Lawyers always desirable
Tribunals give access to justice but of what quality?

Essay 2

Discussion of the purpose of tribunals often begins with The Franks Committee, which was set up in 1957 to examine "Administrative Tribunals and Enquiries" (Franks, 1957). When it brought out its Report, the Franks Committee said that tribunals should be characterised by ". . . openness, fairness and impartiality. . .", clearly implying that the objective of tribunals should certainly be to provide a cheap and effective means for ordinary people to settle their disputes (Franks, 1957).

There are some characteristics of tribunals which make it more likely that they will be accessible to ordinary people who wish to settle disputes. For instance, Tribunals are not staffed solely by judges; the decision-making body is a panel of three people (hence the name "tribunal"). The Chair of the panel is legally qualified, but the two 'wing people' are not; they are lay people who are selected because of their expertise in the area over which the tribunal in question exercises jurisdiction (see, for example, Special Educational Needs Tribunal Regulations, 1995). The absence of judges, and the presence of lay people on the decision-making body, helps to make tribunals more accessible to ordinary people, as does the fact that tribunals are informal in nature. This means that they do not have to follow the same strict rules of procedure as a court does, nor do they have to take evidence on oath (see, for example, Special Educational Needs Tribunal Regulations, 1995).

However, one of the most important points to be made about tribunals is that it is very difficult to make generalisations about them, because there are many different tribunals, set up at different times, mainly during the twentieth century, to deal with specific areas of law; as government action has impinged more and more on society, so the number of tribunals has increased (Wade, 1963). Tribunals tend to have quite specific jurisdictions, and they can operate in quite different ways. For instance, the Special Educational Needs Tribunal makes efforts to be as accessible as possible to litigants in person, and to ensure that it does not have procedures which ordinary people are likely to find intimidating (Aldridge, 1994). On the other hand, research has repeatedly shown that the Industrial Tribunal is so formal that it is virtually indistinguishable from a court (Dickens *et al* 1985, Blankenburg and Rogowski 1986).

There is convincing research which suggests that tribunals are not in fact as accessible to litigants in person as they might at first appear. Genn and Genn (1989) found that litigants' chances of winning a case or making an advantageous settlement were greatly increased if they had a representative, rather than going to the tribunal on their own. This means that although tribunals are *supposed* to be places where ordinary people can go to settle their disputes, in fact they are not wholly meeting that objective, since they are places where ordinary people gain a much more satisfactory outcome if they have a representative, particularly a barrister (Genn and Genn, 1989).

Overall, it is possible to conclude that some tribunals (such as the Special Educational Needs Tribunal) meet the objective of providing somewhere for litigants in person to resolve their disputes without having to use lawyers, but other tribunals, such as the Industrial Tribunal, fail to meet this objective; if ordinary people go to the latter type of tribunal without representation, they are likely to be significantly disadvantaged.

PART 4

8 | Where Next?

This chapter introduces students to questions they should consider when applying to read law as a degree subject and outlines the career options open to students wishing to qualify as lawyers.

LAW COURSES

Law may be studied at degree level at a range of universities and colleges. Law may be studied as a single subject, or in combination with another discipline, such as economics, politics, a foreign language and others. Thus, a student wishing to study law has two different decisions to make, "Do I want to study law on its own?" and "Where do I want to study?" There are currently over eighty institutions offering law degree courses on either a full or part-time basis.

Before making these decisions, it is wise to obtain a wide selection of law prospectuses from universities and colleges. After looking at these, it will quickly become clear that law courses differ radically from institution to institution. There are a wide variety of legal subjects which can be studied, different balances of optional to compulsory subjects, and varying views about the purpose of studying for a law degree.

Begin by asking:

- why do I want to study law? Is it my intention to qualify as a lawyer or am I studying law for other reasons? Am I mainly interested in obtaining a good professional training or am I mainly interested in studying law as an academic subject or am I trying to combine both interests?

- do I want to combine the study of law with the study of some other subject? What other subjects am I interested in? Which combination would suit my interests?

- if I want to qualify as a solicitor or barrister is the degree course I am interested in approved by the Law Society/Bar?

- if I am certain I wish to qualify as a solicitor or barrister do I want to study another subject at degree level to broaden my education and interests?

- what useful information and guidance can I obtain from my school, teachers, family or friends?

Bearing in mind the answers to these questions, read the prospectuses you have obtained and ask:

What reputation has the course, law school and institution got? Why does it have that reputation and is it one which I find attractive? Some universities have a good overall reputation, but an indifferent law school, some universities have a good law school, but a poor overall reputation. You will need to consider what criteria are of most importance to you. Some factors to consider will be highly subjective (*e.g.* geographic location, desire to live at home or away etc). Universities and colleges are submitting themselves increasingly to public scrutiny and assessment of their standards. The Quality Assurance Agency publish Subject Review Reports which assess the quality of teaching in individual law schools throughout the United Kingdom. At the time of writing the Quality Assurance Agency was proposing to publish an updated Subject Review Report in 2001 to replace the current 1994 version. Further information regarding these reports can be obtained from The Quality Assessment Agency, Southgate House, Southgate Street, Gloucester GL1 1UB Tel: 01452 557000 (www.qqa.ac.uk).

The following questions should also be added:

- how much choice does the course offer me and is the law school of sufficient size to offer a wide variety of optional subjects? (Be suspicious of small law schools which claim to offer a wide variety of subjects. Only a few may actually be on offer in any one year). Does the course offer subjects that reflect my career aims?

- what connections has the law school got with the legal profession and the wider world and what are the career opportunities it considers open to its students?

- what guidance does it offer to students on optional choices and careers? Does it offer to help in selecting courses best suited for my intended career?

- how much flexibility does the course give if my motivations or interests change during my three years at college?

- what type of teaching methods are used and what is the mode of assessment?

Eventually, you will have to decide to which university or college to apply. With a few exceptions, applications to full-time courses of higher education are made through a central "clearing house" called UCAS (Universities and Colleges Admission Service). An applicant completes one form only but can make applications to up to six choices of institution/course: the form is reproduced and copied to the admissions tutor of each course selected. Application forms and UCAS Handbooks, which detail application procedures, universities, colleges and courses, are available free of charge via schools and colleges. Local Careers Advisory Services also have stocks. Completed forms should be received at UCAS by December 15 (October 15 if Oxford and Cambridge Universities are included) for those wishing to enrol at University the following autumn. The address of UCAS is Rosehill, New Barn Lane, Cheltenham, Gloucestershire GL52 3ZD. Tel. 01242 222444, 01242 227788 (www.ucas.ac.uk). UCAS publish a guide to the study of law at university, "A Student's Guide to Entry to Law".

In deciding where to apply you should bear in mind the examination grades which the institution may expect you to get if you are given an offer of a place (can you realistically hope to get the required grades?). Do not judge an institution's reputation purely by the grades it demands. Obtain guidance on admission policies and examination grade requirements from your school or college.

A few law schools will want to interview selected candidates before deciding whether or not to give them a place. An interview is not only a chance for the law school to find out about the candidate but a chance for the candidate to find out about the law school. Be prepared to ask questions about the aims of the law degree course, the range and nature of the optional subjects available and current interest in such courses (be aware that some optional courses will not run if there is insufficient interest), and the research interests of the staff. Never ask a question that can be easily answered by reference to material that has already been sent to you or which you should already have obtained. Do not, for example, ask what subjects are taught if this is in a faculty brochure which you have been given. Do ask, if the brochure does not tell you, the philosophy behind a particular course and, for example, its emphasis on traditional legal study or on the study of law in its social context. Asking no questions at all shows that you have not prepared for the interview and perhaps have little interest in the institution. Asking questions that can be answered from available information shows the same thing. Use the information that you have been sent as a basis for asking further, more detailed questions. Some Careers Advisory Services and schools will be able to advise on interview technique and often hold workshops to help develop relevant skills.

Most law schools run open days. Open days offer you an opportunity to look at the facilities that both the law school and its host university has to offer. Typically, you will get an opportunity to talk to both staff and students. You may be able to discuss any particular problems that you have with the law school's admissions tutor.

In many degree courses contract, tort, criminal law, land law, equity and trusts, constitutional and administrative law and law of the European Union (E.U. law) will be studied as compulsory subjects, in either the first or second year. One reason for this is that many academics see these subjects as being basic to the study of English law. Either they contain principles or concepts that are of importance in a wide range of legal subjects or they are about matters which are themselves of general significance. There is also a pragmatic justification for making these subjects compulsory. Students wishing to qualify as barristers or solicitors must normally study these subjects at degree level in order to be exempt from having to take them in professional examinations. The subjects are sometimes referred to as core subjects.

In addition to the seven subjects above, a normal law degree would involve a student in studying another seven or eight subjects. A list of typical subjects might include:

> English Legal System, Labour Law, Commercial Law, Public International Law, Family Law, Jurisprudence, Human Rights and Civil Liberties, Sociology of Law, Revenue Law, Company Law, Law and Medicine, Private International Law and Intellectual Property.

There may be scope for a student to write a dissertation (an extended essay) on a subject of their choice under the supervision of a member of staff as an alternative to studying of one of the optional subjects. Prospectuses should be read so as to get an idea of the context of the courses and the different individual emphases and approaches adopted. Choice of course options is dictated by many factors. The student's own interests, career intentions, the way in which the subject is taught and the folk-lore surrounding it within the institution where a student is studying all play their part. Subjects vary both in content and the style in which they are taught. For example, international law in one institution may involve different material and be taught in a different way from another course labelled international law in another.

Many optional subjects, with the notable exceptions of subjects such as the sociology of law and jurisprudence, have as their starting point principles, concepts and techniques which are acquired in studying the core legal subjects. The core subjects studied tend to place an emphasis on common law rather than statute law, on private law rather than public law and on applying legal principles without considering their origins and social effects in any detail. Some law degree courses seek to redress this balance as there is an argument that the core subjects, with their emphasis on individuals' property and other private rights perpetuate a narrow vision of English law.

No law school can guarantee that it will still be offering the same subjects in its syllabus three years hence. Lecturers may leave, or may lose interest in something which they have taught. Thus, be wary of deciding to go to a particular institution just because of one course, particularly if it is unusual, and particularly if it is taught in the third year. It may not be there when you reach the third year.

LAW AS A PROFESSION

When looking and deciding on your future career, it is vital to make a realistic assessment of the range of career opportunities open to you. This means deciding what are your own aptitudes, preferences and interests, as well as what are the actual jobs on offer. Vacation or other temporary work experience of any sort can be a very useful way in which to test out your prejudices and instincts about different types of work and to help you make an informed choice about them. Such experience will also help you in job applications and interviews for other, more permanent, jobs. Never be afraid to ask teachers and friends about their jobs and career decisions. Use every opportunity to take advantage of careers advice that is available in your school, college or university. Consider whether participating in a placement scheme would help. When you have made a tentative decision and applied for a job, take time in preparing your letter of application, application form and/ or curriculum vitae (resume of your career to date). Get friends and your tutor to read through your applications and ensure that you present yourself in as interesting and as favourable a light as possible. Never hesitate to take advice. Never be diffident about applying for a particular job.

There are a wide variety of jobs with some legal content. The level and kind of prior legal knowledge which they demand (if any) varies from job to job. You will find an extensive list of such jobs, together with addresses to write for more information about them, in the appendix to this book. In the remainder of this chapter we will concentrate on the two areas of the legal profession: solicitors and barristers. The third section of the legal profession, legal executives, is dealt with separately on page 210.

SOLICITORS AND BARRISTERS

The legal profession in England and Wales is divided into three branches (solicitors, barristers and legal executives) all of which have their own entry and training schemes. The majority of lawyers are solicitors. There are over 75,000 solicitors in England and

Wales. Firms of solicitors exist in all large towns, although there is a high concentration in the South East, particularly in London. Traditionally, solicitors were generalists, advising individual clients on a wide variety of legal matters such as Conveyancing, Probate, Personal Injury, Family Law and Criminal Law. Many solicitors continue to perform this role in small firms employing under 40 people, however, there are an increasing amount of private practice firms who advise business and corporate clients on employment law issues, company mergers and acquisitions, contract law and other commercial matters. There are also a growing number of specialist firms who advise on a particular aspect of law such as insurance, shipping, banking, intellectual property and media and entertainment law to name a few. Some of the larger firms have European and international offices where they advise clients on United Kingdom law, E.U. law and foreign law. The largest of these firms have become 'multi-national' businesses employing thousands of lawyers and staff worldwide.

The majority of solicitors are employed in private practice at various levels of seniority up to partner or proprietor (through share option plans). There are, however, around 14,200 solicitors employed in commerce and industry, local government, law centres and other occupations. Their work can be summarised in the following way:

Category of Employment	Total
Commerce/Industry	4,611
Accountancy practice	67
Nationalised industry	78
Trade Union	48
Government Department	49
Local Government	2,845
Court	165
Government funded services	142
Crown Prosecution Service	1,525
Advice service	273
Educational establishment	107
Health service	24
Others	1,110
Not attached to an organisation	3,170
Total	14,254

. . . .

(Source: Law Society 1998)

The majority of the 10,000 plus practising barristers work in central London. The remaining practice on circuit in cities such as Liverpool, Manchester, Bristol and Birmingham. Barristers have restricted access to clients and can normally only represent a client when instructed by a solicitor. However, some professional organisations may brief the bar directly without having to go through a solicitor (through a scheme called 'Bar Direct'). The Bar Council regulates the bodies which have such direct access.

A barrister specialises in giving advice on detailed issues and representing clients in court. The majority work as individual fee-earners on their own account, sharing overheads with other barristers who are members of the set of chambers. However, about a quarter of barristers are not in independent practice but are instead employed by commercial organisations such as the Government Legal Service, the Crown Prosecution Service, local government or the armed forces. Barristers in independent practice have few of the protections which are afforded to solicitors and commercially employed barristers. Their success or failure is linked directly to their own ability, flair, and preparedness to work, luck and connections.

Historically, comparisons have been drawn between the legal and medical professions. Solicitors, in common with general practitioners, are generalists. Barristers, in common with consultants, are specialists. This comparison still has some degree of validity, although it does not give nearly enough emphasis to the highly specialised work undertaken by many firms of solicitors covering such areas as commercial, company and tax law. It also is the case that a considerable number of solicitors currently act as advocates and will do so increasingly due to their rights of audience being extended to the higher courts. Many barristers spend much of their time out of court, advising solicitors and their clients on points of law and drafting pleadings during the initial stages of litigation.

Those primarily interested in advocacy should normally consider becoming barristers. At present, court work undertaken by solicitors tends to involve cases in the lower courts. However, the enhanced "rights of audience" recently granted to solicitors may, over time, change the position. In making a career decision, thought should be given to the relative opportunities at the Bar and in practice as a solicitor. Practice as a solicitor, in the early stages of a person's career, has the attraction of providing some element of predictability and financial security. Newly qualified barristers must be prepared to put up with career uncertainties and fairly modest incomes in their first years of practice.

Choosing between the two branches of the profession in extremely difficult, especially at the present time, when the legal profession is in a state of transition. Changing attitudes towards the function and conduct of the legal profession, the advent of professional advertising, and greater competition between the two branches of the profession, will all change the nature of legal practice and career opportunities within it. Lawyers have less job security than in the past and their range of work and differences in their terms and conditions of employment have grown in recent years. Qualification as a lawyer is no longer (if it has ever been) an automatic passport to a high standard of living or permanent employment.

EDUCATION AND TRAINING OF SOLICITORS

The Law Society's Careers and Recruitment Service (Ipsley Court, Redditch B98 0TD; www.lawsoc.org.uk) issues a series of helpful guidance notes about becoming a solicitor and careers as a solicitor in local government and commerce and industry. Guidance is also given on financial support for students, together with a list of institutions which offer "qualifying" law degrees, postgraduate diplomas in law, the Common Professional Examination (CPE) and the Legal Practice Course (LPC).

The Law Society prescribes the legal education and training required to qualify as a solicitor in England and Wales. This is often updated so you should ask the Law Society for the current version. The main routes to become a solicitor of England and Wales are the law degree route and the non-law degree route. It is also possible to qualify as a solicitor through the legal executive route (see page 195).

Academic Stage of Training

(a) Law Degree Route

This is the quickest and most common way to qualify as a solicitor in England and Wales.

If you decide to take a law degree, you will need to have a good academic record, as competition for places is intense. You should aim for three "A" levels or equivalent. You may study any academic subject. It is important that you try to obtain high grades. Science "A" levels are as acceptable as arts subjects and no one subject is essential for admission to a Law Degree course.

You should study for a qualifying law degree, which covers the seven core subjects required by both the Law Society and the Bar Council, to complete the Academic Stage of Training. These subjects are Constitutional & Administrative Law, Contract, Criminal, Land Law, Equity and Trusts, Tort and E.U. Law. A list of approved degrees is available from the Law Society. You should check that your degree is approved by the Law Society.

(b) Non-Law Degree Route

This is the second most common way to qualify as a solicitor.

If you have a degree in a subject other than law, you are required to undertake a one-year full-time or two-year part-time course leading to the Common Professional Examination, which covers the seven core subjects that constitute the Academic Stage of Training. The course is offered at around thirty five academic institutions across the country and a full list can be obtained from the Law Society. A current alternative to the Common Professional Examination course is the post-graduate Diploma in Law, which also covers the seven core subjects, and will enable you, for Law Society purposes, to complete the Academic Stage of Training. Other alternatives include completing a 'senior status' law degree (a normal law degree condensed into two years) for which an MA or a postgraduate LL.B. is awarded. A list of these alternative courses, which are offered at around thirty institutions, can be obtained from the Law Society or from your local Careers Advisory Service. Courses start in autumn of each year and application is by means of a clearinghouse for most institutions. The closing date for applications is normally in the spring of the year in which the course commences, *e.g.* Spring 2001 for the 2001–2002 course. Competition for places is extremely strong and students who have not obtained an upper second class honours degree or better may find it difficult to gain a place on a course.

Many people ask if they will have problems obtaining employment as a solicitor or barrister if they do not have a law degree. Most employers are keen to recruit law and non-law students and progression in the profession is not normally affected by degree subject.

(c) Student Membership

Upon completion of the Academic Stage of Training, by the Common Professional Examination, Diploma in Law, or a qualifying law degree, you must apply for student membership of the Law Society in order to proceed to the next stage of training. Application forms must be submitted to the Law Society no later than March 31 of the year in which you wish to undertake professional training. You will be asked a number of questions on the form about such matters as criminal convictions. Particular care must be taken in filling in the forms and making certain that you are eligible for membership.

Vocational Stage of Training

Professional training for solicitors is by means of the Legal Practice Course. Anyone wishing to become a solicitor must complete this course unless they intend to qualify via the Legal Executive Route. The purpose of the course is to ensure that trainee solicitors entering training contracts have the necessary knowledge and practical skills to undertake appropriate tasks under proper supervision during the contract. A full-time Legal Practice Course will run for one academic year; a part-time course for two years. The introduction of part-time courses has increased the flexibility of the training scheme and access to the profession. A list of courses, which are offered at twenty-seven institutions, is available from the Law Society (www.lawsoc.org.uk).

The Legal Practice Course (LPC) is made up of four elements: compulsory subjects, electives (optional subjects), general skills and key skills.

There are three compulsory subjects that must be completed by all students: Business Law and Practice, Litigation and Advocacy (including criminal and civil litigation), and Conveyancing. In addition to the compulsory subjects students may choose three optional subjects known as "electives". A student must spend a minimum number of hours on each elective to demonstrate in-depth study.

Further to these elements, the Law Society has established a set of general and key skills which must be emphasised and assessed as part of the Legal Practice Course. The key skills include Interviewing and Advising, Legal Writing and Drafting, and Advocacy and Legal Research. General skills include Professional Conduct and Client Care, Financial Services, Accounts, E.U. Law and Revenue Law. Each course provider must meet the Law Society's standards in these area but has the freedom to be unique in its course content and teaching method. As a result courses are tailored to specific practice area. When choosing an LPC course students should ensure the course content reflects the type of legal career they wish to pursue. Further information about the course can be obtained from the providing institutions. Application forms for the Legal Practice Course can be obtained from the Legal Practice Course Central Applications Board, PO Box 84, Guildford, Surrey, GU3 1YX.

Practical Stage of Training

After successful completion of the Legal Practice Course, you have to undertake a two-year training contract with a firm of solicitors or other authorised organisation. This involves working in paid employment under the supervision of an authorised firm. Finding a training contract is up to you, but help can be obtained from a variety of sources. Competition for training contracts is strong at present and many employers recruit two-three years in advance.

During your training contract you will be required to complete the *Professional Skills Course*. This consists of three core modules: Finance and Business Skills, Advocacy and Communication Skills, and Ethics and Client Responsibility. There is also 24 hours of tuition on optional subjects which can be tailored to the firm's practice areas.

Trainee solicitors

(a) Private Practice

Most training contracts are served with private firms of solicitors. Firms vary considerably in size and type of work; therefore a trainee solicitor's range of experience and salary may also vary considerably. An overview of individual law firms can be obtained from Roset (the register of solicitors employing trainees), John Pritchard's Legal 500 and Chambers Directory of Law Firms. Many large law firms now produce their own recruitment brochures, which should be obtained as they give a good indication of opportunities. Before making an application you need to think of the sort of training you are seeking.

(i) In rural areas, firms will tend to consist of five or six partners at the most, with total staffs often not exceeding fifteen people. Most such firms will be "general practitioners", which means that they will mostly do conveyancing, landlord and tenant, trusts, wills and probate, small-scale commercial and company work, family law, civil and criminal litigation.

(ii) In large towns most firms will also do the kinds of work listed above though there will tend to be some degree of specialisation, (e.g. towards property work and conveyancing, or crime). The larger firms do more commercial work. Some of these firms may have around twenty partners (with some specialising in certain types of work) and staffs of one hundred or more. Generally, in inner city areas, the higher the percentage of legal aid work done and the greater the emphasis of welfare law, (e.g. family employment, social security and housing law). Such firms have been affected by reductions in the availability of legal aid for many people.

(iii) In London and other major cities, there is the greatest degree of specialisation, with the large firms in the City of London concentrating very heavily on company, financial, commercial and shipping work. Such firms are very large with over one hundred partners and staffs of eight hundred or more and with offices around the world. Smaller specialist firms have developed significantly with "niche", specialist practices covering such areas as intellectual property, employment and media law.

(b) Public Service

Legal work in local government covers many aspects of conveyancing and planning and commercial work. Local authorities do a certain amount of prosecuting work both in those areas where they have special law enforcement responsibilities, (e.g. weights and measures or public health legislation) and also sometimes, on behalf of the public. Local authorities are involved in childcare law and social services law.

There are also substantial opportunities for legal careers in Central Government and the Crown Prosecution Service (for relevant addresses see Appendix I).

(c) Industry and commerce

A number of companies and other organisations, both in the private and public sectors have their own legal departments, with qualified solicitors who occasionally take on trainee solicitors. While the work tends to be specialised, large commercial organisations can offer valuable experience in property and commercial work and in areas such as employment, insurance and pension law. Once a person has qualified there are considerable opportunities to work in commerce with a large City of London firm. Limited opportunities also exist to work as a lawyer for a range of trade and employer associations, trade unions, pressure groups and charities.

(d) Law Centres

In the inner areas of a number of cities there are Law Centres, offering occasional opportunities for trainee solicitors seeking to specialise in welfare law. There are opportunities for solicitors to work for Law Centres and similar agencies, especially where they have had an all-round experience of litigation during articles. The development and continuance of many Law Centres have been affected by public spending restraints.

Funding

Students can obtain financial support to fund the Common Professional Examinations (CPE), the Postgraduate Diploma in Law and the Legal Practice Course (LPC). The main sources of funding are as follows:

Sponsorship:

Many of the larger firms of solicitors will sponsor students undertaking the Legal Practice Course (and in some instances those taking the CPE or Post-Graduate Diploma in Law). As a general rule students will complete their training contract with the sponsoring firm and will occasionally have to commit to employment over a longer period of time.

Students hoping to gain sponsorship should apply early. Applications should be submitted to the chosen firm between June and August in the year the applicant hopes to commence the course (two to three years prior to commencing a training contract).

Loan Schemes:

Many of the High Street banks offer loans at favourable rates to fund CPE, Diploma and LPC courses.

Career Development Loans:

These loans are operated on behalf of the Department of Employment for students who are unable to fund the course through other means. Interest on the loan is paid by the Government for the duration of the course and for up to three months after completion (this can be extended to 12 months if the recipient goes in to practical training such as a training contract).

Law Society Bursary Scheme:

The Law Society has a limited fund with which to award support to outstanding students in need of financial assistance. Application forms must be completed by May 10 in the year the applicant hopes to commence the course.

For information on the above and for further sources of funding contact: Legal Education Information Services, The Law Society, Ipsley Court, Berrington Close, Redditch B98 0TD.

Legal Executive Route to Qualifying as a Solicitor (The Non-Graduate Route)

If you have four GCSEs (special provisions apply for those over twenty-one who do not have the relevant qualifications), you can become qualified through the Institute of Legal Executive route.

You should gain employment in a legal office, join the Institute of Legal Executives and over the two years undertake the Institute's Part I Examination. Over the next one to two years undertake the Institute's Part II Examinations which consists of four specialist law papers and one legal practice paper. The choice of law subjects is optional, but you should, if possible, study for three of the six core subjects that constitute the Academic Stage of Training to become a solicitor of England and Wales.

After passing the Part II Examination, you will become a member of the Institute of Legal Executives. You must have served five years (two after membership) in a legal office before you become eligible to be a Fellow of the Institute of Legal Executives.

As a Fellow of the Institute of Legal Executives you must then passed the seven core subjects plus one substantive law paper. You may then enrol as a Student member of the Law Society and attend the Legal Practice course. Where a FILEX has been in continuous legal employment, the requirement to serve Articles of Training may be waived. All FILEX will be required to complete a Professional Skills Course.

Further information on Legal Executives is contained in Appendix I.

EDUCATION AND TRAINING OF BARRISTERS

The academic stage of training for solicitors and barristers (the Bar) is to all intents and purposes the same. The Bar is predominantly a graduate profession. Full details of the entrance requirements can be obtained from The Inns of Court School of Law, 4 Gray's Inn Place, London, WC1R 5DX. More general information is available from The General Council of the Bar, 2/3 Cursitor Street, London EC4A 1NE (www.barcouncil.org.uk).

The academic stage

The academic stage for intending barristers will normally be covered in their degree course, provided that they study the seven core subjects at institutions and on courses approved by the Bar. If the degree does not cover all of the "core" subjects or if the student is a non-law graduate the relevant parts of the Common Professional Examination or Diploma must be completed before entering the Bar Vocational Course.

The vocational stage

Before proceeding to the vocational stage of training, intending barristers must be admitted to one of the four Inns of Court: Middle Temple (Students' Officer, The Honourable

Society of Middle Temple, Treasury Office, London EC4Y 9AT. Tel: 020 7427 4800); Inner Temple (Students' Officer, The Honourable Society of Inner Temple, Treasury Office, London EC4Y 7HL. Tel: 020 7797 8208); Lincoln's Inn (Students' Officer, The Honourable Society of Lincoln's Inn, Treasury Office, 2 Plowden Buildings, London WC2A 3TL. Tel: 020 7405 0138); Grays's Inn (Students' Officer, The Honourable Society of Gray's Inn, 8 South Square, Gray's Inn, London WC1R 5EU. Tel: 020 7458 7800). Once admitted they must comply with certain requirements of the Inn. The most noteworthy of these is the need, prior to qualification, to "keep term", which means attending a certain number of 'qualifying sessions' at the Inn of Court during set periods. This involves 'dinners' which may be combined with events such as moots, advocacy workshops, talks, concerts and training weekends. This requirement is said to enable judges, barristers and intending barristers to meet and get to know each other. Advice should be taken from careers tutors as to the appropriate Inn to join. Much will depend on your career intentions, scholarship opportunities, your likely pupillage arrangements and the contacts which exist between your law department and particular Inns.

For students intending to practice at the Bar, the vocational stage takes the form of a one-year full-time or two-years part-time, compulsory Bar Vocational Course at the Inns of Court School of Law or at one of seven other institutions approved by the Bar Council. For those not intending to practice in the United Kingdom the vocational stage takes the form of the Bar examination, for which there are no compulsory courses.

The Bar Vocational Course places an emphasis on developing practical skills including casework skills (fact management and legal research), written skills (opinion drafting and drafting documents) and interpersonal skills (conference, negotiation and advocacy skills). Other major elements of the course include developing knowledge in criminal and civil litigation, evidence and sentencing with the student choosing a further two optional subjects from a choice of six.

Students applying for the Bar Vocational Course no longer apply to the institution directly. Applications are dealt with centrally through the CACH (Central Application and Clearing House) system. Application packs can be obtained from CACH, 2/3 Cursitor Street, London EC4A 1NE.

Pupillage

Students who pass the Bar Vocational Course examinations are "called to the Bar". They are barristers. In contrast to the solicitor's qualification, the Bar qualification does not entail the successful completion of a period of apprenticeship training. However, barristers intending to practise, rather than teach law or to go on to some other career, must complete a period of apprenticeship ("a pupillage") which takes a period of one-year, split in to two six month periods (sixes). A pupil does not have to stay in the same chambers to complete the second six months. There are a small number of opportunities to undertake a pupillage at the "employed bar" (working as an employed legal advisor rather than as an independent practitioner).

When starting a pupillage, all pupils are assigned a "pupilmaster/mistress", an experienced barrister who will organise training, allocate the work and assess progress. Generally the first six months will consist of assisting the pupil master/mistress by undertaking tasks such as legal research, document reading and drafting, and attending court. On successfully completing the first "six", pupils are issued a certificate allowing them to undertake work for a fee. In the second six pupils will have their own clients, cases and court appearances. During the pupillage, the Bar Council requires all pupils to attend two training courses outside the chambers giving further training in advocacy and managing a practice.

In selecting pupillage a student must have regard not only to the range of training on offer but also to the future prospects in the set of chambers which offers the pupillage. Students should not only consider pupillage in London, but also in sets of chambers in cities such as Manchester or Birmingham. Regard must also be had to the number and amount of pupillage awards and scholarships given by the chambers, to help off-set the living expenses for pupils. Many chambers do a mixture of litigation work covering crime, personal injury litigation and other common law areas. Students wishing to obtain pupillage and to earn a reasonable living at an early stage at the Bar will often choose such chambers. In London, particularly, there is a large number of specialist chambers covering such fields as commercial law, chancery, patents, tax, libel, planning, employment law and so on. Competition is very fierce for places in such sets of chambers. A very good academic record is required and even those students who are offered places are not assured of making a career at the Bar. Even if offered a place for pupillage there is no guarantee that the student will subsequently be offered a position in the chambers ("a tenancy") after its completion.

The *Chambers Pupillages & Awards Handbook*, published by the Bar Council (2–3 Cursitor Street, London EC4A 1NE) gives potential applicants much of the information they need when selecting chambers. Alternatively, if a student wishes to meet and talk with members of a specific chambers before applying, they may consider attending a 'pupillage fair'. To get a feel for the profession students may undertake a 'mini-pupillage' at a chosen chambers. This consists of a period of work experience which may or may not be assessed.

Applying for a pupillage has been made easier by the introduction of PACH (the Pupillage Applications Clearing House), run by the Bar council. Applicants are asked to complete a simple disk-based application form. PACH will then forward the application to up to 12 selected chambers (plus three reserves). Prospective pupils will then have to attend an interview prior to being offered a pupillage. Chambers that do not participate in the scheme can be applied to on an individual basis.

Funding

There is less opportunity to obtain financial support when training to be a barrister compared with trainee solicitors as it is rare for a set of chambers to provide sponsorship to an intending barrister. In addition, pupils are often paid very little during the period of apprenticeship (if at all).

Funding is available for the Common Professional Examination, the Bar Vocational Course and the pupillage year through the individual Inns of Court. Each of the four Inns provide listings of the bursaries and awards available to students who have been admitted to the Inn. As these awards are limited in number the majority of student are self-funded. However, many of the High Street Banks provide loans at favourable rates to fund training.

PRACTICAL POINTS: SOLICITORS AND BARRISTERS

The following points may be of assistance to those considering entering the legal profession:

- Consider when applications need to be made for the various professional examination courses, obtain advice from your tutor, the Law Society or Bar Council and the growing number of institutions offering the professional courses.

- Intending solicitors should give thought to the advantages and disadvantages of choosing either the College of Law or one of the other appropriate institutions for the solicitors' final course. Some local education authorities are willing to give discretionary grants to cover the costs of such courses, only when a student chooses the institution nearest to his home address. Some firms of solicitors will help their prospective trainee solicitors with the course fees and living expenses.

- Intending entrants to the legal profession should assess the total costs of entry, (e.g. tuition and living costs, membership fees and other expenses), the possibility or not of obtaining a bank loan, the availability of scholarships from the various Inns, chambers and law firms and the conditions attached to such awards.

- The desirability of obtaining work experience in a solicitor's office or attached to a barrister's set of chambers during student vacations. Many firms of solicitors and barristers' chambers now organise student placement schemes.

- Advice should be sought to ensure that you obtain a satisfactory apprentice training which reflects your career and subject interests either as a trainee solicitor or as a pupil barrister and that the articles or pupillage is arranged at the appropriate time.

- An assessment should be made of prospects in either branch of the profession and the overall treatment of trainees and new recruits.

- Read regularly the legal recruitment/jobs pages in The Times and other national newspapers, the *Law Society Gazette, The Lawyer* and *Legal Week*. These publications provide an accurate barometer of vacancies, salaries and employment trends in the legal profession.

- Students should make every effort possible to explore career opportunities which are open to them and find out "first-hand" what work as a solicitor or barrister is like whilst they are at university. Do not assume that your interest in the law as a degree subject automatically means that you will enjoy working as a lawyer, or that your disinterest in law as a degree subject means that you will not enjoy working as a lawyer. Appendix I summarises other career opportunities open to students who have studied law or have an interest in a career with a legal content.

QUALIFYING AS A SOLICITOR IN SCOTLAND

This section reproduces material supplied by the Law Society of Scotland in March 2000.

Entering the Legal profession

A law degree is now the accepted means of entering the legal profession. However as an alternative, it is possible to qualify for the solicitor's branch of the legal profession by a combination of the Law Society of Scotland's own examinations and the Diploma in Legal practice.

The Academic Stage

(a) Law Degree Route

A Bachelor of laws Degree can be studied at five Scottish Universities: Aberdeen, Dundee, Edinburgh, Glasgow and Strathclyde. This can be completed as an ordinary degree (three years full time) or as an Honours degree (four years full time).

(b) Non-Law Degree Route (Law Society Examinations)

To qualify as a solicitor without a law degree it is necessary to pass the Law Society of Scotland's professional examinations in order to be eligible to sit the Diploma in Legal Practice. Non-law graduates must be in, or find, full time employment as a Pre-Diploma trainee with a qualified solicitor. Pre-diploma training lasts for three years during which time the trainee will study for the Law Society Examinations and receive training in prescribed areas of law. For admission requirements contact: The Law Society of Scotland, 26 Drumsheugh Gardens, Edinburgh EH1 1RF (www.lawscot.org.uk)

The Vocational Stage

Diploma in Legal Practice

After completing the degree or the Law Society examinations, all intending solicitors are required to take the Diploma in Legal Practice. This seven month course can be taken in Aberdeen, Dundee, Edinburgh or Glasgow. This course teaches the practical knowledge and the skills necessary for the working life of a solicitor. To gain admission to the Diploma Course entrants must obtain passes in certain "core" subjects in their LLB degree and obtain a satisfactory standard in the performance of their LLB or Law Society examinations

Post-Diploma Practical Training

After competition of the Degree/Law Society Professional examinations and the Diploma all intending solicitors serve a two-year post-Diploma training contract with a practising solicitor in Scotland. At the end of the first year, trainees will undertake a block release of four weeks to university to complete the professional competence course which involves more in-depth coverage of professional ethics and legal practice. On completing the first year of training, trainees can apply to be admitted as a solicitor holding a practising certificate. This allows trainees to appear in court for their employer's clients. Towards the end of the two year training period all trainees must pass the Test of Professional competence which is administered by the Law Society of Scotland. If successful the training contract is discharged and the trainee is entitles to apply for a full practising certificate.

Requalifying in Scotland: Solicitors from England, Wales and Northern Ireland

Qualified solicitors from England, Wales and Northern Ireland who wish to be admitted as solicitors in Scotland must apply to the Legal Education Department of the Law

Society of Scotland. Prior to being admitted, a fee must be paid, eligibility must be proved and examinations, covering Conveyancing, Scots Criminal Law and European Community law, must be passed.

For further information: The Legal Education Department, The Law Society of Scotland, 26 Drumsheugh Gardens, Edinburgh, EH3 7YR. Tel: (0131) 226 7411.

QUALIFYING AS AN ADVOCATE (BARRISTER) IN SCOTLAND

An advocate in Scotland undertakes similar work to a barrister in England and Wales. Their primary duty is to represent clients in court and before tribunals. However, advocates train, and often work, as solicitors before going to the Bar.

Intending advocates must obtain a LLB (Honours) Degree in order to proceed with legal training. This must cover the eight core legal subjects. Having completed the law degree it is then necessary to take the one-year postgraduate Diploma in Legal Practice at one of the Law Faculty's Legal Practice Units (Aberdeen, Edinburgh, Dundee, Strathclyde or Glasgow). Intending barristers will then undertake a traineeship for a period of 1–2 years in a solicitors office. Following this period it is recommended, although not essential, to practice as a solicitor before going to the Bar.

On completing the traineeship, intending barristers undertake a period of unpaid practical training with an experienced advocate. Training is completed by successfully completing the Faculty of Advocates' written examinations.

For further information contact: The Faculty of Advocates, Advocate's Library, Parliament House, Edinburgh EH1 1RF.

QUALIFYING AS A SOLICITOR IN NORTHERN IRELAND

Entering the Legal profession

Usually students complete a law degree to enter the profession. However it is possible for students with a degree in another discipline to become qualified.

Academic Stage of Training

(a) Law Degree Route

This is the most common way to qualify as a solicitor. When choosing a degree course it is important to ensure it covers the eight core subjects. These subjects are: Constitutional Law, Criminal Law, Land Law, Law of Tort, Equity, Law of Evidence, Law of contract and European Law.

(b) Non-Law Degree Route

Students from other disciplines can commence training as a solicitor if it can be shown a satisfactory level of knowledge has been achieved in the eight core subjects. The Bachelor of Legal Science awarded by Queen's University, Belfast is accepted as sufficient evidence of knowledge of the relevant subjects. For more information contact: The Queen's University of Belfast, 14 Malone Road, Belfast BT9 5BN (www.qub.ac.ik)

Vocational Stage of Training

Apprenticeship

After completing an acceptable Degree intending solicitors take up a period of apprenticeship. This involves securing both a place at the Institute of Professional Legal Studies and an apprenticeship contract with a qualified solicitor. Applicants to the Institute must sit an entrance examination in the December prior to the year they wish to take up a place at the institute.

The professional education of a solicitor involves a combination of practical in-office training and formal academic instruction. The period of apprenticeship is two years. The first three months of apprenticeship is spent in office, the following twelve at the Institute of Professional Legal Studies and returning to the office for the final nine months. Once the student has passed all the relevant examinations and completed the apprenticeship period, application can be made to be enrolled as a solicitor of the Supreme Court of Judicature in Northern Ireland. Once enrolled a practising certificate can be applied for. Newly qualified solicitors are restricted from acting otherwise than employees for a three-year period (reduced to two by attending the Society's Continuing Legal Education programme)

Contact: The Law Society of Northern Ireland, Law Society House, 98 Victoria Street, Belfast, BT1 3JZ Tel: 028 9023 1614

The Institute of Professional Legal Studies, 10 Lennox Vale, Malone Road, Belfast. (www.qub.ac.uk/ipls)

Requalifying in Northern Ireland: Solicitors from England and Wales

Any practising member of the Bar of England and Wales who has been practising for at least three years can, on payment of a fee and subject to satisfactory references, be called to the Bar of Northern Ireland.

Contact: The Law Society of Northern Ireland, Law Society House, 98 Victoria Street, Belfast, BT1 3JZ Tel: 028 9023 1614

QUALIFYING AS A BARRISTER IN NORTHERN IRELAND

To qualify as a barrister in Northern Ireland it is necessary to attain at least a second class honours degree in law. This must cover the eight core subjects. A non-law graduates who wish to qualify as barrister must complete the Bachelor of Legal Science Studies at the Queen's University of Belfast.

On completing one of the above courses, intending barristers take a one-year Vocational Certificate course at the Queen's University of Belfast before becoming qualified. Barristers then undertake a six-moth unpaid pupillage.

Contact: The Queen's University of Belfast, 14 Malone Road, Belfast BT9 5BN (www.qub.ac.ik)

Appendix I

CAREERS DIRECTORY

This alphabetical list of careers opportunities summarises a selection of those careers which have some legal content or contact with the legal profession. The materials contained in this book are designed to be of assistance to trainees for the vast majority of these occupations. Students who have studied law will sometimes find that they can negotiate exemptions from law examinations in professional courses. In some cases they will automatically have such an exemption. The 50 or so organisations mentioned in the directory were written to in January 2000, and where relevant, their amendments to previous entries have been included. We are extremely grateful to them for their comments. We are also grateful to Jodie Sangster (LL.B., LL.M.) who has helped co-ordinate this process. Most academic institutions and professional bodies now consider a wide variety of qualifications such as BTEC, GNVQ, Scottish Highers and SQA National Units.

ACCOUNTANCY

Accountants are usually thought of in association with companies rather than as independent financial advisors. Whether working for a company or acting as an independent financial advisor, accountants are involved in the day-to-day financial control of businesses as well as larger-scale matters such as the creation of new businesses and the restructuring of established ones.

In recent years the accountancy profession has shown itself to be very adaptable and enterprising. Their work as liquidators and receivers, dealing with the closing down of businesses, has expanded, as has the role of auditors. They have also extended their activities into the more general area of management consultants. An area of accountancy ideally suited to law graduates is tax planning as it involves predicting and applying changes in tax legislation. Due to this, some firms specifically take on law graduates as trainees in this area. Over past decades accountants have increasingly worked closely with solicitors and, in recent years, have expanded their business into areas traditionally the prerogative of solicitors. Many of the larger firms of accountants now own legal practices and are expanding into the legal profession. Although no specific qualifications are required to become an accountant, it is necessary to obtain a professional qualification to become a chartered, certified or management accountant. Many accountancy firms finance the obtaining of such qualifications as part of a graduate-training scheme.

Minimum entry requirements: Entry requirements vary depending upon the qualification sought, however as a general rule a minimum of three GCSE passes plus two A-levels or equivalent are required. Students with a degree may gain exemption from all or part of the Foundation and Certificate Stage papers.

Training period: To become a qualified accountant, a minimum of three years relevant training is required.

Further information:
Institute of Chartered Accountants in England and Wales, Gloucester House, 399 Silbury Boulevard, Central Milton Keynes, MK9 2HL (www.icaew.co.uk)
The Chartered Association of Certified Accountants, 29 Lincoln's Inn, London WC2A 3EE (www.acca.org.uk)
The Chartered Institute of Management Accountants, 63 Portland Place, London W1M 4AB The Chartered Institute of Public Finance and Accountancy, 3 Robert Street, London WC2N 6BH (www.cipfa.org.uk)

ACTUARY

Most actuaries work for insurance and pension fund companies. They calculate matters such as the life expectancies of certain occupational groups and assess a wide range of insurance risks.

Minimum entry standard: 2 "A" levels (one being a B in maths or C in further maths) and 3 "GCSE" levels. This is predominantly a maths graduate profession.

Training period: 5–6 years for graduates.

Further information:
Institute of Actuaries, Napier House, 4 Worcester Street, Oxford OX1 2AW (www.actuaries.org.uk)

ADVERTISING

There is a wide range of job opportunities for graduates in the advertising industry.

Further information:
The Advertising Association, Abford House, 15 Wilton Road, London SW1V 1NJ (www.adassoc.org.uk)
Institute of Practitioners in Advertising, 44 Belgrave Square, London SW1X 8QS (www.ipa.co.uk)

BANKING

The High Street Banks have expanded the range of services they offer to corporate and personal customers. Advice is given on a wide range of services including investments, taxation, securities, loans and leasing schemes. The Banks have substantial trust and probate departments. Merchant banks give specialist advice, manage clients' investments, and advise on company acquisitions, flotations and mergers. They employ a number of lawyers.

Qualifications and training periods depend on the Bank and the relevant traineeship.

Further information:
London Investment Banking Association, 6 Frederick's Place, London EC2R 8BT
The Chartered Institute of Bankers, 4-9 Burgate Lane, Canterbury, Kent CT1 2XJ (www.cib.org.uk)

BARRISTER

See Chapter 8.

BUILDING SOCIETY MANAGEMENT

At present Building Societies have to deal with solicitors over the granting and drawing up of mortgages. They employ a number of lawyers. It is likely that the scope of Building Societies operations will grow in the future to include more commercial initiatives and the provision of a wider range of legal services for their clients. There is also likely to be a greater degree of overlap between the banking and building society businesses.

No mandatory qualification exists for Building Society Management however there is provision to obtain an Associate of the Chartered Institute of Bankers qualification which covers areas such as lending, management and financial services. Other qualifications relevant to Building Society Management, such as CeMAP and the Diploma in Mortgage Lending, may also be obtained from the Chartered Institute of Bankers.

Minimum entry requirements: no formal requirements
Training period: 18 months–4 years

Further information:
The Chartered Institute of Bankers, 4–9 Burgate Lane, Canterbury, Kent CT1 2XJ (www.cib.org.uk)
The Building Society Association, 3 Saville Row, London, W1X 1AF (www.bsa.org.uk)

CHARTERED SECRETARY

Chartered Secretaries are professional administrators with training in finance, law, personnel and information systems. The work will vary depending on the size and function of the organisation. It may include looking after pension schemes, insurance, premises management, liaison between directors and shareholders, company law, committee management and office management.

Minimum entry standard: No academic qualifications are needed for entry but exemptions from professional examinations may be granted for degrees, Higher National Awards and some professional qualifications.

Training period: Variable.

Further information:
Student Services Department, Institute of Chartered Secretaries and Administrators, 16 Park Crescent, London W1N 4AH (www.icsa.org.uk)

CIVIL SERVICE (U.K. AND EUROPEAN)

U.K. Civil Service

The range of jobs in the civil service is enormous; from prison warder to Permanent Secretary. Many have a legal content. The civil service employs a large number of solicitors and barristers. In particular the Government Legal Service employs about 1200 lawyers, who work in both major Departments of State and smaller, more specialised public bodies. Their activities embrace virtually every aspect of law including working with Ministers and Parliamentary Counsel on primary legislation, seeing Bills through Parliament and dealing with public law litigation.

Further information:
Recruitment and Assessment Service, Innovation Court, New Street, Basingstoke, Hampshire, RG21 7JB (www.rasnet.co.uk)
Government Legal Services, Recruitment Team, Queen Anne's Chambers, 28 Broadway, London SW1H 9JS.

European Opportunities

European Institutions:

Regular open competitions are held to recruit staff to institutions such as the European Commission, European Parliament and the European Court of Justice. The majority of opportunities exist within the Commission with the other institutions recruiting on a lesser scale. Open competitions usually consist of a written examination and interview. Full details of all competitions run by the European Commission and the other European Institutions can be obtained by subscribing to the official Journal of the European Communities (Recruitment Notices) through Her Majesty's Stationary Office (The Stationary Office, PO Box 276, London SW3 5DT (www.the-stationary-office.co.uk))

Qualified lawyers are also recruited to the European Commission, Parliament and Council of Ministers through the open competitions. Opportunities at the European Court of Justice are usually confined to lawyer linguists and are rarely advertised.

Minimum entry requirements: Applicants must have good knowledge of two E.U. languages

Further information:
General information about recruitment and open competitions can be obtained from: European Commission, Info-Recruitment, Rue de la Loi 200, 1049 Brussels Tel: +32 2 2993131.

Stages

To enhance prospects of being successful in the open competitions applicants may decides to complete a five month "stage" with the European Commission. A "stage" is a five-month in-service training programme offered to university graduates and public service employees. It consists of a period work experience in one of the commissions services (undertaking tasks such as minute writing, research and assessment of financial, economic and technical co-operation projects) supplemented by lectures and visits to other EU institutions. In some circumstances a "stage" can count towards a training contract or pupillage.

Further information and application forms:
The Traineeships Office, (B68) European Commission, Rue de la Loi 200, B1049 Brussels, Belgium (http://europa.eu.int/comm/stages)
Minimum entry requirements: First or second class honours degree
Training period: 5 months

European Fast Stream

The European Fast Stream Programme is a U.K. Government initiative designed to increase the number of British graduate securing posts in the EU institutions. It offers a four-year period of work experience designed to increase chances of success in the EU recruitment competitions. European Fast Streamers are full time U.K. Civil Servants, working in U.K. Government Departments. Their work has an emphasis on European policy issues, so they learn how the EU machinery works and how Brussels and Member State governments interact. They also get special training to help them get through the EU recruitment competitions. If they pass a competition, they normally resign from the British Civil Service and become employees of one of the EU Institutions.

Minimum entry requirements: A first or second class honours degree, "A" level standard in another EU language. (Must be a British National and no older than 41)

Training period: 4 years

Further information:
European Fast Stream, Room 74/2, Cabinet Office, Horse Guards Road, London SW1P 3AL (www.faststream.gov.uk)
Recruitment and Assessment Service (CAPITA RAS Ltd), Innovation Court, New Street, Basingstoke, Hampshire, RG21 7JB (www.rasnet.co.uk)

CUSTOMS AND EXCISE

HM Customs are responsible for the collection of all indirect taxation (*e.g.* VAT, excise duties) and for enforcing the prohibition against smuggling drugs and other prohibited or restricted items (*e.g.* firearms, pornography).

Further information:
The Solicitor, HM Customs and Excise, New Kings Beam House, 22 Upper Ground, London SE1 9PJ (www.hmce.gov.uk)

ENGINEERING

Most professional engineers study aspects of law during some part of their training; generally this will relate to matters such as contract, employment and building law.

Further information:
EMTA (Engineering Marine Training Authority), 41 Clarendon Road, Watford WD1 1HS (www.eal.org.uk)
The Engineering Council, 10 Maltravers Street, London WC2R 3ER (www.engc.org.uk)
Women into Science and Engineering Ground Floor, Queen Anne's Gate Building, Dartmouth Street, London SW1H 9BP (www.engc.org.uk/wise)

ENVIRONMENTAL HEALTH OFFICERS

Environmental Health Officers work in both the public and private sectors. The work includes responsibility for ensuring that certain food, hygiene, health and safety, environmental protection, public health, housing and other regulatory provisions are complied with. The job includes some involvement with lawyers and the courts and requires detailed knowledge of a number of Acts of Parliament and related statutory instruments.

Minimum entry standard: 2 "A" levels and 5 "GCSE" levels (including English, Maths and 2 science subjects). (Provision for graduate entry).

Training period: 4 year sandwich course leading to BSc (Hons) Environmental Health. 2 year MSc in Environmental Health for science graduates. Some courses offered on a part-time basis.

Further information:
The Chartered Institute of Environmental Health, Chadwick Court, 15 Hatfields, London SE1 8DJ (www.cieh.org.uk)

FACTORY INSPECTOR

Much of a factory inspector's time is spent visiting appropriate premises advising on safety requirements and ensuring that a variety of statutes are complied with. The job involves some contact with courts and lawyers.

Minimum entry standards: Graduate entry plus further experience normally required.

Training period: 2 years

Further information:
The Health and Safety Executive, Room 321, St Hughs House, Bootle, Liverpool L20 (www.hse.gov.uk)
Recruitment and Assessment Service, Innovation Court, New Street, Basingstoke Hampshire RG21 7JB (www.rasnet.co.uk)

HEALTH SERVICES MANAGEMENT

Health service managers play a key role in the organisation, staffing, equipping and functioning of hospitals. Moves towards privatising some services, (e.g. catering and laundering), industrial relations problems, and intricate commercial decisions that have to be taken by hospital trusts have all increased the legal content of the work done.

Minimum entry standards: No set pattern.

Training period: Variable. It is possible to take the Institute of Health Services Management courses but other qualifications such as those in law, accountancy or personnel management may be adequate.

Further information:
Institute of Healthcare Management, 7-10 Chandos Street, London W1M 9DE (www.ihm.org.uk)

HOUSING

Housing professionals work to develop, supply or manage housing and related services. People who work in housing tend to work for a local authority, housing association or a commercial landlord. The work varies according to the particular functions of the housing organisation, its size and location. Social, legal and other changes have expanded the spectrum of work available and skills required in the housing profession. Much of the work has a legal content due to the statutory framework surrounding the field of housing management.

Minimum entry standards: 1 "A" level and 3 GCSE or equivalent.

Training period: 4 years (less for graduates).

Further information:
Chartered Institute of Housing, Octavia House, Westwood Way, Coventry CV4 8JP. Tel: 024 7685 1700 (email: careers @cih.org)

INSURANCE

The insurance field offers a wide range of different employment opportunities. The precise nature of insurance contracts and the wide range of specialist legal rules means there are many openings for lawyers in this area.

Further information:
Careers Information Officer, The Chartered Insurance Institute, The Hall, 20 Aldermanbury, London EC2V 7HY (www.cii.co.uk)

JOURNALISM AND BROADCASTING

This is a wide field offering opportunities not just as a broadcaster or journalist, but also behind the scenes in the administration and management of businesses. Many media companies have "in house" legal departments. The BBC's is probably the largest.

Further information:
BBC Recruitment Service, White City, 201 Wood Lane, London W12 7TS (www.bbc.co.uk/jobs/)
ITV Network Centre, 200 Gray's Inn Road, London WC1 8XS (www.itv.co.uk)
Independent Television Association, 33 Foley Street, London W1P 7LB (www.itc.org.uk)
National Council for the Training of Journalists, Latton Bush Centre, Southern Way, Harlow, Essex CM18 7BL (www.itecharlow.co.uk/nctj/)
Newspaper Society, Bloomsbury House, 74–77 Great Russell Street, London WC1B 3DA (www.newspapersoc.org.uk)
Periodical Publishers' Association, Queen's House, 28 Kingsway, London WC2B 6JR (www.ppa.org.uk)
The Radio Authority, Holbrook House, 14 Great Queen Street, Holborn, London WC2B 5DG (www.radioauthority.org.uk)

LEGAL CAREER OPPORTUNITIES

Solicitors and Barristers are covered in Chapter 8. This entry reproduces material supplied by the Law Society in January 2000 on other careers in the legal profession.

(a) Legal Executives

Legal executives have their own status and role within the legal profession. They work as assistants to solicitors, predominantly in the area of private practice. To qualify as a legal executive they must take the examinations of the Institute of Legal Executives (ILEX). To qualify as a Fellow of the Institute they must also have at least 5 years experience in legal work. They do a wide range of legal work and often develop their own individual specialisations (particularly in the field of conveyancing, accounts, trusts, wills and litigation). It is possible to qualify as a solicitor through the Legal Executive route by taking further examinations. Some people are employed by solicitors to do the same work as legal executives although they are not qualified as such.

Entry qualifications: 4 GCSE levels in approved subjects or the ILEX Preliminary Certificate in Legal Studies or the ILEX para legal training qualification.

Further information:
The Institute of Legal Executives, Kempston Manor, Kempston, Bedford MK42 7AB (www.ilex.org.uk)

(b) Outdoor Clerks

Many large firms of solicitors employ school leavers as Clerks who deliver statements of case or attend court to pay fees and have documents stamped. Careers offices, Job Centres and newspapers advertise vacancies for Outdoor Clerks. Qualifications required range from two to four GCSE's including English Language

(c) Barristers' Clerks

Barristers' Clerks manage the diaries, court lists and fees of barristers in practice.

Further information:
Institute of Barristers' Clerks, 4a Essex Court, London EC4Y 9AJ (www.instbclerks.org)

(d) Legal Secretaries

Legal Secretaries provide the secretarial and clerical backup for solicitors, barristers, law courts, civil service, and banks. They deal with large amounts of correspondence and the preparation of documents such as wills, divorce petitions and witness statements.

Further information:
Association of Legal Secretaries, The Mill, Clymping Street, Clymping, Littlehampton, West Sussex BN17 5RN.

(e) Legal Cashiers

Legal Cashiers are usually employed in solicitors' practices, and their main duties are to keep solicitors up to date with the financial position of the firm and to maintain records. A cashier often deals with the payment of salaries, pensions, National Insurance contributions and Income Tax. Cashiers are increasingly using computerised accounting systems.

Further information:
The Institute of Legal Cashiers, 2nd Floor, 146 Eltham Hill, Eltham, London SE9 6SN (www.ilca.org.uk)

(f) Law Costs Draftsmen

Law Costs Draftsmen ensure that the firm's clients are properly charged for the work that has been done on their behalf. They are concerned with all areas of law and deal with every type of legal matter that passes through solicitors' hands. They are not therefore restricted to one narrow area of law but must acquire a knowledge of law to enable them to deal with the files. A knowledge of legal procedure is vital.

Further information:
Association of Law Costs Draftsmen, Church Cottage, Church Lane, Stuston, Diss, Norfolk IP21 4AG (www.alcd.org.uk)

(g) Licensed Conveyancers

Licensed Conveyancers are involved in the preparation of transfers, conveyances, contracts and other documents in connection with the selling and buying of property or land. To become a Licensed Conveyancer you need a minimum of four GCSEs including English Language, and must be prepared to sit and pass further examinations and undergo further practical training.

Further information:
The Council for Licensed Conveyancers, 16 Glebe Road, Chelmsford, Essex CM1 1QG.

(h) Justices' Clerks

Justices' Clerks are barristers or solicitors who manage the magistrates' courts service and are responsible for providing legal advice to lay magistrates. They also train newly appointed magistrates and act as secretary to management and selection committees. They are widely involved in liaison with other professionals in the criminal justice system.

Further information:
A.R. Heath, Honorary Secretary, The Justices' Clerks' Society, Liverpool Magistrates Court, 107 Dale Street, Liverpool, W1P 6DD (www.jc-society.co.uk)

(i) Court Clerks

Court Clerks work in Justices' Clerks' offices and advise lay magistrates on law and procedure in court. They are also responsible for the Licensing and Betting and Gaming Committees, which involves visiting premises with a Magistrate. Court Clerks often have to be on standby at weekends just in case it is necessary to set up an emergency court.

Further information:
The Association of Magisterial Officers, 231 Vauxhall Bridge Road, London SW1V 1EG.

(j) Crown Prosecution Service

The Crown Prosecution Service is an independent body responsible for the prosecution and review of criminal proceedings instituted by the police in England and Wales (with the exception of cases conducted by the Serious Fraud Office and certain minor offences). The Crown Prosecution Service is part of the Civil Service, and all staff are civil servants. Cases are prosecuted by solicitors, barristers or designated caseworkers who are assisted in the preparation of papers by caseworkers and support services.

Further information:
The Crown Prosecution Service, 50 Ludgate Hill, London EC4M 7GG (www.cps.gov.uk)

(k) The Government Legal Service

The GLS consists of around 1,200 qualified lawyers employed in approximately 30 government organisations. There may be anything from 1 to 200 lawyers in a single organisation. Whilst GLS lawyers are employed by the department in which they work, they also benefit from the corperate approach that their departments membership of GLS brings, including career and training opportunities. The work undertaken by GLS lawyers covers most aspects of law covered by the private sector.

Further information:
Government Legal Services, Recruitment Team, Queen Anne's Chambers, 28 Broadway, London SW1H 9JS.

(l) The Lord Chancellor's Department

This office, part of the Civil Service, employs civil servants, some of whom are lawyers, to deal with matters relating to the administration of the courts. The Department also deals with policy matters concerning the legal profession.

Further information:
Lord Chancellor's Department, Selborne House, Victoria Street, London, SW1E 6QE (www.open.gov.uk/lcd)

(m) Armed Forces

There are a number of vacancies for lawyers in the armed forces.

Further information:
Army Legal Services, Trenchard Lines, Upavon, Pewsey, Wiltshire SN9 6BE (www.army.mod.uk)
RAF Legal Services, RAF Innsworth, Gloucestershire, GL3 1EZ (www.raf.mod.uk)

LIBRARY, INFORMATION AND TRAINING SERVICES

An increasing number of the larger firms of solicitors have specialist departments covering legal information and practice developments, library services, precedents, education and training programmes, research and publications.

These departments are often staffed by lawyers.

Further information:
Library Association, 7 Ridgmont Street, London WC1W 7AE (www.la-hq.org.uk)
The British and Irish Association of Law Librarians, 26 Myton Crescent, Warwick CV34 6QA (www.biall.org.uk)

LOCAL GOVERNMENT

Some specific careers in local government are listed in this appendix under the appropriate headings. There are a wide range of careers in local government either as a lawyer or in management. For information about them you should consult the appropriate department of the Town Hall or Council Office in the area in which you wish to work.

MANAGEMENT

Most companies in industry, commerce and the financial sectors have graduate recruitment programmes. A good law degree will often be considered a suitable background to a career in management. Please consult your own Careers' Advisory Service on particular opportunities, when to apply, and to obtain an overview of a career in management.

Some companies will actually come to your university or college to interview prospective trainees and employees.

PATENT OFFICE

Patent agents advise on all aspects of the protection of ideas through patents, copyright and trade marks. Registration of a patent or industrial design is a way of preventing anyone copying your invention without them first paying an appropriate fee. The job involves a knowledge of both science and law and is particularly suitable for a science or engineering student with an interest in the law.

Minimum entry standard: Science or engineering degree.

Training period: 3–4 years.

Further information:

Chartered Institute of Patent Agents, Staple Inn Buildings, London WC1V 7PU (www.cipa.org.uk)

PERSONNEL MANAGEMENT

The continual development of employment law and health and safety legislation over the past decades has resulted in an increased need for some personnel managers to have a specialist knowledge of law so that they can advise their companies on such matters and, if necessary, represent them in industrial tribunals.

Minimum entry standard: Varies (provision for graduate entry).

Training period: Variable.

Further information:

Institute of Personnel Management, 35 Camp Road, Wimbledon, London SW19 4UX (www.ipd.co.uk)

POLICE

The Police force offers a variety of careers suitable for law graduates. All entrants to the police force must complete a two year period as a uniformed Constable within a police station. On completion of this period there is scope to progress through the police ranks or work for one of the specialist squads such as the Air Support Unit or the Public Order Branch. Graduates may apply for the Accelerated Promotion Scheme for Graduates (APSG) which provides enhanced career progression.

Further information:

The Police Recruiting Department, The Home Office, 50 Queen Anne's Gate, London SW1H 9AT (www.police.uk or www.homeoffice.gov.uk/police.htm)

The Metropolitan Police Recruitment Department, 26 Aybrook Street, London, W1M 3JL (www.met.police.uk/recruitment)

For graduate entry: Police Graduate Liason Officer, Room 556, The Home Office, 50 Queen Anne's Gate, London SW1H 9AT (www.homeoffice.gov.uk/hmic/apshome.htm)

PUBLIC RELATIONS

Many of the largest firms of solicitors now employ external or internal public relations advisers to help them with their overall "image" and relations with the media, clients and prospective clients.

Further information:
Institute of Public Relations, The Old Trading House, 15 Northburgh Street, London EC1V 0PR (www.ipr.org.uk)

PUBLISHING

Some law publishers, such as Butterworths and Sweet & Maxwell, are interested in employing law graduates and newly qualified lawyers in their editorial and marketing departments. If you are interested in working for a particular legal publisher you should contact them directly. Your law tutor should be able to advise you about which law publishers you should approach.

Further information:
Publishers' Association, 1 Kingsway, London WC2B 6XF (www.publishers.org.uk)
Butterworths, Halsbury House, 35 Chancery Lane, London WC2A 1EL (www.butterworths.co.uk)
Sweet & Maxwell, 100 Avenue Road, Swiss Cottage, London NW3 3PF (www.sweetandmaxwell.co.uk)

RECRUITMENT CONSULTANTS

There is some scope for law graduates and lawyers to work for the recruitment consultants for the legal profession. To obtain an idea of the "market leaders", read the legal job vacancy pages of the national newspapers, the *Law Society Gazette*, *Legal Week* and *The Lawyer*.

SOCIAL WORK AND PROBATION

Social work

The majority of social workers are employed by local authorities. They provide a social work service to families, children, the elderly, the sick, those with disabilities and the community at large. They are employed in a variety of settings; hospitals, residential homes and in the community. Some are specialists working in such areas as mental health or child care where a good knowledge of the relevant area of law is particularly important. Other elements of social work include providing advice and support where a general awareness of the law is frequently required.

Probation

Probation officers are social workers with special responsibility for offenders. They prepare social inquiry reports to assist the courts in determining sentences, supervise probation orders and community service orders, and provide an aftercare service for former prisoners. Through the Divorce Court Welfare Service, probation officers also provide services for families involved in marriage breakdown. They assist with conciliation of parties and prepare welfare reports for use in resolving custody disputes. A legal background in this work is helpful though not essential.

Minimum entry standard: A Diploma in Social Work is needed to practice as a qualified social worker. The entry standard for this varies.

Training period: For graduates and non-graduates 2 years.

Further information:
CCETSW (Central Council for Education and Training in Social Work) Derbyshire House, St Chad's Street, London WC1H 8AD (www.ccetsw.org.uk)
Probation Unit, Home Office, Queen Anne's Gate, London SW1H 9AT (www.homeoffice.gov.uk/cpd/probu/probu.htm)

For graduates and non-graduates:
Social Work Admissions Systems (SWAS), Rose Hill, New Barn Lane, Cheltenham, Gloucestershire, GL50 3SH (Tel: 01242 544600)

STOCK EXCHANGE

Graduates with either law or law-related degrees may find jobs in firms of stockbrokers working in their research and investment analysis departments. There is no formal training for these positions.

The London Stock Exchange organises and regulates the activities of its 400 plus member firms which range from large international securities houses to small two-partner firms of brokers.

It is the member firms, rather than the Exchange, which employ stockbrokers. You should contact the firms directly as recruiting requirements vary. Most reference sections of business libraries hold the London Stock Exchange Member Firms Book, which gives the names and addresses of stockbroking firms.

The London Stock Exchange itself runs a Graduate Training Scheme. For further information write to: Human Resources at the Stock Exchange, London EC2N 1HP (www.londonstockexchange.com)

There are also a number of securities industry courses and exams. For more information, write to: The Securities Institute, Centurion House, 24 Monument Street, London EC3R 8AJ (www.securities—institute.org.uk)

SURVEYING AND AUCTIONEERING

Membership of the Royal Institution of Chartered Surveyors requires study of a number of subjects which have a legal content, covering such topics as contract, agency and land law.

Further information:
Royal Institution of Chartered Surveyors, 12 Great George Street, London SW1P 3AD (www.rics.org.uk)

TAX INSPECTOR

Those who are interested in tax law or the tax system and who have a good degree or an accountancy qualification may be interested in this career option. Progress in the tax inspectorate depends on both the ability to pass internal revenue examinations and the willingness to be mobile. Some tax inspectors later leave the service in order to start work as tax consultants with firms of accountants.

Minimum entry standard: First or Second class honours degree or equivalent.

Training period: 4–7 years.

Further information:
Inland Revenue (HRD), PO Box 55, Mowbray House, Castle Meadow Road, Nottingham, NG2 1BE (www.inlandrevenue.gov.uk)
Recruitment and Assessment Service, Innovation Court, New Street, Basingstoke, Hampshire, RG21 7JB (www.rasnet.co.uk)

TEACHING AND POST-GRADUATE OPPORTUNITIES

If you are interested in either of the above options you should consult your law tutor or your local Careers Advisory Service. The majority of university law faculties have facilities for post-graduate research and/or run taught post-graduate courses. You normally need a second class honours degree to obtain a place on such a course. Most of these courses can either be studied full-time or part-time. Some are run on a "distance learning" basis. It is very difficult to obtain scholarships or state grants for such courses. Some universities are able to offer scholarships or other forms of assistance. A post-graduate degree is of some assistance to anyone wishing to teach law. The majority of university law lecturers have an upper second class honours degree or better. Many also have a professional qualification, further degree or both. Although opportunities to lecture in law are limited there are more openings than in many other disciplines.

It is possible to pursue post-graduate research in foreign countries, particularly in the United States and Canada and, increasingly, with the European Union.

Further information:
For further degrees and diplomas by examination or research write direct to a range of law faculties. Diplomas and higher degrees can be obtained in a vast array of legal and law related subjects on a part-time or full-time basis at a wide range of institutions.

Study in the United Kingdom:
Grants Information: The British Arts and Humanities Research Board (AHRB), 10 Carlton House Terrace, London, SW1Y 5AH (www.ahrb.ac.uk)
Law Commission, Conquest House, 37-38 John Street, London WC1N 2BQ (for research assistant positions) (www.open.gov.uk/lawcomm)

The Economic and Social Science Research Council, Polaris House, Swindon SN2 1ET (www.esrc.ac.uk)

Overseas Opportunities:
Association of Commonwealth Universities, John Foster House, 36, Gordon Square, London WC1H 0PF (www.acu.ac.uk)
The British Council, Bridgewater House, 58 Whitworth Street, Manchester, M1 6BB (www.britishcouncil.org)
Commonwealth Legal Education Association (CLEA) c/o Legal and Constitutional Affairs Division, Commonwealth Secretariat, Marlborough House, Pall Mall, London SW1Y 5XH

For the USA:
The U.S. Educational Advisory Service, The Fulbright Commission, 62 Doughty Street, London WC1N 2LS (www.fulbright.co.uk)

TRADING STANDARDS OFFICER

Trading standards officers are responsible for the enforcement of a wide range of legislation including the Trade Descriptions Act 1968, the Consumer Credit Act 1974, the Consumer Protection Act 1987 and other regulatory provisions covering food, drugs, weights and measures. They are also often involved in the provision of advice and assistance to traders and to consumers. They are employed by local authorities.

Minimum entry standard: A Consumer Protection Degree via one of four approved university courses (The Manchester Metropolitan University, University of Teeside, Glasgow Caledonian University and University of Wales Institute, Cardiff) or accreditation of prior experience and learning (APEL).

Further information:
Institute of Trading Standards Administration, PO Box 2714, The Croft, County Hall, Lewes, East Sussex BN7 1AL

Appendix II

ABBREVIATIONS

The short list below contains some of the standard abbreviations that you will find most frequently referred to in books and case reports. It is not exhaustive. It will help you whilst you are beginning your study of law but, if you intend to acquire a more detailed knowledge of law, you will need to consult one of the detailed lists found in the books mentioned in the section, "General Reference," in Appendix III.

A.C.	Appeal Cases (Law Reports).
All E.R.	All England Law Reports.
C.L.J.	Cambridge Law Journal.
Ch.D.	Chancery Division (Law Reports).
C.M.L.R.	Common Market Law Reports.
Conv.(n.s.)	Conveyancer and Property Lawyer (New Series).
Crim.L.R.	Criminal Law Review.
D.L.R.	Dominion Law Reports.
E.L.R.	European Law Reports.
E.L.Rev.	European Law Review.
E.R.	English Reports.
Fam.	Family Division (Law Reports).
Fam. Law	Family Law (A journal which also contains notes about cases).
H. of C. or H.C.	House of Commons.
H. of L. or H.L.	House of Lords.
I.L.J.	Industrial Law Journal.
K.B.	King's Bench (Law Reports).
L.Q.R.	Law Quarterly Review.
L.S.Gaz.	Law Society Gazette.

M.L.R.	Modern Law Review.
N.I.L.Q.	Northern Ireland Legal Quarterly.
N.L.J.	New Law Journal.
P.L.	Public Law.
O.J.	Official Journal of the European Communities.
Q.B.D.	Queen's Bench Division.
R.T.R.	Road Traffic Reports.
S.I.	Statutory Instrument.
S.J. or Sol.Jo.	Solicitors' Journal.
W.L.R.	Weekly Law Reports.

Appendix III

FURTHER READING

The number of books about law and legal rules increases each day. They range from simple guides, written for the GCSE student, to thousand-page, closely argued texts, written for the academic. Some are encyclopedias; others are exhaustive surveys of a very small area of law. This short list of further reading is intended to be of use to those readers who want to take further specific themes raised in this book. The list is not a guide to legal literature as a whole. Readers who have specific interests should consult their library catalogues for books in their area.

Introductory books

Atiyah, P. Law and Modern Society (2nd. ed. 1995) Oxford University Press. Intended for the law reader, rather than the student already studying for a law degree, this is an introduction both to the legal system and ideas about law. It is written in an accessible style and is suitable for those contemplating studying law at degree level as well as anyone with a general interest in law.

Waldron, J. The Law (1990) Routledge. Another general introduction to law. The author is a political scientist and philosopher. The book is particularly concerned with questions about the relationship of politics and law in the United Kingdom.

Books on the English legal system

Bailey, S. and Gunn, M. Smith and Bailey on the Modern English Legal System (3rd. ed., 1996) Sweet and Maxwell.
Cownie, F and Bradney A. The English Legal System in Context (1996) Butterworths
White, R. The English Legal System in Action (3rd ed., 1999) Oxford University Press.

These books are primarily textbooks for law degree students studying an English Legal System course. They give the reader a basic background in the institutions and rules of the system but concentrate more on how the system actually works in practice.

Ward, R. Walker and Walker's English Legal System (8th ed., 1998) Butterworths.

Like the books above this is a textbook for law students studying legal systems courses. However, this book focuses much more on the rules of the system rather than on the way in which they operate in practice.

Cross, R. Precedent in English Law (4th ed., 1991) Oxford University Press.
Cross, R. Statutory Interpretation (3rd ed., 1995) Butterworths.
   These are standard textbooks on traditional doctrinal theory (the theory of the way in which judges use previous judgments and statutory material) for students and practitioners.

Goodrich, P. Reading the Law (1986) Basil Blackwell.
   Like the books by Cross above, this book is concerned with the nature of legal reasoning in the English legal system. However, it takes its inspiration from studies of literature and theology. It is the best introduction to the newer analyses of legal reasoning.

Bibliographical techniques and dictionaries

Dane, J. and Thomas, P. How to Use a Law Library (3rd ed., 1996) Sweet and Maxwell. A very detailed account of the different techniques used in finding and updating legal material. The title is somewhat misleading since the book also gives guidance in how to find material outside the confines of the law section of a library. Useful for those interested in advanced study.
   Osborn's Concise Law Dictionary (1993) Sweet and Maxwell. A good pocket guide.

Appendix IV

EXERCISE ANSWERS

Exercise 1

1. Section 1 creates an offence of unlawful marketing of knives; section 2 creates an offence of publishing material in connection with the unlawful marketing of a knife.

2. With the exception of s.8 which does not apply to Northern Ireland, it applies to the whole of the United Kingdom (s.11(7)).

3. Only s.11 entered into force on the date of Royal Assent so it is necessary to find out whether any commencement orders have been made under s.11(3) and which parts of the Act they bring into force; see commencement orders 1997 S.I. 1906.

4. The terms of the offence in s.1(1) and (4) are satisfied but Jonathan has a defence under s.3(1)(a)(i) providing he can also satisfy the conditions in paras (b) and (c).

5. No. In order for there to be an offence the marketing or publication must be 'likely to stimulate or encourage violent behaviour involving the use of the knife...' (ss.1(1)(b), 2(1)(b)). Skinning or gutting live animals is not 'violent behaviour' within the definition in the Act (s.10).

6. The court has a power to order the forfeiture of the sword and knives, s.6(1)(b) because they were in Wally's possession when he was arrested (s.6 (5)(a)). Gurpul may apply for a recovery order under s.7(3) but he will have to satisfy the court of the conditions in s.7(6) and s.7(7).

Exercise 2

1. Section 4A was added by the Dangerous Dogs (Amendment) Act 1997 which came into force on June 8, 1997. The Current Law Statute Citator entry for the 1991 Act refers to 1997 c.53 *i.e.* the 1997 Act. The entry for this lists the Commencement Order SI 97/1151.

2. Neither Act applies in Northern Ireland: 1991 Act, s.10(5); 1997 Act, s.6(2). There is a power in s.8 of the 1991 Act to extend that Act to Northern Ireland. It would be possible to make such an order in terms which corresponded with the amended Act so no further power is required in the 1997 Act.

3. No but it does list, in s.1(1), types of dog which it is illegal to possess etc. The Secretary of State is also empowered in s.1(1)(c) to add other types of dog if they have been bred for fighting or have the characteristics of a dog bred for fighting. The Secretary of State can also designate any other type of dog which present a "serious danger to the public" s.2(1).

4. Pugsy is a dog to which s.1 applies. It is an offence for Peter to breed, sell, or give Pugsy to anyone else in England, Wales or Scotland; he may not have Pugsy in a public place without a lead and muzzle or abandon him, s.1(2). Unless Peter complies with the registration and exemption scheme made under s.1(5) Pugsy will have to be destroyed. Destruction can also be ordered if Peter commits any of the offences in s.1(2). If Peter wants to bring Pugsy back to England he should comply with the exemption scheme, make sure Pugsy is muzzled and on a lead in public.

5. The maximum penalty for Peter's offence is a fine not exceeding level 5 and 6 months imprisonment s.1(7). The court can order destruction, s.4(1) and disqualify Peter from keeping a dog. Originally the court had no discretion regarding the dog's destruction but the Dangerous Dogs (Amendment) Act 1997, s.1 which adds a new subsection 1A to the 1991 Act, s.4 removes the requirement to order destruction if the court is satisfied about certain conditions. Peter will need to satisfy the court that Pugsy is not a danger to public safety and that he had a good reason for not having registered Pugsy.

6.   (i) If Becks can be said to have been "dangerously out of control" Barbara has committed the aggravated offence in s.3(1). "Public place" is defined in s.10(2) and includes a park to which the public have access.

        (ii) If Stan was in charge of Becks when the incident happened, Barbara would have a defence under s.3(2) providing she reasonably believed that Stan was a fit and proper person to have charge of Becks.

        (iii) Under s.6 the head of the household of a dog owner under the age of 16 is also an owner and is thus potentially liable for the offence in s.3(1). It makes no difference to the offence that the injured person was the owner.

7. The 1997 Act abolished the mandatory order for the destruction of a dangerous dog; the court now has discretion not to order destruction if the three conditions in s.4(1A) are satisfied. The 1997 Act, s.2 also created a new power to make a contingent order for destruction by adding s.4A to the 1991 Act; s.3 added s.4B which empowered the court to order destruction of a dog even though no one had been prosecuted for an offence.

Exercise 3—Case 1

1. Mr. Khan. See paragraph 3 of the decision.

2. See the formulation by Lord Woolf M.R. in paragraph 1 of the decision.

3. (a)   1. Two hearings took place in the Employment Tribunal ("ET").
          See paragraph 2 of the decision.
       2. An appeal was heard by the Employment Appeal Tribunal ("EAT").
          See paragraph 2 of the decision.
       3. The reported decision is in relation to a hearing before the Court of
          Appeal (Civil Division).
          See the information set out at the head of the report.

   (b) Civil proceedings.

   (c)   1. The Employment Tribunal ("ET") decided (a) that the appellant had
            unlawfully victimised Mr. Khan and (b) that an award of £1,500
            damages should be made to him (*i.e.* Mr. Khan won).
            See paragraph 2 of the decision.
         2. The Employment Appeal Tribunal ("EAT") dismissed the appeal
            (*i.e.* Mr. Khan won).
            See paragraph 2 of the decision.
         3. The Court of Appeal (Civil Division) dimissed the appeal unan-
            imously (*i.e.* Mr. Khan won).
            See paragraph 33 of the decision, setting out the conclusion of Lord
            Woolf M.R. together with the following agreements by Lady Justice
            Hale and Lord Mustill.

   (d) No.

4. See the four grounds set out in paragraph 7 of the decisions.

Exercise 4—Case 2

1. (a)   1. Queen's Bench Division of the High Court.
            See at page 567F in the report of the Court of Appeal decision.
            See at page 463e–f in the report of the House of Lords opinions.
         2. Court of Appeal (Civil Division).
            See at page 566E–F in the report of the Court of Appeal decision.
            See also the "running header" of the published law report.
            See at page 463e–f in the report of the House of Lords opinions.
         3. House of Lords.
            See at page 462a–b in the report of the House of Lords opinions.
         4. Note also that the case had come before the Appeal Committee of
            the House of Lords on 18 December 1997 in respect of an application
            for leave to appeal. See at page 463e in the report of the House of
            Lords opinions. This results from the refusal of the Court of Appeal
            to grant leave to appeal. See at page 594G–H in the report of the
            Court of Appeal decision.

(b)   1. Claim dismissed (*i.e.* The claimant lost)
      2. Appeal allowed by 2–1 majority (*i.e.* The claimant won)
      3. Appeal allowed by 4–1 majority (*i.e.* The claimant lost)

2. First, as regards the report of the Court of Appeal decision, compare the judgment of Swinton-Thomas L.J. at page 585F with the judgment of Stuart-Smith L.J. at page 591H and the judgment of Waite L.J. at page 594G. Secondly, in relation to the report of the House of Lords opinions, compare the opinion of Lord Steyn at page 467f with the opinion of Lord Hope at page 480c and the opinion of Lord Slynn at page 464f. Then note the opinion of Lord Goff at page 463h together with the opinion of Lord Jauncey at page 463j.

3. See the judgment of Stuart-Smith L.J. at page 573G–H, 574B–C, and 574D, where he identifies "three issues".
    Note also the judgment of Waite L.J. at page 592A–B, where he identifies "5 questions".

4. See the report of the Court of Appeal decision at page 568A–B.

5. First, a misdirection on "causation". See at page 593B in the report of the Court of Appeal decision. Secondly, a misdirection OR a finding which was "against the weight of evidence". See at page 593F–594C in the report of the Court of Appeal decision.

Exercise 5

1. It is possible to see the focus of the author's interests in a number of different ways. One might say, broadly, they are concerned with how well models of criminal justice, such as those of Packer, describe what is happening to the British criminal justice system (pp. 502–505). More narrowly, one might say that they are concerned with the function of arrest has changed over the last two decades (pp. 505-518). However, if your answer has taken this latter form then you need to ask yourself why they are interested in this question.

2. The authors deal with this question at page 505. They note both the legal consequences of an arrest (being taken into custody and detained, for example) and its social consequences (the impact that being arrested will have on a person's reputation, for example). Most importantly, they argue that, whilst arrest was once the culmination of an investigation, it is now merely part of the process. Note that they are not primarily concerned with the legal rules but, rather, with the way that the rules operate in practice. They therefore rarely give strict legal authorities for their propositions about what the law says; they assert (correctly) what the legal consequences of an arrest are. You would need to look at another source if you wanted to find the correct legal authorities for what they suggest is the case.

3. Hillyard and Gordon are interested in the fact that arrest rates differ from area to area. However, arrest rates are simply the record of the number of arrests within a particular area. The fact that such rates vary from area to area is of little significance in itself. If all murders were fortuitously concentrated in one area one would expect the arrest rate for murder in that area to be high and the

corresponding rate in other areas to be low. The likelihood of somebody being a criminal is known to correlate with certain demographic factors (for example, age and gender). It is thus possible to calculate an arrest rate that one would expect in a particular area, given its demographic characteristics, and compare that with the actual arrest rate (see pages 510-51) Arrest rates which are above the rate that one would expect given the area's demographic characteristics require an explanation.

4. Broadly, you should have suggested two different kinds of reasons. One is that such areas might objectively be linked with higher rates of crime. There could be a variety of reasons for this. Poverty might mean that crime seems to be an appropriate way of getting hold of material or goods or social deprivation might mean that people lack the educational qualifications to enter into employment and thus lead them to crime. Reasons like these would mean that such areas need closer policing. Alternatively "closer policing" might be the result of an inaccurate perception that there was greater criminality in a particular area. Such a perception would probably be self-justifying to some degree. Paying closer attention to an area would tend to uncover a much higher percentage of such crime as did in fact exist. What is important at this stage is that you note both possibilities and do not dismiss either, whatever personal feelings you have. Both arguments can be investigated further to see what merit there is in them. Both may be accurate in whole or in part or neither may be correct. The great danger in analysing material is to do so on the basis of what we already believe before we read the study and before we look at the evidence. "Doubt everything" (including our own most cherished beliefs) is generally the best advice.

5. This question goes to the very heart of why law is important (if it is). On the one hand there is the argument that legal rules establish and protect our rights within a civilized society. They tell us what we can do and what we can expect other people to do? This applies as much to the conduct of the police as it does to anyone else. The emergence of an informal rather than a formal system of justice is therefore a failure of law. On the other hand legal rules can never cater for every situation. We always fail to imagine the full complexity of what things might be like. People sometimes praise informal systems as catering much for the real needs of people, as being more flexible and thus as being more just. To what degree do we expect the law to perfectly describe how we should behave, whether we be police or anyone else?

Index